1000

Why

Illustrations
for
Preaching
and
Teaching

G. Curtis Jones

BROADMAN PRESS
Nashville, Tennessee

To my wife,
Sybil Nettleton Jones,
whose daily witness is a
contagious illustration of
the Christian life.

Library of Congress Cataloging-in-Publication Data

Jones, G. Curtis (George Curtis), 1911-
    1000 Illustrations for preaching and teaching.

    Includes index.
    1. Homiletical illustrations.   I. Title.
II. Title: One thousand illustrations for preaching and teaching.
BV4225.2.J66   1986   251'.08   83-70843
ISBN 0-8054-2249-8 (pbk.)

Contents

Acknowledgments

In reality, every book is a symposium, that is, it represents the collaboration and skills of many persons, some of whom are no longer with us, yet from their lives and witness we siphon strength and gain perspective. Among those who have generously participated in the gestation and production of this book are: my friends at Broadman Press; Mr. Charles Palmer, Elmira, New York; Dr. Marvin G. Osborn, Holmes Beach, Florida; Dr. Howard E. Short, Saint Louis, Missouri, for their counseling and editorial expertise. To our son, Paul H. Jones, doctoral candidate, Vanderbilt University, for valuable research; to Sybil, my loving critic and spouse of forty-eight years, for her constant support; and to my efficient secretary, Judy Hurley, for preparation of the manuscript, I voice my indebtedness and gratitude.

Copyrighted material is indicated in the notes section, as well as a number of courtesy references for those who wish to explore a given source more minutely.

If there have been omissions, either through inability to locate original sources or because we did not realize a given reference required permission, we apologize and voice gratitude to both author and publisher for said material.

Introduction

Living in the country, we frequently experience electrical power outages. The temporary inconvenience—which sometimes extends into hours—is caused by a thunderstorm with accompanying lightning, a tree limb falling over a line, or a squirrel tripping a fuse or becoming entangled in a relay. And then there are occasions when power failures are due to overloads. Whatever the cause, it is an exasperating experience.

Public servants, especially preachers and teachers, are often victims of overloads. Mentally, emotionally, physically, and spiritually their circuits are jammed beyond their abilities to respond effectively. Time-watching, schedule-oriented Americans are forever searching for labor-saving devices.

It is hoped that *1,000 Illustrations for Preaching and Teaching* will in some measure free up a little time for busy persons, as well as fuel their creativity and production. Having been in the pastoral ministry for almost fifty years, I know how time-consuming it can be to find a stimulating Scripture for a given occasion or the exact quotation or illustration to flesh out a sermon or a lesson. We all need help in the preparation of our presentations.

No one volume could possibly contain appropriate anecdotes and illustrations for every conceivable need. Within the context of fifty categories, however, we have endeavored to provide a wide range of adaptable material. In addition to the alphabetized illustrations, each section is highlighted by provocative scriptural references and epigrams. The general index will also assist in identifying available information. It is hoped that my work will make your work easier, more enjoyable, and effective.

G.C.J.

Action

1 Samuel 17:31-50; Esther 4:14-17; Daniel 11:30-32; Luke 4:18-19

> Let us then be up and doing,
> With a heart for any fate;
> Still achieving, still pursuing,
> Learn to labor and to wait.
>
> —Henry Wadsworth Longfellow

> If you love Him, why not serve Him?
> Soldier of the cross.
>
> —Black Spiritual

Adventure

Writing in *The New Yorker,* January 1954, Dr. R. B. Robertson reported the fascinating experience of accompanying a group of men on a whaling ship. Later he tried to analyze why these highly successful men would leave their businesses, comfortable homes, and loved ones for such a hazardous, yet joyous experience. He concluded they were psychopaths—not in a sick, inferior sense, but in a superior sense! He said they were men whose minds and spirits were so healthy that they could not accept the civilization into which they had been born.

Be Ready

The English journalist, G. K. Chesterton, reminded us of a practice among certain Christian knights of the medieval period. Before leaving for battle, they would receive the sacraments with one foot in the stirrup.

Comments

If you would not be forgotten,
As soon as you are dead and rotten,
Either write things worth reading
Or do things worth the writing.
                    —Benjamin Franklin

The great end of life is not knowledge, but action.
                    —T. H. Huxley

The Human Situation

All of humankind is torn between choices for good or evil. The Apostle Paul grappled with this dichotomy, this being torn between good and evil, superior and inferior. He cried out:

I do not understand my own actions. For I do not do what I want, but I do the very thing I hate. . . . I do not do the good I want, but the evil I do not want is what I do. Now if I do what I do not want, it is no longer I that do it, but sin which dwells within me (Rom. 7:15,19-20, RSV).

Focusing the Light

During the days of the American Civil War, Henry Ward Beecher became very unpopular because he was constantly fighting the sins of slavery. On one occasion, two young slave sisters tried to escape and were captured and returned to New Orleans for sale. The price was one-thousand dollars apiece. Since their labor was not worth anything like that amount, their fate was obvious. The father of the girls got word to Dr. Beecher, whereupon the courageous preacher assembled his people and read the auctioneer's bill of sale advertising the girls. It began with their physical qualifications and health. Their moral qualifications were limited to obedience, and finally this supreme compliment, "They are prayin' Methodist niggers!" When Beecher had finished reading the notice, he had bought their freedom.

The church of Jesus Christ must be careful to tend the light of human decency!

Follow the Dream

The Greek philosopher Heraclitus once said, "You could not step twice in the same river." It is never the same. Life is very much like a rolling river. We can never relive a day. Life is forever moving and without a moment's rest. Therefore it behooves us to give a good account of ourselves every moment of every day. Whatever his station, a Christian will strive to give an honest day's work for an honest day's pay. He will work as with a dream possessed, for in the words of Gerald Kennedy, "To be human means to be captured by a dream."

Forgetting Self

Lenny Skutnick, twenty-eight, watched while a people in a helicopter tried to rescue a stewardess struggling to survive an airplane crash in Washington, D. C. Twice she slipped from the rope dropped to her and fell back into the icy Potomac. Seeing that her strength was gone, Skutnick shed his coat and boots, jumped into the water, and swam thirty yards to her rescue. Questioned by the press afterward about his motivation, Skutnick replied: "I had been there all that time and nobody was getting in the water. . . . It's something I never thought I would do, but in looking back, I guess I did it because I didn't think about it. Somebody had to go in the water."

Humble Growth

Benjamin Franklin developed a set of disciplines which he hoped would enable him to attain moral perfection. He drew up a list of twelve virtues which he considered essential to achieving the good life. He ruled each page with seven lines. Daily he appraised and recorded his behavior. During a conversation Franklin shared his profile of excellence with an old

Quaker, who quietly informed him he had omitted the virtue of humility.

I Owe a Debt

Paul Green, in his *Burma Diary*, told of an American ambulance driver whose carrier was heavily loaded. En route, Chinese soldiers swarmed all over the vehicle, for it was their last means of escape before the advancing Japanese. The order came that no more men should be taken. Reluctantly, the driver got out of his machine and pushed the wounded off the ambulance. Later the troubled driver went to China, for as he said, "I owe the Chinese a debt."

No one can contemplate seriously what transpired at Calvary without acknowledging his or her own dept.

It Starts with You

Elton Trueblood relates the story of a man who had the crazy idea he wanted to walk a tightwire across Niagara Falls, pushing a wheelbarrow with a man in it. The aspirant erected a simulated practice situation in his backyard. Daily the determined person practiced, first with a balance bar, later without it. Eventually, after long, arduous weeks of hard work, the "wire-walker" became very good. At last the day arrived for the hazardous undertaking. Neighbors and persons from the press assembled. Looking nervously across the rushing water the stuntman said to an admiring friend, "Joe, do you believe I can do it?"

"I absolutely believe you can."

The performer looked out over the falls one more time: "Joe, do you really believe . . . ?"

"I really believe you can."

"Fine, you're my man. Get in the wheelbarrow."

The Cross—A Call to Action

"And they crucified him. . . . And sitting down they watched him there" (Matt. 27:35-36). Like those Roman soldiers, many of us merely lapse into inaction. But the cross of Christ is infinitely more than a showcase, an exhibit to arouse curiousity. It is a clarion call to action, commitment, and discipleship.

Making the Impossible Easy

George Balanchine, the great choreographer, died April 30, 1983, at the age of seventy-nine. "Mr. B," as he was affectionately known by his dancers, possessed a magical power over his performers. "He showed them how to make the impossible seem easy."[1]

Shadow of a Machine?

Helmut Thielicke, noted German theologian and preacher, tells how Lawrence of Arabia handled his crushing disappointment at the outcome of his efforts in World War I. Sir Winston Churchill once cited Lawrence as one of the greatest hopes of the British Empire. Following his brilliant desert campaign on behalf of the Arabs, who adored him, the world-famous colonel, humiliated by the meaningless results of their sacrifices, dehumanized himself by enlisting as a common soldier in the Royal Air Force. "I do it," he said, "in order to serve a mechanical purpose, not as a leader, but as the shadow of a machine. . . . It is a blessing to be only a part of a machine. You learn that it doesn't depend entirely on you."[2]

Struggle and Strength

It is claimed that Descartes was not heroic, Leibnitz a fawning courtier, Will Gibbs a recluse, Gauss cold and secretive. Notwithstanding his abilities, Pasteur is believed to have been tainted with chauvinism and racism. A dubious religiosity apparently clouded the magnificent minds of Newton and Pascal.

But the lives of Marie and Pierre Curie were beautifully different. Their supportive and compatible lives were shining examples of purity and productivity.

> The story of Marie Curie is not merely that of a poor Polish governess who struggled against adversity and became a triumphant success. The story of Marie Curie lies precisely in the fact that she was happiest during her struggles and least happy when a vulgar world acclaimed her.[3]

Strutting

Vanity is a great weakness of mankind in general, but it seems especially ludicrous when it appears among the professionally religious. The contradiction between human humility before God and human beings strutting before each other is a perfect opening for ridicule, and Jesus employed it to perfection in the twenty-third chapter of Matthew's Gospel.[4]

The Twelfth Man

It was November 23, 1935; the place, Princeton's Palmer Stadium. The snow was falling so heavily that the marker lines were obliterated and a dry ball was needed after each play. Undefeated Dartmouth was playing Princeton for the Ivy League championship. Late in the fourth quarter, with Princeton leading 19-6 and in possession of the ball on Dartmouth's six-yard line, the Indians made their last stand. They held Princeton to three yards in two tries.

Just before the ball was snapped on the third down, a spectator jumped from the stands, sprinted across the end zone, and joined the Dartmouth line before officials could stop either him or the play. Even so, Princeton gained another two yards.

Police hurried onto the field and removed the mysterious defender. Although Dartmouth lost 26-6, to this day no one can be certain who the twelfth man was for the Indians.

"We Had to Get Through"

Jack is a wiry Hebrew whose face bears the marks of suffering and sacrifice. As he drove me from Tel Aviv to Jerusalem, on approaching a designated section of road he said, "This is Courage Way." I inquired as to its meaning. He declared that during the war of 1948, the old road to Jerusalem was cut off and a new way had to be found. This road was built by men, women, and children who were unable to take up arms. "A lot of our people," he said, "were killed building this road."

As we neared the sharp, corrugated hills overlooking the Holy City, he said, "This, too, is a reminder of the bitter days of 1948 when a part of our army was sealed in Jerusalem. They needed supplies and food. The Arabs were advantageously ensconced in the hillsides and had every advantage. At last it was decided to organize a fleet of one hundred armored trucks to carry necessary equipment to the marooned soldiers. There was one driver and one gunner in each truck. Our orders were to keep driving. If one were killed, he was left, and if one were severely wounded, he was left to die while the caravan moved forward. It was a long, hard, grueling fight which eventually spelled victory for the Jews."

My driver told me that over the entire campaign he was wounded seven times and seven times returned to action, even with the loss of an eye. Then, with obvious feeling, he said as he pointed to the destroyed trucks, "The drivers of those trucks were strong men. . . . We had to get through."

Viewing History

The biblical writers, because they worshiped a dynamic God, confronted us with a dynamic view of history. They did not interpret history as a theatrical performance to which we can contribute only as an audience. They saw it rather as the arena of the action of the sovereign Lord of "life, death and destiny." They saw it as the sphere in which God accepts and rejects people and nations on the basis of their response to His gracious offer of faith and freedom in fellowship.[5]

Waving to the World

Unless the weather is very inclement, James Snellings, age seventy-two, stands at the corner of Maple Avenue and Bremo Road, Richmond, Virginia, waving good morning to motorists. This self-appointed ambassador of goodwill assumes his station about 7:15 and remains until 9 o'clock. Not as spry as he once was, he frequently rests his right arm on a mailbox while steadying himself with a cane.

Women, he says, return his greetings more generously than do men. One day he reported 180 women waved to him, only seventy-five men. "I do this for the fun of it," he says. "I try to be nice to everybody. Most wave. Some don't. The don'ts don't worry me a bit."

America

Daniel 11:30-32; 2 Kings 17:29; Matthew 21:43; Luke 4:18-19

A nation is born stoic and dies epicurean.
—Will Durant

Democracy substitutes election by the incompetent many for appointment by the corrupt few.
—Bernard Shaw

The American Flag

We were going out to dinner with two of our Floridian friends. As we rode along the elderly man allowed: "I had a puzzling experience today." Knowing of his tremendous business background and ministries of compassion, I pricked up my ears and asked, "I'm interested, tell me about it." In a troubled mood he replied, "I went to four prominent stores today to buy an American flag, and couldn't find one."

Bankruptcies

Writing in *The Wall Street Journal* of May 24, 1982, Thomas Petzinger, Jr. declared businesses that filed for bankruptcy during the first three months of 1982 represented thirty-six for every hour of the business day, a rate that would total 74,676, the largest in U. S. history.

Battles Never Fought

The noted Southern journalist Harry Ashmore wrote a definitive book which he called *An Epitaph for Dixie* (W. W. Norton & Co., 1957). In it he refers to the South's history as something of a personal tragedy. "It seems to me that the tragedy lies not in the battles we lost, but in the battles we never fought."

Beyond Criticism

Despite caustic criticisms, in 1948 Charles Scribner's Sons brought out a little book entitled *Of Flight and Life* which told of the heroic and gratuitous services of Charles A. Lindbergh, Jr., to his country in counseling with the builders of fighter planes at Willow Run and testing these sky speedsters. He actually flew combat missions as a civilian.

Business Failures

Business failures reached all-time highs in 1982-1983. Dun & Bradstreet reported that the week of February 17, 1983, hit a post-Depression record of 713 failures. An increasing number of individuals—about half a million—are taking the recovery advantages provided by our present bankruptcy laws. Some of these persons are making in excess of one-hundred thousand dollars a year.

Democracy for Sale?

A new power broker has entered the political arena—Political Action Committees (PACs). Included are special interest groups that contribute to campaigns of political candidates who favor their posture on given issues. This is a relatively new phenomenon which may ultimately dislodge big business as the determiner of many elections.

Media reported that PAC members spent $182 million in the 1982 elections. Senator Jesse Helms' (R-NC) Congressional Club is said to have spent $9.6 million; the National Conservative Political Action Committee, $9 million; the Fund for a Conservative Majority, $2.5. The largest amount raised by a liberal group—the National Committee for an Effective Congress—was $2.2 million.

Economically Speaking

President Gerald Ford once observed that an economist is a person who tells you there is definitely not going to be a hurricane. Then shortly thereafter, he volunteers to repair and rebuild your roof.[1]

The Gun Craze

A handgun is sold in America every thirteen seconds, adding about two million annually to the nation's estimated arsenal of fifty-five million automatics and revolvers. This works out to be one pistol for every four citizens. America has one of the worst murder records in the world. Consider these facts: In the United States there are 9.7 murders a year per 100,000 people; in Japan, 1.6; in Britain, 1.3; and in West Germany, 1.3.[2]

Honoring the Future

No society is smaller than the one that sees no obligation to later generations. A society earns its place in history by respecting the unclamorous claims of the unborn.[3]

Lest We Forget

Visitors to Honolulu usually see Pearl Harbor. Two hundred years ago Hawaiians called it Wae Momi, "Water of Pearl." In 1861 the United States Navy constructed a fueling station in Honolulu. By 1916 it was the tenth most important naval base in the world. Eventually it became the Fourteenth Naval District, center of Pacific operations. However, we chiefly remember Pearl Harbor as scene of the surprise, dastardly air attack by the Japanese on Sunday morning, December 7, 1941, at six o'clock. On that infamous day, 2,335 American servicemen lost their lives; 1,143 were wounded.

Eighteen of the ninety-seven ships along "Battleship Row" were sunk. The *Arizona* sank in nine minutes with eleven-hundred men aboard. To this day this rusting hulk now a memorial—continues to give off oil, even as memory of the attack alienates thoughtful citizens.

Living in a Pluralistic Society

In commenting on the pluralism of values in America and how technology is reshaping the status quo, Professor John J. Conger of the University of Colorado says: "What we are moving to are values adopted to new relations. We can't get by with just situational ethics. But if we can be tolerant of each other and also care about each other, I can see a very bright future developing in the 1980s."[4]

The Magic of Freedom

On April 8, 1983, before a live audience and on television, in a dramatic effort to illustrate the tragedy that would ensue should America lose her freedom, David Copperfield, the renowned magician, created the illusion that the Statue of Liberty had disappeared. Following the incredible feat, the young man spoke briefly, spontaneously. He declared that he was a son of immigrants, and that his mother pointed with pride to

France's gift of the statue to America. The unveiling was October 28, 1886. That which impressed David Copperfield's mother was not its enormity—the statue and pedestal is 305-feet, six-inches tall and weighs two-hundred-twenty-five tons—but a portion of the poem by Emma Lazarus articulating the basic philosophy of American democracy, especially these two lines: "Give me your tired, your poor,/Your huddled masses yearning to breathe free."

Mr. Copperfield continued that America would remain free so long as people remembered to communicate, to care, and to show compassion. True freedom, he declared, "is magic."

A Man of Letters

The twenty-fifth President of the United States, Theodore Roosevelt, was a powerful and resourceful person, a graduate of Harvard (1880) who was intrigued by history and politics. He is most frequently referred to as a controversial, power-loving President who believed in the "big-stick" approach to problems and who earned the name of "trustbuster." He also won a Nobel peace prize. He was a man of written communications. It is declared that he wrote one-hundred-fifty thousand letters.

No Country

Media reported that one Meyer Lansky, seventy years of age, with a shadowy record, went to Israel in 1969. Eventually, he was refused citizenship and deported from Israel. He went to Zurich, but Switzerland did not want him. Then he flew to Rio de Janeiro, Argentina, Paraguay, Bolivia, Peru, and Panama. Even though he is reputed to have been willing to give a million dollars for citizenship in a country, no one wanted the disclaimed man being sought for several crimes. Eventually he returned to Miami where the FBI awaited him and where he was placed in a hospital with an ailing heart.

It is amazing how little the best of us regard our country until we desperately need it.

Perception

Toward the close of the Civil War, the Confederate cavalry mounted a desperate charge against Washington. President Lincoln rode out to observe the skirmish, near what is now Walter Reed Army Hospital. At six-feet-four-inches, the Chief Executive was a sizable target. Whereupon a Union Army lieutenant shouted, "Get down, you fool." The next day Lincoln wrote to thank the officer, future Supreme Court Justice Oliver Wendell Holmes.[5]

A Political Phenomenon

It is said that Charles Evans Hughes was governor of New York, justice of the Supreme Court, presidential nominee, secretary of state, and chief justice of the United States without lobbying in his own behalf, without spending so much as a postage stamp. Mr. Hughes never sought an office; the office sought him.

Questionable Justice

"Not guilty by reason of insanity." This was the unbelievable sentence recited by Judge Barrington Parker following each of the thirteen charges leveled against John Warnock Hinckley, Jr., for the attempted assassination of President Ronald Reagan. The trial is said to have cost $2.5 million. As would be expected, reactions to the verdict varied from clever maneuvering of language to a travesty of justice. Arthur Eads, district attorney of Bell County, Texas, declared: "Only in the U. S. can a man try to assassinate the leader of the country in front of 125 million people and be found not guilty." Many echoed the sentiments of Eads that the verdict was symptomatic of a runaway leniency in the justice system.[6]

Room for an Immigrant?

In 1894 a ship of the Holland-American Line glided into New York Harbor. It was laden with immigrants. Among them stood a boy holding his father's hand. The sight of the city overwhelmed the youngster, who began to ask questions. "Father, do you know anybody in America?" The sympathetic answer was, "No." "Do you have a job awaiting you?" the lad continued. Against a soft, "No," the troubled youngster asked, "How much money have you, Father? . . . If you don't know anybody in America, and if you haven't a job, and only $450, what are we going to do if you don't get a job and your money runs out?"

"My boy," the father explained, "this is America. It was in this country where a boy, born in a one-room cabin with a dirt floor and lighted by a single window, climbed to the greatest gift within the power of the American people to confer: the presidency. In a land where such a thing could happen, there must be room for a Dutch immigrant who has faith in God and is not afraid to work. There must be a place for us."

And what a place! The little boy who asked so many questions that day later became the powerful preacher and educator of the Reformed Church in America, the Reverend Joseph R. Sizoo.

A Shocking Proposal

In an effort to ease tension between Indians and whites, Patrick Henry, in 1784, proposed intermarriage. The eloquent orator stipulated that when free white males or female Virginians married Indians, the couples would receive ten pounds immediately and five pounds more at the birth of each child. They would also be recipients of tax breaks and free education for their male children up to age twenty-one. With Patrick Henry's persuasiveness the bill passed its first and second readings. However, by time of the third reading, Henry had been elected governor, and without his overt participation, the bill ultimately failed.[7]

How would racial tensions throughout the history of our country been affected had this proposal been approved?

Surviving

In 1959 Dr. Laurence M. Gould, president of Carleton College in Minnesota, gave an address entitled "Why Men Survive." He pointed out that nineteen out of twenty-one notable civilizations had died from within. He asserted that if America is to grow great we must stop gagging at the word *spiritual*. Our task is to rediscover and reassert our faith in the spiritual, nonutilitarian values on which American life has really rested from the beginning.

Awareness

Exodus 33:14-17; Song of Solomon 6:12; Matthew 16:5-12; Mark 16:1-8; Luke 1:46-49; John 14:25-26; Acts 3:19-21

He who is conscious of a debt that he can never repay will be forever paying it.

—G. K. Chesterton

Listen to voices in the upper air,
Nor lose thy simple faith in mysteries.

—Henry Wadsworth Longfellow

Answering the Critics

In the sixteenth century the Italian artist, Raphael Sanzio, was commissioned to paint likenesses of Peter and Paul. When at last the work was finished, the reviewing cardinals of Rome complained "they are too ruddy." Courageously Raphael replied, "They blush on seeing the Church governed by such men as you."

Awareness of His Presence

Dr. Howard Thurman tells of preaching in the chapel at Tuskegee Institute, where he met Dr. George Washington Carver. Sitting in his usual pew, the great scientist and Christian focused on the preacher. "There was the customary rose in his lapel, a Bible in his lap, and a light in his eyes that seemed to be controlled by some inner dimmer switch."[1]

Can You Hear the Good News?

Lloyd C. Douglas had a friend who was a violin teacher. Although not too successful, the old man was imbued with considerable wisdom. One day Douglas asked his friend, "Well, what's the good news today?"

The music master went over to a tuning fork suspended from the ceiling by a cord and struck it with a mallet. "There is the good news for the day," he said. "That, my friend, is 'A.' It was 'A' all day yesterday. It will be 'A' all day tomorrow, next week, and for a thousand years. The soprano upstairs warbles off key; the tenor next door flats his high ones; and the piano across the hall is out of tune. Noise all around me, noise; but that, my friend, is 'A.' "

Comments

These people, Donatus, are the Christians—and I am one of them!
—Cyprian

Thou hast touched me and I am on fire for Thy peace.
—Augustine

Coping in Crisis

On the day of the premiere of *The Nutcracker* in 1954, at five in the afternoon, George Balanchine, the master choreographer, discovered that some of the costumes were not ready. Instead of throwing his weight around or screaming orders to the seamstresses, he picked up a needle and thread and began sewing.[2]

Fairness?

Exclusive sweaters by designer Ralph Lauren, retailing in the United States for approximately four-hundred dollars, are knitted by British pensioners for from $10 to $27 per garment.[3]

Keep at It!

During the 1960 presidential campaign, John Kennedy concluded a moving speech with the story of a judge in Hartford, Connecticut, who was presiding in court one morning in the middle seventeenth century when an eclipse of the sun occurred. The courtroom began to panic. Whereupon the judge rapped for order and said: "If this be the end of the world, let us at least be found doing our duty. Bring in the candles!"

Let the Lanterns Glow

The Swedish painter, Högfeld, back in the sober thirties, illustrated a happy party, with mandolins and Chinese lanterns, joyously floating downstream in their small craft, while from the riverbanks piercing eyes of hungry beasts were waiting for them to step ashore. Surrounded by light and music, the singers were unaware of danger. For better or for worse, most of us go through life this way, giving little thought to danger so long "as the lanterns glow."

Listen for Your Tune

"If a man does not keep pace with his companions," declared Henry David Thoreau, "perhaps it is because he hears a different drummer. Let him step to the music which he hears, however measured or far away." The temptation, of course, is to do the opposite. The Christian, like everyone else, lives under constant pressure to conform, to do what others do, and to have no real individuality.

Living with a Duty

Dag Hammarskjold's staff gave him a surprise birthday party in April of 1958. After a statement of gratitude, he concluded with a line from the Swedish poet Gunnar Ekëlof: "Will the day ever come when joy is great and sorrow small?" The secretary general added these trenchant words: "On the day we feel we are living with a duty, well fulfilled and worth our while, on that day joy is great and we can look on sorrow as being small."

Nonsensical People

In his play, *Our Town,* Thornton Wilder described the atmosphere in a New Hampshire village at the turn of the century. Observing all the pettiness, personal idiosyncrasies, and tragedies of normal life, he wrote: "Wherever you come near the human race, there's layers and layers of nonsense . . ."

Personal Attitude

In *A Practical Guide to Transactional Analysis—I'm OK—You're OK.,* Thomas A. Harris, M. D., projects this emotional stance which is worthy of review:

I'm not OK—You're OK
I'm not OK—You're not OK
I'm OK—You're not OK
I'm OK—You're OK

These attitudes reflect the delicate balance, the psychological ticking that goes on in an individual. Hopefully such an analysis will lead one to a more open self-accepting, self-permitting, healthy, I'm OK-you're OK emotional stance.

Realization

Dr. William Sloane Coffin, Jr., shares an experience at Idlewild Airport. He was having breakfast in one of the small diners, when suddenly there appeared a disheveled, desperate-looking Cuban, waving a beer bottle. In a rasping voice, and in broken English, he harangued his audience to pay more attention to Cuba. He was so obnoxious that finally a waitress said, "This is a business establishment. We don't want no trouble. Now get out!" Obediently, the crestfallen man left. All returned to their breakfasts except an American sailor, who sat staring at his coffee. He said to the waitress, "Look, he wasn't trying to make you no trouble. He was trying to tell you, you *got* trouble."

Rejection of Labels

Chaplain Howard Rice, who is professor of ministry at San Francisco Theological Seminary, himself a victim of multiple sclerosis, says, "Persons with disabilities are not disabled. . . . We are people who are unable to do something which others consider normal. . . . Part of what society means when it calls someone 'normal' is independent. . . . People who are not independent are defined as abnormal." Professor Rice continues, "For people with disabilities, the beginning of freedom is the rejection of the labels and stigmas which others put on us."[4]

Unaware of the Apparent

Paul's defense before Roman Governor Festus and Jewish King Agrippa was mind-boggling to the Roman. But Paul felt that surely Agrippa, being a Jew, should have understood. "For the king knows about these matters, and I speak to him also with confidence; since I am persuaded that none of these things escape his notice; for this has not been done in a corner" (Acts 26:26, NASB).

Self-Awareness

"In the depth of winter, I finally learned that within me there lay an invincible summer."
—Albert Camus

Symbols Of Wholeness

Three objects in the study of the late John Baillie depicted his Christian character: the desk where he wrote, the chair where he read, and the pad where he prayed.

Take Care of Your Parents

There's another, selfish side of taking care of your parents when they're old. If we put our parents away, our children watch and remember. The example we live out before them in treating our parents with love and regard is the example they will follow in treating us when we reach old age. If we mistreat our parents or ignore them in their time of need, our children notice that as well. The example we set may be our own doing.[5]

Take off the Mask

Sven Killsgaard, an enlisted man in the Marine Corps stationed at Camp Pendleton, California, met with a horrible accident while driving through a fog bank, leaving him paralyzed for two months. He has made remarkable progress, but must live with disabilities the rest of his life. Even so, he graduated from seminary in 1983. Sven says, "Those of us who live with disabilities must learn to take off our mask of bitterness."

World Anger

Anatoly Shcharansky, a prisoner of the Soviets accused of being a CIA spy, reminds us of "the universal gravity of souls." He maintains the existence of a bond between persons and the influence of one soul on another.

This declaration was universally confirmed by the reaction of civilized souls to the barbaric shooting down of the Korean Airlines Flight 007 by an alleged Soviet SU-15 August 31, 1983, with 269 persons aboard. Instantly, thoughtful persons asked:

How can America, indeed any peace-loving nation, hope to achieve peace with the paranoid Soviets?

The Bible

Isaiah 30:8; John 1:1; John 1:14; Hebrews 4:12-13

Our Bible is not an amulet, a magical charm, but a book to be read, marked, inwardly digested, and translated into life.
—The late Professor J. Philip Hyatt,
Vanderbilt Divinity School

If I read this book [Bible], I cannot read that book.
—John Ruskin

The Bible

We search the world for truth. We cull
The good, the true, the beautiful,
From graven stone and written scroll,
And all old lower-fields of the soul;
And, weary seekers of the best,
We come back laden from our quest,
To find that all the sages said
Is in the Book our mothers read.
—John Greenleaf Whittier

An Authentic Portrait

In front of old Trinity Church in Boston stands a statue of Phillips Brooks, its great preacher. Behind the figure of the New England minister and bishop, Christ is portrayed standing with his hand on Brooks' shoulder. The story is told of a working woman who paused to gaze upon the figures and asked, "Who is that standing back of Dr. Brooks?" A stranger replied, "That is Christ." The dear soul replied, "It doesn't look like Him."

The only authentic picture we have of Christ is in the Bible, and we miss the whole point of it when we try to make the Bible an ethical scrapbook or a handy, do-it-yourself manual. It is the revelation of Christ.

Difficult Passages

A man once complained to Mark Twain that the Bible was all jumbled up, inconsistent, and filled with passages he could not understand. The humorist replied, "I have more difficulty with the passages I do understand than with the passages I do not understand."

Distributing Bibles

The well-known organization, the Gideons, was founded by three traveling salesmen. Over a twenty-year period, they distributed one-million Bibles! Now it is claimed they distribute a million copies of the Bible every seventeen days!

Don't Lose the Bible in Church!

During the reign of King Josiah, who lived seven centuries before Christ, the law had become hopelessly mixed up with common opinions. Idolatry was flourishing; contempt for theology was common. There was little or no resistance to moral erosion. Josiah, who was made king at age eight, was worried. He desired to be a good king and he was. He wanted to lead his people out of darkness. He turned to the Temple for help. The results were disappointing. The Word of the Lord could not be found! A renovating program on the Temple was started. At last the high priest, Hilkiah, said to Shaphan, his secretary, "I have found the book of the law in the house of the Lord" (2 Kings 22:8).

God's Word

And so, I thought, the anvil of God's Word
For ages the skeptics' blows have beat upon,

But though the noise of falling blows was heard
The anvil is unchanged; the hammers gone.
                                            —John Clifford

The Enduring Word

Scholars generally agree the Bible was written over a span of about twelve-hundred years. We do not have a single book in the handwriting of the original author, but only copies of copies of copies. This by no means lessens its authenticity; it testifies to its indestructibility.

Here It Is!

In his book, *Is God in There?*, Dr. Charles Leber shares a moving experience from a youth meeting in Sao Paulo, Brazil. His interpreter was an American Christian, a college president, and a splendid student of the Portuguese language. During the course of his prepared address Dr. Leber spontaneously interjected, "Not by might, nor by power, but by My Spirit, saith the Lord."

The interpreter hesitated and Leber slowly repeated the sentence. Finally, the interpreter quietly said, "I'm sorry, friend, I've forgotten how to translate that," and turning to the audience asked, "Does anyone here know enough English and Portuguese to translate what the speaker just said?" No one responded.

Dr. Leber whispered, "Skip it, skip it. Let's go on."

As they came down from the rostrum, an enthusiastic boy about twelve years of age pushed through the crowd and joyously exclaimed, "Here it is, mister! Here it is, mister!"[1] The lad had found the sixth verse of the fourth chapter of Zechariah. "Not by might, nor by power, but by my spirit, saith the Lord."

This is the parable of our day. It symbolizes our despair and our hope. When we are able to find and translate God's Word into life, then and only then do we know the Bible.

Holding Up the Bible

A critic of Billy Graham once said: "All he does is to hold up the Bible and shout!" This comment, of course, is capable of more than one interpretation. Positively speaking, however, what more could an evangelist, indeed any Christian, do than hold up the eternal principles and teachings of the Bible, especially the life of the One who fulfilled it?

Like a Mighty Army Moves . . .

There were fourteen generations between Abraham and David; fourteen more between David and the deportation of the Jews to Babylon; and still another fourteen generations before the appearance of the Messiah, but something highly significant was quietly going on in the bloodstream of history.

Looking for Loopholes

Just before W. C. Fields's death, a friend visited his hospital room. The great American comedian was doing something out of character—thumbing through a Bible. "What are you doing, Bill?" asked the caller. Fields thoughtfully replied, "I'm looking for loopholes."

Read Before Acting

When The Bible House was dedicated in Canberra, Australia, the prime minister, Sir Robert Gordon Menzies, shared an interesting experience. He said that while reading law with an eminent constitutional lawyer, whenever a question involving the Constitution of the Commonwealth came up, the seasoned barrister would say, "Now, Menzies, the first thing we ought to do before we become too involved in the decisions given by the courts is to read the Constitution again." The men would sit down and read the legal instrument from beginning to end, saturating themselves in the letter as well as in the spirit of the law before attempting to concentrate on the forthcoming case. To Menzies it illustrated an old Latin maxim: "Melius est petere fontes quam sectare rivulos." ("It is better to seek the fountainhead than to divide up the little streams.")

Read with Diligence

What Francis Bacon, the seventeenth-century English philosopher, said about reading in general applies with peculiar relevancy to the Bible: "Some books," he maintained, "are to be tasted, others to be swallowed, and some few to be chewed and digested"; that is, some books are to be read only in parts; others to be read, but not curiously; and some few to be read wholly, and with diligence and attention. The Bible belongs in the last group.

Some Comments

To me the gospel is just one great figure standing with outstretched arms.

—Phillips Brooks

There is only one Book.

—Sir Walter Scott

Bible stories are like empty cups for people to fill with their own experiences and drink from them over and over again.

—Anne Morrow Lindbergh

Still the Best-Seller

Even though over one-thousand new books are published every day—not counting pamphlets, booklets, and government reports—the Bible remains the world's best-seller. It has been translated into more languages and dialects than any other book. Yet, the Bible is not read as often or with as much understanding as its wide circulation might suggest.

Their Rhetoric

Delete the influence of the Bible from the writings of Blake, Thoreau, Emerson, T. S. Eliot, and Winston Churchill, and their contributions would be different. The addresses of Lincoln, the measured prose of Washington, and the inspired speeches of Patrick Henry had their roots in the Bible.

To Start Something

We need to go back to the Bible, we who have not read a word of it for many years. We need to buy a modern printing and translation and read the old, old Word as if it were intended only for ourselves. We are not to be surprised if it does not put an end to all our problems; for the Bible was not intended to finish anything but to start something.[2]

What If Napoleon?

It is claimed that once Napoleon Bonaparte toyed with the idea of becoming a book merchant. Such a probability stirs the imagination. What if Napoleon had devoted himself to selling books—including the Bible—instead of waging war!

Where It Begins

"The Story of the New Testament," says Dr. M. Jack Suggs in *The Layman Reads His Bible,* "begins with a Man who wrote no part of it but was responsible for all of it."

Wycliffe's Royalty

John Wycliffe and his colleagues, using the text of Jerome, produced the first complete translation of the Bible in 1382. Wycliffe's translation was a lasting contribution to Christendom. His reward for sharing the Scripture? Critics dug up and burned his bones.

Celebrations

Psalm 33:12a; 1 Timothy 3:15-16a; 2 Timothy 2:15; Luke 17:15-16

The red-letter days now become, to all intents and purposes, dead-letter days.

—Charles Lamb

Children's Day

Inspired Action

In October, 1880, when J. H. Garrison was editor of *The Christian,* a weekly publication of the Disciples of Christ, he was invited to address the national convention meeting in Louisville, Kentucky. The night before his departure, as they were having family prayers, Garrison asked for God's guidance at the convention and mentioned the needs of people around the world. Afterwards his two boys, six and ten, and a little niece who lived with them, "gathered up their pennies and nickels and tied them up in a little bag and brought them to me, wholly unsolicited, saying, 'Here is all the money we have and we want it to go to the people who have never heard about Jesus.' "

The amount? $1.13.

Deeply moved, Garrison referred to the experience during the course of his address in Louisville. He dramatically asked, "Brethren, what will you do with these children's offerings? At present you have no place for it—no fund in which I can place it."

Result? The Foreign Missionary Society of the Christian Church (Disciples of Christ) was born. Isaiah's words, though in another context, are nonetheless pertinent: "And a little child shall lead them" (11:6).

A Star Is Born

I heard Red Skelton tell this story. It concerned his boyhood in Vincennes, Indiana. He was eight years old. One evening as he stood selling his papers, a stranger appeared and asked what was going on in town. Politely he replied that a comedian was giving a show down at the theater. The stranger inquired if the lad planned to go. Young Skelton indicated he would like to, but first he had to sell his papers. Persisting, the gentleman asked if he would go if he had a ticket. Thoughtfully the lad said he would have to ask his mother. Whereupon the kind man bought all of Red's papers and agreed on a meeting place before the show.

The grateful and excited boy had a seat in the center balcony. When the curtain went up, Red peered down and, to his utter amazement, there stood the man who had bought his papers—Ed Wynn! Red Skelton was so thrilled that at intermission he made his way through the crowd to backstage to see Mr. Wynn, who showed him many things. Indeed, the comedian held up the little fellow to a peephole in the curtain so he could see the audience.

Skelton declared that in that high moment he knew he wanted to be a comedian.

Father's Day

"Love, Father"

Dr. Burris Jenkins was a popular preacher and writer of a generation ago. When his son went to college, Jenkins admonished him not to join a certain fraternity. This, of course, was the very fraternity young Jenkins joined. For months he lived with the secret. Then, as he spoke to a church youth group one night, he was smitten by a sense of unworthiness. Returning to his room, he wrote his father in detail of his disobedience. Two days later he received this wire: "It's all right. I forgive you. I knew it two days after you did it. Love, Father."

Too Late

"'O my son Absalom, my son, my son Absalom! Would I had died instead of you, O Absalom, my son, my son!" (2 Sam. 18:33b). The sun and wind of the centuries have failed to dry the tears or still the anguish of this exceedingly sorrowful cry. Who was this distraught person? A neurotic parent? No, a king—King David!

David was the first king in history to be selected according to ability rather than birth. He was courageous. His character crowned him king. He was considerate and in many ways magnanimous. Twice he spared the life of his enemy Saul. In spite of his sins, the people of Judah loved him. David was a good ruler, a fine soldier, and a wise statesman. He did not fail as king. He failed as father. He was too involved in royal responsibilities to relate adequately to his family.

While young Absalom was on reconnaissance with his father's troops, his long hair became entangled in the limbs of a tree, making him an easy prey for the enemy. The king was crushed by the news of his son's death because he realized the accident could have been avoided. David's anguish was increased by the knowledge that he had not been a worthy example.

This is a continuing and familiar pattern of busy fathers. They have a way of coming too late to the needs of their children.

Independence Day

Do You Share the Dream?

Dr. George McLeod of Scotland once defined a Confucian as "one who pays occasional visits to the shrines of his ancestors." This is commendable and therapeutic, provided one does not reminisce too long or become mesmerized by past glory.

On July 4, 1776, our forefathers signed the Declaration of

Independence. We need to reexamine the vision and philosophy of those who fashioned a dream in Philadelphia.

When citizenship seems purchasable, politics puissant, and the image of America distorted, let us view our country with clearer hearts.

Drama and Dedication

During the Continental Congress of 1776 the committee selected a tall, rangy, auburn-haired Virginian named Thomas Jefferson to draft a proposition paper. He secluded himself and, with minimum help, within about seventeen days produced one of the most profound and beautiful political documents ever penned. British Prime Minister William Gladstone later said it was an "inspired instrument." Congress debated the document, made a few changes, and then signed it with great fanfare, ringing of the Liberty Bell, the making of clever speeches, and costly commitments.

Caesar Rodney, ill with a malignant disease that covered part of his face, rode all day and all night from Dover, Delaware, in time to stride, booted and spurred, into the Assembly Hall in Philadelphia to bark: "I vote for independence."

John Hancock led off the formal signing with his bold signature, saying he wanted George III to be able to read it without his specs.

Benjamin Franklin quipped: "We shall have to hang together, or assuredly we shall all hang separately."

Among many magnificent statements in this eloquent and comprehensive document, that which most succinctly characterizes the American stance and spirit is this impeccable sentence:

> We hold these truths to be self-evident, that all men are created equal, that they are endowed by their Creator with certain unalienable Rights, that among these are Life, Liberty and the pursuit of Happiness.

Shared Purpose

Toward the end of the Declaration of Independence we find a summary sentence which places everything in perspective: "And for the support of this Declaration, with a firm reliance on the protection of Divine Providence, we mutually pledge to each other our Lives, our Fortunes, and our sacred Honor."

This is a unique creed. The signers believed something very special was happening and that God would see them through. It was a new and courageous covenant, men mutually pledging their lives, their fortunes, and their sacred honor! This is breathtaking and inconceivable in the fermentation of today's world.

Have we forgotten the high price some of our founding Fathers paid for their freedom? Have we forgotten that nine signers of the Declaration of Independence did not survive the war? Many lost their homes and fortunes.

Thomas Nelson of Virginia directed bombardment of his own mansion at Yorktown. It was occupied by Cornwallis. Nelson also undertook to raise $2 million to repay the French fleet for its assistance. The war notes he redeemed cost him his fortune. He died in poverty. This was his sacred honor.

Francis Lewis, a wealthy New York trader, lost everything he had. His wife was thrown into prison and died shortly after her release.

Richard Stockton of New Jersey, a Princeton graduate, lost his wealth, property, and magnificent library. He was imprisoned and died following the war.

These illustrations of sacred honor should suffice to remind us that the Fourth of July commemorates a costly freedom, one that documented the rhetoric of the signers of the Declaration of Independence.

Labor Day

God's Labor Union!

Despite reported acts of violence, exploitation, and corruption, much has been accomplished to improve and dignify American workers since June 28, 1894, when congress designated the first Monday in September as Labor Day, a legal holiday. Today's labyrinth of labor unions covers virtually the entire spectrum of society, professions included.

Whatever your likes or dislikes regarding labor unions, I believe they are here to stay. But long before the Coal Miners' Act of 1911, obliteration of sweat shops, child labor, and refinements in negotiations and working conditions, God's labor force, the church of Jesus Christ, was at work! The Lord is depending on the committed community to bring in a better day. Two admonitions will suffice:

> The harvest is plentiful, but the laborers are few; pray therefore the Lord of the harvest to send out laborers into his harvest (Matt. 9:37-38).
>
> We must work the works of him who sent me, while it is day; night comes, when no one can work (John 9:4).

Hollywood Hallucinations

Aspiring actors and actresses look to Hollywood as the eternal panacea. Yet, according to Screen Actors Guild with a membership of some fifty-two thousand, 81 percent earned less than five thousand dollars in 1982. The big-money people —fifty thousand dollars and more—constitute only 2.6 percent of the membership. Television commercials provide performers with about half their annual income. Furthermore, the Guild, as reported to the press, declares 85 percent of its members are unemployed on any given day of the year.

Making a Living or Making a Life?

Moses was a herdsman; David was a shepherd; Paul a tent-maker; Luke a physician; Lydia a merchant; and Jesus a carpenter. Carey was a cobbler; Beethoven a musician, and George Washington Carver a chemist. God's labor union is all-inclusive and is concerned with far more than bargaining strategy, hours and wages, and economic battering rams. It is compassionately concerned with the nature, needs, and destiny of persons.

Labor Day Sunday compels us to face the perennial problems associated with making a living and making a life. Paul's admonition to the Corinthians is altogether pertinent, "each man's work will become manifest" (1 Cor. 3:13).

Show Him Your Hands!

During the illustrious career of S. Parkes Cadman, a spacious and sincere soul who was a preacher of unusual abilities and pastor of Central Congregational Church, Brooklyn, New York, he was called to a humble home. There, on a thin, clean bed lay a dying woman. She was a member of Cadman's church. She was nearing the border and craved words of comfort from her minister before starting the Jerusalem journey. The pastor sat listening to his distressed and dying parishioner as she recounted her life. For many years she had been breadwinner for a large family. Her days were long, laboriously spent, earning money to pay the bills. In fact, she was the charwoman for the neighborhood.

After confessing her unsung career, she turned to her minister and wistfully asked, "When I stand before my Maker, what shall I do?"

Cadman, who had already noticed her calloused hands, and realizing now, more than ever, that they had been used unselfishly for others, said in an affectionately, comforting voice, "Show Him your hands!"

Memorial Day

Flatter Their Souls with Deeds

How shall we honor them, our Deathless Dead?
With strew of laurel and the stately tread?
With blaze of banners brightening overhead?
Nay, not alone these cheaper praises bring:
They will not have this easy honoring.
How shall we honor them, our Deathless Dead?
How keep their mighty memories alive?
In him who feels their passion, they survive!
Flatter their souls with deeds, and all is said![1]

We Still Remember Them

There is a handsome bronze plaque on the south front of the rotunda at the University of Virginia honoring its students who made the supreme sacrifice in World War I. Conspicuously clear and haunting are these lines:
They shall grow not old, as we that are left
grow old;
Age shall not weary them nor the years condemn.
At the going down of the sun and in the morning
we will remember them.[2]

Mother's Day

A Loving Mother

Charles W. Eliot, Harvard's esteemed president of yesteryear, was born with a disfiguring birthmark. At first it was most difficult for his mother to accept. All the while, however, she was schooling herself in the art of loving her unattractive child, saying as she met his needs, "He is my son, he is my son."

With the passing years, Mrs. Eliot had every right to say, and with pride, "He is my son." One honor after another marked

Eliot's achievements until at last, in 1869, the son of Boston's mayor was elected president of Harvard University.

What if he had not been loved in his home?

A School in the Home

Samuel and Susanna Wesley were dedicated Christians. Samuel was a rector and his wife was a daughter of the manse. Altogether they had nineteen children. John was the fifteenth child and Charles, the eighteenth. Eleven of their children died; eight lived. Think of their heartaches!

There were precious few conveniences in those days: no automatic washers; no electric refrigerators; no running water in the home; no telephone; no radio; no quick means of communication or travel. Yet we read that Susanna Wesley expected each child to know the alphabet by the time he/she was five years old. At six, he/she started to school in their big living room. Susanna taught her children six hours a day—from nine to twelve and from two to five. Later, of course, they went to various formal schools, including Oxford.

Furthermore, she gave one hour a day each week to each child's spiritual development. It made such a profound impression on her children that later, in times of distress, her sons declared that they wished they might have the privilege of counseling with their mother again.

New Year's Day

High Resolves

The New Year is traditionally a time of high resolves and vocal intentions. Today this is even more imperative. If there was ever a time when we need to scrub our slates, make reparations for our reprisals, and offer penitence for our sins, it is now. It is essential to begin with God. In Him we begin; in Him we end.

The curtain of time has rung down on another year. No

amount of agonizing will rewrite the witness of your life and mine. But God has brought us to the land of beginning again, and through His grace we may yet experience a more perfect day.

All aspirants should heed and be heartened by Isaiah's assurance: "Though your sins are like scarlet, they shall be as white as snow; though they are red like crimson, they shall become like wool" (Isa. 1:18).

Leftovers!

Perry Barlow's provocative cartoon of a man and wife visiting a year-end automobile sale is pertinent. The weary husband, fatigued from Christmas pressures, sits reading a sign in a showroom, "A Leftover Model." And so are we all, thank God!

Thanksgiving

The Founders

On December 20, 1606, three bold boats sailed down the Thames in London, embarking on a voyage to search for a safe port along the shores of Virginia. *Susan Constant,* flagship of Sir Christopher Newport's fleet, 110 feet, 7 inches long, was by far the largest vessel. Though she had only nineteen bunks, she carried fifty-four passengers and a crew of seventeen. She was a sturdy ship with the crudest of accommodations. No one had any privacy except the captain. There was no galley. When weather permitted, food was cooked in sand pots on deck.

The second largest ship in this history-making voyage was the *Godspeed.* It was 69 feet, 2 inches overall, and had cramped sleeping quarters for twelve, yet she listed thirty-nine passengers and a crew of thirteen.

Quite appropriately, one of the boats used by the founders was the *Discovery.* This small sailing craft displaced about twenty tons of water and measured 50 feet, 2 1/4 inches from stem to stern. The rough "below" was partitioned for four bunks. Yet she brought over twelve passengers and a crew of nine.

It required 128 days for the voyage. The founders arrived at Cape Henry, Virginia, April 26, 1607, at four o'clock in the morning. On this windswept shore, the grateful settlers raised a "large wooden cross" and thanked God for their safe arrival. Jamestown was selected as their site on May 14. These were dark and daring days. The disease-infested swamps, together with Indian warfare, claimed many. Food was scarce. Several hundred colonists came to Virginia in the first six years of her founding, and at one point only sixty persons survived.

On June 7, 1610, it was decided to abandon the settlement. The colonists sailed down the James River once again to challenge the Atlantic. Next morning, Sir Thomas Gates, lieutenant governor of the colony, received word that Lord De la Warr had arrived at Point Comfort with settlers and supplies. Governor Gates returned to the empty fort and, falling on his knees, thanked God the colony had been saved.

The Pilgrims

Dramatic and significant is the story of the Pilgrims. On December 21, 1620, the voyaging *Mayflower* dropped anchor in Plymouth Bay, with Captain Christopher Jones at her helm. It had been a grueling voyage, taking the one-hundred-twenty-ton-capacity ship sixty-six days to make the perilous crossing. There had been disease, anxiety, and childbirth among the 102 courageous passengers. Furthermore, they arrived on the bleak New England shore during a hard winter which ultimately claimed half of their number. However, when spring came and the captain of the *Mayflower* offered free passage to anyone desiring to return, not a single person accepted.

The fidelity of the forty-one men, who while still aboard the *Mayflower* had signed the famous Compact beginning with the words, "In ye name of God Amen," was taking on visible meaning. These chivalrous souls had dedicated themselves to the total causes of freedom. They had come to a wilderness to carve out a better way of life. Faith prompted the voyage; faith sustained the Pilgrims and their religious convictions constrained them to raise their voices in praise. Their hardships, sacrifice, devotion, concept of government, and vigorous religion all remind us of those who sought a country.

Christlikeness

Exodus 2:1-6; Isaiah 49:15; Matthew 15:32; Luke 10:33-34;
Romans 1:1-7

Life is an adventure in forgiveness.

—Norman Cousins

Christ the transforming Light
Touches this heart of mine
Piercing the darkest night
Making His glory shine.

—J. Wilbur Chapman

Beyond Self

During the early days of the Confederacy, Robert E. Lee was severely criticized by General W. H. C. Whiting. Most persons would have retaliated. One day, President Jefferson Davis invited General Lee to share with him his appraisal of General Whiting. The noble Virginian commended Whiting in highest terms. Whereupon, an officer took General Lee aside to remind him of General Whiting's verbiage against him. To which Lee replied: "I understood that the President desired to know my opinion of Whiting, not Whiting's opinion of me."

Call Me Eccentric

When narcotic detectives raided a loft apartment in a depressed neighborhood in New York City, their eyes and hearts were shockingly opened. The dark corridors and dingy rooms were crowded with twisted, ill-fed, and ill-clothed derelicts. Out of this human scrap heap, the police arrested six men for carrying hypodermic needles and heroin. Apprehensive of the host of this heterogenous company, the detectives charged him with harboring drug addicts.

At police headquarters, the meek-looking and mild-mannered man claimed that he had chosen to live among these people to provide them with food, shelter, and clothing. His door was open to all. He did not realize he was breaking the law in extending compassion. Investigation revealed that the operator of this strange hostel was neither a vagrant nor a drug habitue. The dedicated man turned out to be John Sargent Cram, a millionaire, who had been educated at Princeton and Oxford. To avoid the "rigmarole" of organized charity, he had moved into the undesirable neighborhood and had gone to work.

After his trial and acquittal, Cram was admonished not to take in drug addicts. Later he said to a reporter, "I don't know if my work does any good, but I don't think it does any harm. . . . I'm quite happy, you know. I am anything but a despondent person. Call me eccentric. Call it by reason for being. I have no other!"[1]

Compassion

Jean Bourgeois, age forty-five, a Belgian mountain climber, on December 30, 1982, fell a distance of 164 feet from a height of 19,800 on the Tibetan side of Mount Everest. Presumed dead, Bourgeois eventually showed up in a Tibetan village. The villagers asked, "Are you a Yeti (Abominable Snowman)?" After he explained his plight to them, the villagers provided food, shelter, and medical care for this stranger and arranged transportation to Nepal.

Discernment

During the most difficult days of Abraham Lincoln's mercantile adventure with his partner Barry, he demonstrated a remarkable characteristic: sensitivity. The store was not going well. In fact, they were gradually going broke. Barry said, "Abe, how long do you think we can hold out?" He is reported as saying: "I don't know. . . . If we have to sell out I should hope we would have enough left for me to buy *Blackstone's Commentary on English Law*."

A few days later, a rickety, dust-covered wagon stopped in front of their store. A weather-beaten, gaunt man stuck his head out. By his side was the pinched face of his wife and two small children. The travelers declared they were headed west and had run out of money and wanted to know if the merchants would be interested in buying a barrel. There were many empty barrels in the store, as well as barrels of merchandise they could not sell, but as Lincoln looked into the faces of anxiety and need, he said, "Well, I guess a fellow could always use a good barrel. What do you want for it?"

"Fifty cents."

Lincoln reached into his pocket and gave the man fifty cents, reputed to have been practically his last dime.

"Dr. Witten's Boys"

Elsewhere in this volume I mentioned the phenomenal physician who made a home for boys from difficult and deserted situations. During the course of preparing this book I was invited back to our first parish, Tazewell Christian Church, Tazewell, Virginia, to participate in its centennial celebration. One evening was designated "Dr. Witten's Boys." A goodly number of his adopted sons were present. There were movies

and testimonials. One of the "boys"—a handsome businessman—was moderator. This is his story:

Dr. Jack Witten was born in Tazewell County, attended local
schools and The Medical College of Virginia, where he left an
enviable academic record. He chose to practice medicine in the
hills of southwest Virginia. Being disappointed in love, he
never married. One night as he was ministering to a dying
mother in a humble home, she plaintively asked, "Who will
take care of my little boy?" "I will," said Dr. Witten. And that
was the beginning of his boy collection.

Even though they lived in a spacious house with an adequate
supporting staff of workers, each boy had a specific responsibility. Beneath the rather martial atmosphere that permeated
the place, there was bonding love. The master of ceremonies
declared that 300 boys crossed Witten's threshold, and 150 of
them received housing and schooling, many attending prestigious colleges and universities. Think of it!

In a voice heavy with emotion, the spokesman said, "Doc
will always live in our hearts."

What implementation of the Lord's words: "Truly, I say to
you, as you did it to one of the least of these my brethren, you
did it to me" (Matt. 25:40).

Forgiveness

Near the end of Irving Stone's powerful novel, *Love Is Eternal,*
about Mary Todd and Abraham Lincoln, there is a moving
conversation between Mrs. Lincoln and the President's body-
guard, Parker, who had been summoned to Mrs. Lincoln's
room.

"Why were you not at the door to keep the assassin out?"
she demanded.

With head bowed, Parker replied, "I have bitterly repented
it. But I did not believe that anyone would try to kill so good
a man in such a public place. The belief made me careless. I was

attracted by the play, and did not see the assassin enter the box."

"You should have seen him. You had no business to be careless." With this, Mrs. Lincoln fell back on her pillow and covered her face with her hands, and from deep emotion, said: "Go now. It's not you I can't forgive; it's the assassin."

Tad, who had spent that miserable night beneath his father's desk in the executive office, drawled, "If Pa had lived, he would have forgiven the man who shot him. Pa forgave everybody."[2]

The comment is reminiscent of Another who, having given His all to reveal love, was rejected by His own and killed by those who should have protected Him. Yet in the agonies of death He prayed: "Father, forgive them; for they know not what they do" (Luke 23:34).

A Friend Indeed!

When in Rhodesia, now Zimbabwe, I asked a friend why Cecil Rhodes did not participate in the gold rush days to augment his fortune in diamonds. "The story goes," he said, "that during the early leasing of the better gold fields, a friend of Rhodes lay desperately ill. The popular and immensely wealthy Rhodes denied himself the privilege of participating in the bidding to sit by his friend's bed, day and night, until he died."

Good Samaritan

The December 27, 1971 issue of *Time* featured an article entitled, "The Do-Gooders." In reality, it is a modern interpretation of the good Samaritan. It reminds us of individuals who are committed to serving others. Do-gooders are not popular. They never have been, except when needed. Currently the term is frequently used sarcastically or in some derogatory manner. Often it is associated with insincere church members whose stance and spirit in the world fail to coincide with their

Sunday profiles. This is a pity, because believers are supposed to be do-gooders, not in a sentimental, sensational, self-righteous way, but in the truest sense of compassion.

Greater Love Has No One . . .

Various persons have observed that no one has any more religion than he or she can demonstrate in an emergency. This was certainly true of Arland D. Williams, Jr., a bank examiner with the Federal Reserve System in Atlanta, who was aboard the ill-fated Boeing 737 that crashed in the frigid Potomac River shortly after taking off from Washington's National Airport, January 13, 1982.

Identification of the hero was announced in June of 1983. Representatives from the Coast Guard said when a helicopter lowered a line to survivors, Williams indicated he was trapped (it was later discovered his seat belt was jammed) and passed "the line on to other injured persons." By his not grabbing the rescue line, thus saving valuable time, other passengers were saved.

In presenting the medal to Williams's mother, Virginia L. Williams, Mattoon, Illinois, his teenage son, Arland D. Williams, III, and daughter, Leslie Ann Williams, President Reagan said: "You can live with tremendous pride in your father." (Read John 15:13).

How Do You Think Jesus Looked?

A minister filling in for a teacher of a young boys' class asked, "What do you think Jesus was like?"

Doubtless the pastor expected an answer like: He was a good man; He was a poet; He was a carpenter; He was like God. But no.

One little fellow raised his hand and replied, "I think Jesus was like my Sunday School teacher."

Has anyone ever compared your demeanor and deeds to those of Jesus?

Humble Hero

Lenny Skutnik, a fourteen-thousand-dollar-a-year congressional clerk, was praised by the president, received a thundering ovation from congress, was the personal guest of at least two governors, and received thousands of letters from admirers. All this was because he threw off his coat, dived in the icy Potomac River, January 13, 1982, and rescued Priscilla Tirado from the ill-fated Air Florida Boeing 737 that crashed after hitting a bridge and sank in the waters below. The shy, soft-spoken Skutnik, not overly impressed with himself, commented: "It could have been anybody, I just happened to be there."

Judge Not

A strange but commendable custom existed among the Omaha Indians. When a brave left the bounds of his tribe and would be gone for a while, a campfire council was held on the eve of his departure. Just before the embers fell into ash, the nomad was asked to stand; his great physique silhouetted against the dying flames. At last the warrior was implored to pray: "Great Spirit, help me never to judge another until I have walked two weeks in his moccasins."

A Life at Stake!

G. Ray Jordan relates this story in *Religion that Is Eternal* (Macmillan, 1960). It centers around the life of the late Rabbi Cohen of Texas during the presidency of William H. Taft. The noted Jewish leader did not sleep well one night because he was concentrating on how to help a certain refugee. Next morning he said to his wife: "Pack my bag; I am going to Washington." On arriving in the capital city he was sorry to learn that the Department of Labor still insisted the case of Lemcauk, the refugee, was one of obvious illegal entry.

The rabbi then called his congressman, insisting that he give him an entree to the President of the United States. Although

President Taft was kind and friendly, he told the rabbi that the Lemcauk case was in the hands of the Department and that they had rendered a decision. Realizing that he had lost, the rabbi stood up to leave and thanked the President for seeing him.

"I am sorry this had to happen to you, Rabbi Cohen," President Taft said, "but allow me to say that I certainly admire the way you Jews help each other—to travel all the way from Galveston, Texas, when a member of your faith is in trouble."

"Member of my faith? This man is not a Jew," said the rabbi, "he is a Greek Catholic."

The President's face changed, and in low tones he said: "You mean to say you traveled all the way up here at your own expense to help out a Greek Catholic?"

"He is in trouble; they are going to deport him on the next ship. . . . He will face a firing squad when he gets back to Russia. He is a human being, Mr. President. A human life is at stake, that is the way I see it."

"Sit down, Rabbi," said the President. He rang for his secretary and gave this wire: "To the Chief Inspector of Immigration at Galveston: Hold Lemcauk in Galveston and release in the custody of Rabbi Cohen on his return." Then he added, "They'll hear direct from the Department."[3]

Loving Spirit

Jonathan Edwards was born September 5, 1703, in East Windsor, Connecticut, where his father was minister of the village church for sixty-four years. Jonathan was a bright boy. He entered Yale at thirteen and graduated at seventeen. Eventually he became assistant to his grandfather, Solomon Stoddard, pastor of the Congregational Church in Northampton, Massachusetts. When Dr. Stoddard died, Jonathan succeeded him at the age of twenty-six. Five years later he stepped into pulpit fame as one of America's most provocative theologians and preachers.

In 1744 controversy developed in his congregation. Gossip made its rounds. Not a single soul united with his church for four years. Agitation for a new minister spread. Personal animosities grew. Finally, in 1750, the church dismissed its minister. Edwards was then forty-seven and had a wife and ten children to support.

The members of Northampton Church soon discovered that their pastor was not easily replaced. His stature was far larger than they had surmised. A bit chagrined, officers of the congregation asked Dr. Edwards if he would supply until his successor was determined. With remarkable grace and effectiveness, Jonathan Edwards returned to the pulpit from which he had been dismissed. After this interim service, the only parish available to the deposed pastor was a small one near Stockbridge, Massachusetts, where he also served as missionary to the Housatonic Indians.

Despite economic hardship and personal embarrassment, the dedicated minister maintained a beautiful and forgiving spirit. It was in this obscure parish that Jonathan Edwards wrote some of his most important works, including *The Freedom of the Will.* Seven years after his dismissal from the prominent pulpit in Northampton, he was called to the presidency of the College of New Jersey, which is now Princeton.

Personal Peace

Show Me the Way to Go Home was Red Barber's spiritual autobiography, a pilgrimage of faith. This noted sports announcer of a few years ago shared his anger with God for taking his mother when she was quite young. Red was so resentful that he stayed away from church for ten years. Eventually, through touch-and-go experiences with his wife, who lost two babies and almost the third, he came to himself. Ultimately he attained the distinction of becoming a lay leader in the Episcopal church.

Red Barber's father was railroad engineer in North Carolina, a good man, quiet, who became increasingly stolid after his wife's death. When his own death was imminent, none of the relatives could remember if the old man had ever been baptized. Deafness made conversation difficult. With his father sitting up in a chair and all but oblivious to what was going on, after the custom of the Episcopal Church, Red baptized his father.

The next day, to everyone's astonishment, the senior Barber raised his head and stuttered, "I want to see a preacher." Being in a Baptist home, they sent for a Baptist pastor who read Scripture and prayed. Afterwards the young minister took the old man's hand for a moment. William Lanier Barber looked him in the eye and with steady voice said, "All my life I have loved God Almighty. That will have to be enough for me now."

Red Barber declared it was the most beautiful, complete confession of a man's faith he had ever witnessed.

Later that afternoon Mr. Barber said three things to his son. "Walter, I want you to have my watch; you are the only one in the family with any sense of time."

Then he said, "Walter, I love you."

His final admonition: "Walter, go on back to your job."

How human can you get? How Christian can you become? The essence of being yourself is when you are yourself before God! Before your family! Before death!

Prophets of Peace

In *Chronicle of a Generation*, Raymond B. Fosdick, referring to the continuing influence of the American prophet of peace, Woodrow Wilson, wrote, "From his grave his ideals have ruled the future." In a far greater sense, the resurrected Christ seeks to serve and save our world.

Reconciliation

In his book *Roads We Travel*, the late Frank Pippin, of the Community Christian Church, Kansas City, tells the story of a famed French artist who lived a considerable distance from Paris and who lured a famous Parisian physician to come to his estate under the pretext of a serious illness. When the doctor arrived, he discovered no one was seriously ill but the family dog had a broken leg and he was asked to fix it. Though outraged, the eminent doctor said not a word but set the dog's leg and returned to the city.

Months later the noted physician, in an effort to get even, invited the artist to Paris to do some painting for him. The artist responded. Upon arriving at the given address, the doctor, in an arrogant mood, gave him a bucket of yellow paint saying, "There is a bookcase with no glass doors. . . . Please paint the wooden doors with yellow paint. That's all."

The artist, sensing the physician's spirit of tit for tat, was not enraged, but accepted the challenge and did a breathtaking scene on each of the wooden doors. When finished the doctor was enthralled, as was every patient who entered his office. The doctor apologized to the artist and the artist to the doctor.

Jesus said, "The kingdom of God is not coming with signs to be observed; nor will they say 'Lo, here it is!' or 'There!' for behold, the Kingdom of God is in the midst of you" (Luke 17:20*b*-21).

Saint of the Streets

In *Something Beautiful for God*, Malcolm Muggeridge refers to Mother Teresa of Calcutta as "blest with certainties." This saintly soul, struggling against inconceivable odds, is committed to bringing light, hope, and love to derelicts of India. A growing confidence in God and faith in the presence of Christ keep her going. She claims that whenever a homeless child cries she hears the Babe in Bethlehem.

Suffering Love

Wilfred Grenfell was once asked what influenced him to give himself unreservedly to Christian missions. Slowly he told this story: "Into a hospital where I was a resident physician, a woman was brought one night terribly burned. Immediately it was evident there was no hope for her. Her husband had come home drunk and had thrown a paraffin lamp over her. The police were summoned and at last they brought in the half-sobered husband. The magistrate leaned over the bed and insisted that the patient tell the police exactly what happened. He impressed upon her the importance of telling the whole truth as she only had a little while to live.

"The poor soul turned her face from side to side, avoiding facing her husband, who stood at the foot of the bed. Finally her eyes rested on his strong hands, following them up his arms and shoulders and then across to his face. Their eyes met. Her expression of suffering momentarily disappeared, as tenderness and love colored her countenance. She looked at the magistrate and calmly said, 'Sir, it was just an accident,' and fell back on her pillow, dead."

Grenfell added: "This was like God, and God is like that. His love sees through our sins."

Unmaking Enemies

Time's cover story for April 25, 1983, featured the amazing congressman from Florida, Claude Pepper. Well into his eighties, he continues to work long days and nights. Back in the 1950s he fell on hard times in his party, and was soundly beaten for his senatorial seat by George Smathers. While the tough and tender old politician is not known for holding grudges, it was not until 1982 that he fully forgave Smathers for his campaign tactics.

It came about in this way: An aide suggested that they ask Smathers' law firm for a campaign gift. Reluctantly, the good

Baptist agreed and was surprised to receive a check for three-hundred-fifty dollars. Later, in the House dining room, Pepper approached Smathers and solemnly said, "You know that check you sent in for my campaign? Well, it bounced." It had not, of course, and when George Smathers realized Claude Pepper was joking, "both knew that their enmity was over."

Christmas
Isaiah 9:6; Matthew 2:1-6; Matthew 2:10-12; Luke 2:1-20

Glory to God, this wondrous morn,
On earth the Saviour Christ is born.
　　　　　　　　　—Bliss Carman

Have you seen God's Christmas tree in the sky,
With its trillions of tapers blazing high?
　　　　　　　　　—Angela Morgan

Advent, a Season of Expectancy

Advent, the penitential period embracing the four Sundays before Christmas, is a time of reflection on ancient promises and preparation for the continual coming of Christ's spirit into the world. An appropriate epistle for any Advent Sunday: Romans 13:11-14.

An Ancient Greeting

The Italian architect-believer, Fra Giovanni, wrote in 1513:

I salute you. There is nothing I can give you which you have not;
　　but there is much that, while I cannot give you, you can take.
No heaven can come to us unless our hearts find rest in it today.
　　Take heaven . . .
No peace lies in the future which is not hidden in the present.
　　Take peace . . .

The gloom of the world is but a shadow; behind it, yet within our
reach is joy. Take joy . . .
And so at this Christmas time I greet you with the prayer that for
you, now and forever, the day breaks and the shadows flee
away.[1]

Another Bethlehem!

Oklahoma City made startling and shocking news Sunday
morning, December 6, 1964. A thirty-one-year-old mother
gave birth to a child on the sidewalk at the corner of Sheridan
and Broadway. A curious crowd "watched without helping."
The woman and her baby lay on the pavement for about forty-
five minutes in a temperature of about thirty-four degrees.

A visitor from Tulsa summoned a taxi. When the cab
arrived, however, the driver refused to take the mother to the
hospital. Then the helpful stranger called the police, to no
avail. During the time the woman lay on the sidewalk, two
patrol cars passed the scene and neither stopped.

A former state representative chanced that way, stopped and
called the fire department for an ambulance. He also sent a man
across the street to a hotel to borrow a blanket, but a porter
refused him. Meanwhile, the rescue squad arrived. While waiting for an ambulance, Captain Bill Latham of the fire department and the former representative, Bob Cunningham,
decided to take the mother and her child to the hospital in the
latter's car. And they did.

This unbelievable story, heralded across America Monday,
December 7, and doubtless around the world, is reminiscent of
what happened in ancient Bethlehem, when another woman
was heavy with child. "And she gave birth to her first-born son
and wrapped him in swaddling cloths, and laid him in a manger, because there was no place for them in the inn" (Luke
2:7).[2]

The Awe of Christmas Eve

It may come as a surprise to learn that among Albert Einstein's talents was a gift for music. He played the violin and often joined in chamber music sessions in the homes of neighbors and friends. When well past sixty, he decided to give up his participation in chamber ensembles because it was too demanding on his time and digital reflexes. Even so, he continued to play for his own pleasure.

An exception occurred one Christmas Eve when choristers appeared at the Einstein home—112 Mercer Street in Princeton, New Jersey. Hearing the singing, the noble man picked up his violin, went out on the chilly porch, and provided accompaniment for the carolers.

The contagion of Christmas is irresistible! Its charm surrounds and inspires young and old, rich and poor, wise and simple. Grateful souls are impelled to join in carols of praise, even the pious Jew.

Babies Make the Difference

A remarkably revealing article appeared in the August 15, 1983, issue of *Time* entitled, "What Do Babies Know?" Michael Lewis, a psychologist, presides over the data being gathered by the Institute for the Study of Child Development at Rutgers Medical School, New Brunswick, New Jersey.

Among the startling facts: Babies are born "legally blind." Although unable to see, a newborn nevertheless holds up a hand, as if examining it, within seven minutes after birth. Their ears function well. Within a few weeks they recognize the sound of their mother's voice. Incidently, babies seem to prefer the tone of the female voice over that of the male. At twelve hours old, an infant which has never tasted anything, not even his/her mother's milk, gurgles with satisfaction on receiving a drop of sugar water. At twenty-three days of age the baby can imitate adults.

Beyond risks and costs of rearing children today, having a baby is an act of faith and hope. "It represents a belief in better things to come."

When a wrong needs righting, a truth needs telling, a song needs singing, a soul needs saving—God sends a baby into the world to accomplish it.

Before the Song Started

Before the song started,
The world, brokenhearted,
Was dreamlessly passing the long empty days;
Then a dark, lonely hillside was spangled with light
And a song burst into the night!

A new Word was spoken,
And chords that were broken,
Wove gently together to make a new song.
It was more than a carol to greet the new morn—
The Source of all music was born. . .

He started the whole world singing a song—
The words and the music were there all along!
What the song had to say
Was that Love found a way
To start the world singing a song.[3]

Christmas in August!

I shall forever remember the awe that enveloped me as our small party entered the Church of the Nativity in Bethlehem. Guides provided slender tapers to light our way down the winding steps to the grotto where tradition says Jesus was born. (*How absurd*, I thought, *to be carrying a candle while looking for the Light of the World!*) Upon reaching the designated spot, I found myself standing by a tall, dark man from Sudan. The aura of universal faith and visible ecumenicity generated a holy silence; a silence that constrained us. Presently, a lady, obviously from Europe, without any prompting began to sing, "Silent Night, Holy Night." Within seconds, each joined in singing the carol in his or her own tongue. It was a redemptive moment. Christmas in August!

Christmas: The Harbinger of Peace

Christ of the Andes is an impressive symbol of peace. Once Chile and Argentina were enemies and fought constantly. At last they decided it was in their mutual interest to live in peace. So, high upon their natural boundaries, the Andes Mountains, they erected a great statue of Christ with outstretched arms. The inscription reads: "Sooner shall these mountains crumble into dust than the Argentines and Chileans break the peace sworn at the feet of Christ the Redeemer." Christmas reminds us of the coming of peace to earth.

Jesus was known as the Prince of peace. His motives, manner, and ministry all reflect peace. He said, "Happy are those who make peace, for they will be known as sons of God!" (Matt. 5:9, Phillips).

The Christmas Spirit

Five days after an arsonist destroyed Christmas Village in Bridgeport, Connecticut, December, 1982, city officials and community leaders assembled to see what could be done. For twenty-six years children had come to the "Village" to see animated Christmas scenes, visit with Santa Claus, and receive a toy. The fire had destroyed much of the one-hundred-forty-foot-long building, including many handmade scenes, and about fourteen thousand dollars worth of toys that were to be given away by the Police Athletic League, sponsors of the annual event. Frank Parlatore, a sixty-five-year-old retired factory worker who has been Santa Claus at the Village for twenty-five years, sat near the ruins weeping. A seven-year-old child was among the children who feared Santa had died in the fire.

Meanwhile the community committed and calibrated itself beautifully to restore the building in time for Christmas. With fantastic cooperation and contributions from institutions, trade unions, and individuals, the project went forth. Soon the site was teeming with workers; volunteers with every needed expertise worked around the clock in freezing temperatures. Through remarkable supportiveness and participation, the "Village" was ready for reopening twenty-four hours ahead of schedule.

The mayor of Bridgeport, Leonard S. Paoletta, called it "a miracle." Santa Claus proclaimed it "the best Christmas ever." President Reagan called from Camp David to congratulate the community and to say this is "one of the most inspiring Christmas stories I have heard in years and years and years."[4]

Did Christ Come Too Soon?

Reflecting on the Christmas season with its sacredness, sentimentality, and commercialism brings to mind Maxwell Anderson's provocative drama, *The Wingless Victory*.

The story is laid in Salem, Massachusetts, in the winter of 1800. Nathaniel McQueston and his wife, Oparre, are the principal characters. Nathaniel, a sea captain, returns home a wealthy man. He brings with him his wife, a Malay princess who saved his life. The McQuestons and their children encounter rebuffs, mingled with self-righteousness. Once a worshiper of tribal gods, Oparre was drawn to the gentle Christ by her husband. Believing in the power of Christianity, she tries to win the love of her husband's people and prejudiced neighbors. Disillusioned and rejected, Oparre repudiates Christ and once again embraces the tenets of her early upbringing. Resolving to die, she returns to the ship with a broken heart. Oparre takes poison and kneels in prayer to the gods of yesterday. While waiting for death she says:

The earth rolls toward the dark,
and men begin to sleep. God of the children,
god of the lesser children of the earth,
the black, the unclean, the vengeful, you are mine
now as when I was a child. He came too soon,
this Christ of peace. Men are not ready yet.
Another hundred thousand years they must drink
your potion of tears and blood.[5]

Divine Insanity

Everybody has seen babies and most people like them. If God wanted to be loved as well as feared, He moved correctly here. If He wanted
to know His people as well as rule them, He moved correctly here, for
a baby growing up learns all about people. If God wanted to be inti-
mately a part of man, He moved correctly here, for the experience of
birth and familyhood is our most intimate and precious experience.

So it comes beyond logic; it is what Bishop Karl Morgan Block used
to call a kind of divine insanity. It is either all falsehood or it is the
truest thing in the world. It either rises above the tawdriness of what
we make of Christmas or it is a part of it and completely irrelevant.[6]

The Gift of a Letter

My wife, Sybil, is a prolific letter writer. She will average
two notes a day to acquaintances, family, friends, and former
employees. She thoroughly enjoys it, and keeps a detailed
diary of events and anniversaries. She is not much on beauty
parlors and parties, but great on keeping in touch with people.

The letter, especially a good one, is rapidly disappearing.
Even though it is easy "to reach out and touch someone" by
telephone, perhaps it is too easy. It takes time and effort to
produce a personal letter, and they last, and last.

In writing to the brethren at Corinth, Paul said: "You yourselves are our letter of recommendation, written on your
hearts, to be known and read by all men" (2 Cor. 3:2). We not
only produce letters, we are Christ's letters of recommendation
or repudiation. Since Christmas is the birthday of our Lord,

why not send someone who would least expect to hear from you a Christmas letter!

Hoping It Might Be So

Thomas Hardy wrote a poem called *The Oxen*. In it is expressed the belief by country folk that on Christmas Eve, at twelve o'clock, animals kneel in their stalls in memory of the wondrous birth in a stable in Bethlehem. The poem concludes with Hardy saying if someone told him that in a farm that very night animals were kneeling in the straw, and asked him to come and see, "I should go with him in the gloom, Hoping it might be so."

Keeping Watch Over His Own

Dumas Malone writes in *Jefferson, the Virginian* (vol. 1, p. 21) that the earliest reference to Thomas Jefferson was his being "carried on a pillow by a mounted slave on the journey from Shadwell (his birthplace) to Tuckahoe," a distance of approximately fifty-eight miles.

This dramatic sentence describing the precarious method of transporting a future President, and the principal architect of the Constitution of the United States—the utter confidence in the slave's ability to deliver the child safely—is reminiscent of a journey made by Joseph and Mary from Nazareth to Bethlehem. It would seem that the destiny of the world rode on the surefootedness of an ass.

Loving Christ

On Christmas Day some years ago, a little boy was seen going in and out of his church several times. When asked, "What gift did you ask of the Christ child?" he replied, "I didn't ask for anything. I was just in there loving Him for a little while."

The Manger and the Cross

Dag Hammarskjöld, former secretary-general of the United Nations, wrote in *Markings,* a manuscript that was published after his death: "How proper it is that Christmas should follow Advent. For him who looks towards the future, the manger is situated on Golgotha, and the cross has already been raised in Bethlehem."

Unique Gifts

A friend told me of an extraordinary manufacturer who gave each of his employees a hanging mirror and a handsome reproduction of the head of Christ for Christmas one year. The Christian businessman presented the gifts personally with these instructions: "Hang the mirror on one side of the room and the picture of Christ directly across the room, so that when you look in the mirror you will see the face of Christ along with yours." Then this pensive admonition: "It's going to take both to get you through."

What Does He Want?

The late Paul Ehrman Scherer, celebrated Lutheran preacher, told the story of a college professor who sat reading a book in the waiting room of a maternity section of a hospital while his own child was being born. When at last a nurse appeared and said, "It's a boy!" the teacher scarcely looked up, but grunted, as was his custom when interrupted by a student, "Ask him what he wants."

Christmas is a good time to ask the Lord what He wants from us on His birthday!

What Do We Mean?

In 1952 pupils in a New York public school were invited by their teacher to mention things associated with Christmas. The children responded spontaneously: "Santa Claus," "Reindeer,"

"Christmas trees," "presents." Then a pensive little girl said, "The birthday of Jesus."

"Oh, no," the teacher replied quickly, "that's not what we mean."

Where Does God Fit In?

A schoolteacher in England tells a charming story. At Christmastime she supervised the construction of a manger scene in a corner of the classroom. The children participated happily in the project. They also enjoyed casting characters for the drama depicting the Nativity.

The teacher noticed one boy was particularly enamored by it all and was forever going back and forth to the scene. At last she asked him if there was anything bothering him. He said, "No." She said, "Are there any questions you would like to ask?" "Yes," he said, "what I'd like to know is—where does God fit in?"

The Church

Isaiah 54:2; Matthew 16:13-19; Acts 2:1-24,43-47; Colossians 1:18

The church is her true self only when she exists for humanity.
—Dietrich Bonhoeffer

Antithesis

The church has buildings but little boldness.
The church has numbers but little nerve.
The church has comfort but little courage.
The church has status but little spirit.
The church has prestige but little power.[1]

Carrier of the Faith

Through the ages Christians have looked upon the church as the company of the committed, the visible followers of Christ, members of His body in a broken world, pilgrims en route to New Jerusalem. The vast majority of believers consider the church to be God's conduit, the carrier of the faith from one generation to another.

Lay Participation

Worship in our churches normally dictates for the pastor to officiate. Yet, the New Testament church was filled with lay participation. "When you meet together, each contributes something—a song of praise, a lesson, a revelation, a 'tongue,' an interpretation? Good, but let everything be for edification" (1 Cor. 14:26, Moffatt). Nothing would do more to enliven the services of a church than to give laypersons a significant part.

Conviction Builds the Church

There is a perceptive story told of Heinrich Heine, the German poet, who was standing with a friend before the cathedral of Amiens in France. "Tell me, Heinrich," said his friend, "why can't people build piles like this anymore?"

"My dear friend," replied Heine, "in those days people had convictions. We moderns have opinions. And it takes more than an opinion to build a Gothic cathedral."[2]

Dead or Alive?

Once there was a hermit who was very wise. He articulated answers to troublesome questions. This aggravated some of the youth, who decided to trick him. They captured a small bird. And this was their plan: One would approach the guru with the little creature clutched in hand, asking if the bird were dead or alive. If the oracle said "alive," the bird would be crushed. If he said "dead," it would be released to fly away.

Eagerly awaiting the encounter, the youngsters approached the wise man. One boy asked, "This bird that I hold in my hand; is it dead or alive?"

Quietly the perceptive sage replied, "As you will, my son, as you will."

Definitions

The church is not a sheltered sanctuary for saints. Rather, it is a survival station for sinners.   —Joseph Jay

Perceptive Christians have insisted that they must differentiate between the organization and organism, between the visible and invisible church, between statistics and Spirit.

Devotion to Church

Several preachers have told of a deaf member of a church and a rather typical-minded American churchman who asked, "Why do you come to church each Sunday when you cannot hear the service?" The humble man replied, "I come each week to let people know which side I am on."

Do You Go to Sunday School?

The late Pierce Harris, a prominent Methodist minister in Atlanta, told this story. He was to preach at a prison camp. The men were dressed in their usual garb and sat in a semicircle on the ground beneath the trees waiting for the service. One inmate stood in the back of a truck to introduce the preacher.

In substance, the inmate said: "Several years ago, two boys lived in the same community in North Georgia, attended the same school, played with the same fellows, and went to the same Sunday School. One dropped out of Sunday School because he felt he had outgrown it. The second boy kept on going, because he really believed in it. The boy who dropped out is making this presentation today. The boy who kept going is the distinguished preacher of the morning."

Gifts that Cost

When King David was searching for a site to build the Temple near Jerusalem, he found a very attractive piece of land that belonged to a man named Araunah. When the Jebusite learned who it was that wanted his land, he offered to give it to the King, as well as oxen and wood for the sacrifice. But David said, "No, but I will buy it off you for a price; I will not offer burnt offerings to the Lord my God which cost me nothing" (2 Sam. 24:24).

Interfaith

The Longboat Island Chapel, Florida, an interfaith community church, prints the following affirmation of faith in its bulletin and repeats it in concern during worship:

Love is the doctrine of this church;
The quest of truth its sacrament;
And service is its prayer.

To dwell together in peace,
To seek knowledge in freedom,
To serve mankind in fellowship,
To the end that all souls shall grow
Into harmony with the Divine.

Thus we covenant with each other,
And with God.[3]

It Belongs to Me

Chris Emmett, in describing the life of Shanghai Pierce, the owner of an enormous plantation, reports that the tycoon decided to introduce religion to his ranch and built a church. While driving around his acreage, a visitor asked, "Colonel Pierce, do you belong to that church?" Emphatically he answered, "(Expletive deleted.) The church belongs to *me*!"

Think it over, without the expletive. Do we really belong to the church, or do we presumptuously believe that it belongs to us?

The Landmark

Years ago a tornado destroyed a little church on the coast of England. The congregation was too poor to replace it. One day a representative of the British Admiralty called on the local minister. The official inquired if his people planned to rebuild. The pastor explained their situation. Whereupon the caller said, "If you do not rebuild the church, we will. That spire is on all of our charts and maps. It is the landmark by which the ships of the seven seas steer their courses."

The Moravian Seal

The beautiful seal of the Moravian Church features a lamb, encircled by the Latin words: *Noster Agnus Vincit; Sequamur Eum.* The English rendering is: Our Lamb Has Conquered; Let Us Follow Him.

The One Longed For

The late Dr. George Truett, who was pastor of First Baptist Church, Dallas, used to say: "God will not ask you what sort of a church you have lived in, but God will ask you what sort of a church you have longed for."

The Open Door

Squire Hughes was one of the first settlers west of the Miami River in Ohio. He would ride twenty miles on horseback to worship at the Presbyterian Church in Cincinnati. The first time he entered the church and walked down the aisle, all the pew doors were closed. No one invited him in. As he returned from the front of the church seeking a seat, a few opened the doors of their pews. He scorned their belated hospitality, went out of the church, found a board, carried it back down to the front, and sat down on it. After the benediction he picked up the plank, put it on his shoulder, and strode out, mounted his horse, and rode away. The next time the pioneer came to old First Church, every pew was opened to him. A stranger had taught the congregation a lesson in Christian courtesy.

Where Are Kings and Empires Now?

O where are the kings and empires now
Of old that went and came?
But, Lord, Thy Church is praying yet,
A thousand years the same.

We mark her goodly battlements,
And her foundations strong;
We hear within the solemn voice
Of her unending song.

For not like kingdoms of the world,
Thy holy Church, O God;
Though earthquake shocks are threat'ning her,
And tempests are abroad.
Unshaken as eternal hills,
Immovable she stands,
A mountain that shall fill the earth,
A house not made by hands.[4]

Sectarianism

The great evangelist, D. L. Moody, once declared: "If I thought I had one drop of Sectarian blood in my veins, I would let it out before I went to bed; if I had one Sectarian hair in my head, I would pull it out."

Sound of Its Singing

The world is my church;
I cannot go beyond the sound of its singing.

Around its open doors grow hedges of mercy;
Tall, graceful trees, with leaves of healing

define its entrance,
While from its windows pour pure sunshine,
encouraging growth
and fragrance
of its flowers
of pure affection;
So to its altars I would go and daily kneeling
sometimes in rapture,
Lay there my heart and all its fears and plans;
Then eat the sacred Bread of Life, offered on silver trays
of listening;
Drink there the wine of Christly inspiration.

Listening and affirming,
I then can view united Heaven and Earth;
Can find myself to be
Lifted from despair to praise.[5]

Strength and Growth

In the sixteenth century, Martin Luther strengthened the church by exposing its corruption and artificiality. He enunciated its structural sins. In Britain in the eighteenth century, a man named William Law enlarged the place of the church by exposing the piety of its members. And John Wesley and his colleagues lengthened the cords of the church to embrace neglected masses. The twentieth-century American church has endeavored to be all things to all people. It has produced fascinating materials, specialized in dialogues, programs, and projects; but the spiritual life of professing Christians has not always been in proper balance.

Witnessing to the World

In Liverpool, England, Saint Nicholas Church graces the harbor. Into this harbor come a variety of ships, especially those laden with wheat, food for the peoples of the world. Before the war, the church faced away from the harbor, so that when you entered you turned your back, as it were, on the world. The church building was destroyed by bombs during World War II, and when it was rebuilt, it was made to face the harbor. Can this be the symbol and the witness of the church today?

Commitment

Ruth 1:15-18; Luke 9:62; John 21:15-18; Romans 10:8-9

Christianity not only saves you from sin, but from cynicism.
—E. Stanley Jones

Beyond the Body

Norman Cousins, in his book, *Anatomy of an Illness*, tells of a visit to the great cellist, Pablo Casals, when Casals was ninety years old. His infirmities were enormous and crippling. Yet, almost miraculously, he was able to rise above his body because of his love for his art. A daily session with his cello was like cortisone for his stiffening joints.

Bosom of the Church

A few miles out of Paris, Kentucky, is the old Cane Ridge Meeting House, the scene of many revivals. It is where Barton W. Stone gave a mighty impetus to the Disciples of Christ denomination. There is also a graveyard on the top of the hill. On one of the stones is this inscription:

Here lies Nathaniel Rogers who was born in 1755. He was a member of the convention that formed the constitution of Kentucky in 1799. But what is of far more consequence, he was a member of the church of Christ in the bosom of which he died.

Called to Follow

Divine dreams are the taproot of enthusiasm. So, we are called to join God's kingdom. You and I are called to be modern disciples of Jesus. We are called to think of the possibilities God has for us. We are called to deny ourselves, take up our cross, and follow Him.[1]

Cheerful Sacrifice

I shall never forget a visit to a leprosarium in Kimpese, Zaire. A young Scotsman was the missionary in charge. The pale-faced man, his wife, and their baby lived a few paces from the hospital. He was a strong man, physically. His mind was keen, his heart was warm, and he obviously loved his work. I had met him at a prayer meeting the night before. With great pride, he showed me their facilities and some of their people. All the while I secretly remembered what a missionary from another communion had told me about their dire poverty, of how their sponsoring group had not been able to pay them with any regularity. Yet there was not the slightest trace of resentment or discontent.

The young man showed me some of his experiments with vegetables and fruit trees. Fresh foods are at a premium in this section of Zaire. As I shared the generous hospitality of their home, I felt as if I were stealing from hungry people.

This moving experience brought to mind the frontispiece of a book by Stephen Graham. On it is pictured a lighted candle, with these words: "May I waste so that I show the face of Christ."

Committed to Care

The small village of Humlikon, Switzerland, sustained an unbelievable tragedy September 4, 1963. Forty-three men and women, all dirt farmers, boarded a plane for a one-day excursion to Geneva, where they were to inspect a fertilizer plant.

The airplane crashed en route and all were killed. Imagine one generation from a small community obliterated at once! Jakob Zindel, elderly town clerk, faced the dreadful task of notifying the next of kin.

The following day, Pastor Konrad Niederer, from the nearby village of Andelfingen, came to offer assistance. Day after day he, his people, and volunteers from as far away as England, assisted with the children and crops.

Jakob Peter, seventy-four, former councilman from Zurich, was chosen leader and coordinator of the bereaved community. More than eighteen-hundred gifts from around the world, totaling three-hundred-fifty thousand dollars, came in as a tidal wave of love. Orphaned children, of course, were given first consideration. Equipment was purchased to expedite the harvesting of potatoes and beets. A Humlikon farmer said, "We have suffered a great misfortune, yes, but we have good fortune, too, for we have learned that the world has a heart."

Creativity

One of the most brilliant, inventive persons of our day was the late Buckminster Fuller. Inventor of the geodesic dome, and holder of 818 other patents in fifty-five countries, he was the recipient of forty-five honorary degrees. While an octogenarian, he lectured twice a week to students. One admirer said: "I have known very few people who came away from listening to Bucky who did not feel they had been under a starlit sky."

Don't Get Knocked Out

J. B. Phillips renders the ninth verse of the fourth chapter of 2 Corinthians to read: "We may be knocked down but we are never knocked out!"

A Fellowship of Beggars

The year 1983 marked the five-hundredth anniversary of the great reformer, Martin Luther, whose stature increases with time. Found by his deathbed, scrawled in German and Latin, was this declaration: "We are beggars: That is true."

This statement may have inspired D. T. Niles to say, "Evangelism is one beggar telling another beggar where he can find a piece of bread." Not a sweet roll and a cup of coffee, but a bite of the staff of life—bread!

The church is a fellowship of beggars, receiving and offering love, support, and hope. Committed Christians acknowledge their dependence upon God and their interdependence on one another. They are always in the bread line, if not receiving, then giving.

Giving One's Best

A few years ago I was privileged to visit with the popular violinist Benno Rubinoff. During the conversation he said that when he was not on tour he practiced some eight hours a day, and when on the road he often rehearsed between concerts. I asked him why. He patiently replied, "Well, I strive for perfection. I doubt if my audience would know the difference if I lightened up on rehearsals, but I would. Music is my life. Music is in my heart. I must always give my best."

Incredible Obedience

Take your son, your only son Isaac, whom you love, and go to the land of Moriah, and offer him there as a burnt offering upon one of the mountains of which I shall tell you (Gen. 22:2).

Abraham turned pale, sick. This was not only the son of his old age but the one designated to be his "seed." Had God lied? Was this the demand of a rational God? Surely old Abraham, bubbling with emotion, longed to talk it over with someone. Why not Sarah? But as Professor Roland H. Bainton has suggested, had he discussed it with anyone, "he would be dissuaded and prevented from carrying out the behest."

The designated spot for the sacrifice, Mount Moriah, was

some distance away. Abraham rose up early in the morning, saddled his ass, strapped the prepared wood on the beast, and with two servants and his son Isaac, started the sad journey. Not even those of us who have lost a son can begin to know the impact of the command to offer a son as a "burnt offering." One's blood turns cold, the demand is inconceivable. Everything in Abraham died, except his obedience. The agony lasted three days!

Arriving at the place of execution, preparations were made. All the while Isaac was asking heartbreaking questions. Faithful Abraham built the altar, placing the wood on it, and finally his bound son. With trembling, upraised hand Abraham drew the knife "to slay his son." The boy was horrified! If God had winked, Isaac would have been dead.

But in that awful moment an angel cried out, "Abraham, Abraham!" And he said "Here am I." The angel said, " 'Do not lay your hand on the lad or do anything to him; for now I know that you fear God' " (Gen. 22:12).

Never has history recorded such obedience, save that demonstrated at Calvary.

I Will Come

It is moving to remember when Booker T. Washington discovered the brilliant George Washington Carver on the faculty of Iowa State College, Ames, Iowa, and how each man attracted the other. Washington was so impressed with the scope of Carver's work that the young scientist was invited to join the faculty of Tuskegee Institute in Alabama. During the negotiations, Washington said in substance to Carver, "I cannot offer you a large salary but some day you will have it. I cannot offer you fame, for soon you will be famous. All I can offer you is immortality." Characteristically, Carver laid the matter in the lap of the Lord. Eventually, he wrote across the letter of invitation the simple words, "I will come."

Keeping the Promise

Many have seen the Passion Play in the Bavarian village of Oberammergau. It is usually a once-a-decade spectacular involving practically all forty-eight hundred villagers and much of their livestock. The 1984 presentation marked its three-hundred-fiftieth anniversary. The eight-hour performance ran five days a week for one-hundred days, beginning May 20.

The origin of the play goes back to the time of the Thirty Years War. European powers were constantly skirmishing across Germany, bringing destruction, famine, and plague. Oberammergau records of 1632 reveal that at least eighty-four villagers died from the plague.

The villagers are said to have sought relief by promising God that they would stage a drama reenacting the life and death of Christ if Oberammergau were spared. It is said that from that day the Black Death did not claim a single soul in the community.

In 1634 the villagers of Oberammergau made good on their promise and staged the first Passion Play in the cemetery.

Let Down Your Bucket

An unforgettable experience of my college days was to hear a series of lectures by George Washington Carver. His life is a chronicle of sacrifice, humility, brilliance, good deeds, and dedication. He stated his personal philosophy in these simple words, "Let down your buckets where you are." He encouraged us and everyone not to go through life dodging issues, complaining, and criticizing, but to contribute something.

This was illustrated time and time again in Dr. Carver's own career, but never more dramatically than when he was offered one-hundred-seventy-five thousand dollars a year to work with Thomas A. Edison, and declined. His reason: "I felt that God was not through with me in Tuskegee; there was still plenty of work to do for Him there."

National Commitment

The Russian writer, Boris Pasternak, became famous with the appearance of his novel, *Doctor Zhivago*. This exposé of the Communist system was smuggled out of the country and published in Italy. Pasternak was declared a traitor, and saved from death only because of world acclaim. *Doctor Zhivago* won for Pasternak the Nobel prize for literature in 1958. The government advised the celebrated author if he accepted the prize he would be deported. After six days of painful struggle, Pasternak wrote Premier Krushchev: "Leaving the motherland would equal death for me. I am tied to Russia by birth, by life and work."

And so he declined the coveted prize, and lived out his years in official disrepute. Although we may disagree with his decision, Pasternak was a loyal patriot; he did not seek political asylum for financial or personal advantage.

Personal Allegiance

Dietrich Bonhoeffer, the amazing Christian martyr of Germany, said, "Discipleship means allegiance to the suffering Christ." Great leaders have always demanded personal allegiance. King Arthur bound his knights to him by rigid vows. Giuseppe Garibaldi, nineteenth-century Italian patriot, offered his followers hunger, death, and Italy's freedom. Sir Winston Churchill's stirring speech in the House of Commons, May 13, 1940, is best remembered by the dramatic words: "I have nothing to offer but blood, toil, tears, and sweat."

Personal Involvement

Henry Dunant was born to wealthy parents in Switzerland in 1828. Deeply compassionate, he devoted considerable time assisting and encouraging young people, especially the poor. When only about eighteen, he founded a Young Men's Christian Union.

Eventually, this sensitive person journeyed to Italy to have an audience with Emperor Napoleon III, who was busy driving the Austrians out of Northern Italy. Arriving shortly after a horrendous battle, Henry Dunant could not believe what he saw. Some forty thousand men—wounded, dying, and dead—lay scattered over a bloody terrain for vermin and vultures to consume.

Forgetting his personal agenda, Dunant pitched in, doing whatever he could to help the overworked doctors. He subsequently wrote and spoke on the horrors of war. At last the Geneva Convention of 1864 convened to consider common problems. Twenty-two nations participated, and signed accords acknowledging the neutrality of medical personnel in time of hostility. They chose a red cross on a white field for their banner and symbol.

And so the Red Cross was born!

Staying Power

When Cortez disembarked his five-hundred men upon the eastern coast of Mexico, he set fire to the ships. As his warriors watched their means of retreat burn, they knew they were committed with their lives to conquer the new world for Spain.

Similarly, everyone who sets foot on the shore of discipleship is called upon to burn his own ships in the harbor. We Christians cannot spend our days looking back. We must move forward. Jesus said: "No one who puts his hand to the plow and looks back is fit for the kingdom of God" (Luke 9:62). There is no compromising center, no relaxed position. The Christian life is one of tension and triumph.

When the great Quaker, George Fox, was put in prison because of his activity against war and slavery, he immediately launched a crusade for prison reform. Christian discipline results in a dedicated, determined life and when one door closes, God causes another to open.

An Unpurchasable Person

Dr. Reid Vipond of Canada shares a story of an oil company that needed a suave public-relations man for its office in the Orient. After interviewing several candidates, the officials decided to ask a local missionary to take the position. Company executives met with this man of unusual gifts. Whatever their proposition, his answer was always "No."

"What's wrong?" asked one interviewer. "Isn't the salary big enough?"

The missionary replied, "The salary is big enough, but the job isn't."

Unquenchable Light

The sixteenth-century English bishop, Hugh Latimer, was one of the first preachers of social righteousness in the English-speaking world. He was imprisoned for his courage and enunciations. While in the Tower of London, he wrote, "Pray for me, I say pray for me; at times I am so afraid that I could creep into a mousehole." This was the same Latimer who later walked bravely to the stake in Oxford, saying to his companion, Nicholas Ridley, as he went, "Play the man, Master Ridley; we shall this day light such a candle, by God's grace in England, as I trust shall never be put out."

What Can I Do?

The minister of a metropolitan congregation shared the inspiration gained from a phenomenal layman. The man was a business magnate. As a conscientious and generous steward, he gave one building in their church complex without fanfare, while continuing to be the largest contributor to the local budget. That which pleased the pastor most, however, was not the man's monetary gifts, magnificent as they were, but the giving of himself. Following Sunday worship, this marvelous soul would ask, "Pastor, what can I do for our church this week?"

Courage

Joshua 1:6-7; Luke 9:51; 2 Timothy 3:7; Hebrews 12:12

Screw your courage to the sticking-place, And we'll not fail.
—William Shakespeare, from
Macbeth

Good Courage

Second Samuel 10 records a seemingly impossible impasse for the armies of David. David's commanding general, Joab, "saw that the battle was set against him both in front and in the rear." Then he and his brother, Abishai, vowed to support each other and to leave the results in the hands of God. Joab reinforced Abishai with these courageous words:

If the Syrians are too strong for me, than you shall help me, but if the Ammonites are too strong for you, then I will come and help you. Be of good courage, and let us play the man for our people, and for the cities of our God; and may the Lord do what seems good to him (2 Sam. 10:9,11-12).

Brace Yourself

During the dreadful days of 1940 Winston Churchill, in summoning cooperation and support for survival, declared, "Let us . . . brace ourselves to our duty, and so bear ourselves that, if the British Empire and its Commonwealth last for a thousand years, men will still say: 'This was their finest hour.' "[1]

The Bravest of the Brave

Dr. Barney C. Clark, age sixty-one retired dentist from Des Moines, Washington, made medical history in December, 1982, by becoming the first patient to receive a permanent artificial heart. The six-feet, two-inch Clark was suffering from cardiomyopathy, a progressive weakening of the heart that inevitably leads to congestive heart failure.

The eyes of the world focused on the University of Utah Medical Center, Salt Lake City, where surgeon William DeVries, with a team of fifteen doctors, nurses, and attendants, performed the seven-and-one-half-hour operation. Dr. De-Vries described the operation as being "almost a spiritual experience."

Dr. Jeffrey Anderson, the Utah cardiologist who had arranged the first meeting between the patient and DeVries, says that when Clark's heart had been carefully cut out and placed on a stainless steel tray: "It was an irreversible step. From then on everyone was going on faith that the machine would work."

During the Christmas season of 1982 the courageous Clark, tethered to 375 pounds of power equipment, joked with nurses, and listened to Handel's *Messiah* as sung by the Mormon Tabernacle Choir.

Christians as Contestants

The handwriting was on the wall. Paul was in a pensive mood. There is nothing subtle or ambiguous about his language. It is crystal clear. In simple, penetrating words, the apostle declared, "I have fought the good fight, I have finished the race, I have kept the faith" (2 Tim. 4:7). J. B. Phillips translates this valedictory sentence to read, "The glorious fight that God gave me I have fought, the course that I was set I have finished, and I have kept the faith."

The Courtesy of Courage

In *A Spiritual Autobiography*, William Barclay told of his admiration for John Swinnerton Phillimore, professor of Latin at Glasgow University. Having won a prize in his class, young Barclay went to the home of Dr. Phillimore to select a complimentary book. The professor was the epitome of kindness. "There was surely unparalleled courtesy in the heart of the man who gave all of himself to a student an hour before he was to go out to die." Could you be as courteous knowing your death was at hand?

Faith and Hope

During World War II, a pharmacist's mate, Wheeler B. Lipes, Jr., performed a lifesaving appendectomy on Seaman Darrell Dean Rector aboard the submarine, *Sea Dragon*. Maneuvering behind enemy lines in the Pacific, the closest thing to a doctor on board was pharmacist's mate Lipes, a lab technician by training, who had witnessed an appendectomy.

Facing certain death if not operated upon, Rector agreed to Lipes correcting the situation. Without surgical instruments, Lipes used a knife blade for a scalpel, a tea strainer to administer ether, and spoons from the galley to keep the incision open during surgery. The crude tools were sterilized with alcohol from a torpedo.

Surgery was performed in the officer's quarters on September 11, 1942, the first appendectomy aboard a submerged submarine. Rector resumed his responsibilities in thirteen days.[2]

Glimpses of Courage

Courage asserts itself in myriad ways: toddlers taking their lumps while learning to walk; octogenarians living alone; paraplegics in wheelchairs participating in a marathon; astronauts walking on the moon; a Rose Kennedy living with family tragedies; single parents coping with children and jobs; Lech

Walesa challenging the harshness of the Polish government; college students facing a spate of new temptations; unemployed persons desperately seeking work; and, that strong Man struggling uphill with a cross. From these and other profiles of courage we glimpse the resiliency of the human spirit—daily battlegrounds faced and conquered.

Hang On

Analyzing certain British victories over the French, the Duke of Wellington said: "British soldiers are not braver than French soldiers, they are only brave five minutes longer."

In Decline

Speaking at the 1978 Harvard commencement, Alexander Solzhenitsyn referred to "a decline in courage" and the "spiritual exhaustion" of the West. His remarks incensed many, including several national leaders. We know, however, that clandestine activities, corruption, and deliberate deception by leaders document Solzhenitsyn's declaration.

Instant Sacrifice

Alistair Anthony of Glasgow, Scotland, while visiting his parents in Blackpool, England, dived into the stormy sea to rescue his Jack Russell terrier, Henry, and was lost. The dog, chasing a ball along the promenade, was swept away by vicious twenty-foot waves. Three members of the police force who participated in the rescue attempt also lost their lives. An editor for *The Daily Mail,* one of Britain's national newspapers, wrote: "Often and glibly, we talk of duty and of service and of the human bonds that hold our society together. In the face of courage and sacrifices such as this, we can only fall silent."

Jesus said, "Greater love has no man than this, that a man lay down his life for his friends" (John 15:13).

Are dogs not included among our friends?[3]

Luther's

When Luther walked into the presence of Charles V and other powerful persons at the Diet of Worms, April 1521, to answer charges of heresy and to hear a possible death sentence, an old knight was heard to say: "Little monk, I like the step you take but neither I nor any of our battle comrades would take it."

Consider that little Augustinian monk who shocked Christendom by his defiance of papal authority and who, at last, stood trial for his life. During a high moment in the trial, Martin Luther exclaimed:

> I do not accept the authority of popes and councils, for they have contradicted each other—my conscience is captive to the Word of God. I cannot and I will not recant anything, for to go against conscience is neither right nor safe. God help me. Amen.[4]

Not to Compromise

In his autobiography, *Donahue,* Phil Donahue, shares an experience from Holden, West Virginia. He and a CBS television crew had gone to this Appalachian community to cover rescue attempts of thirty-eight miners. They had planned to be there one night but stayed three, eating doughnuts and drinking Red Cross coffee in bitterly cold weather.

At last the rescue teams emerged, covered with soot and grime, weary beyond words. Relatives of the miners were waiting in the snow. Gathered around a smudge pot, a preacher said, "Dear God, let us pray." They joined hands and sang, "What a Friend We Have in Jesus." Donahue says it gave him goose bumps. It was beautiful! He knew it would make a great film for CBS, but the camera was frozen; by the time it was warmed up, the service was over. At 2:30 in the morning, Donahue approached the pastor with a request.

"Reverend, I am from CBS News. Would you please go back

through your prayer again? We have 206 television stations across the country who will hear you pray for these miners."

The humble minister looked at him and said, "Son, I just couldn't do it. I have already prayed to my God, and any further praying at this time would be wrong. No sir, I just can't do it."

Donahue was shocked that anyone would turn down a chance to be on CBS News. At last he made his way to a pay telephone to report to New York: "The _____ won't pray!"

Donahue claims that the preacher's stand was the greatest demonstration of moral courage he has ever encountered. The man would not "show biz" for Jesus. He would not sell his soul—not even to CBS. Donahue says he often thinks of that preacher and that night. "I don't know where he is now, but if he isn't going to Heaven, no one is."[5]

Some Definitions

Where true fortitude dwells, loyalty, bounty, friendship, and fidelity may be found.

—Sir Thomas Browne

Courage, the footstool of the Virtues, upon which they stand.

—Robert Louis Stevenson

The World Stood Up

When Rosa Parks sat down in the segregated bus in Montgomery, Alabama, the world stood up!

To Be Gracious

Gene Smith, in *When the Cheering Stopped*, pictures a vivid and moving scene just three days before the retirement of Woodrow Wilson from the White House. He had held his last cabinet meeting. Much courage and discipline had been manifested. When asked what he was going to do, Wilson thought for a moment and said: "I am going to try to teach ex-presidents how to behave. There will be one very difficult thing for me to stand, however, and that is Mr. Harding's English!"

To Confront

Dr. Theodore Ferris tells of a young Presbyterian minister who was in charge of a large city church. The most active and generous member was a woman whose wealthy husband never attended. With the passing of the years, the young cleric felt impelled to do something about it. He finally made an appointment with the industrialist. The businessman seemed even more austere as he sat quietly behind his great desk. Awkwardly, the young man came to the point of his visit. In very simple language he set forth the Christian proposition and then added, "I think you ought to do something about this one way or another." The man did not answer. Carefully the minister reiterated his conversation. Again there was silence. A third time the preacher rephrased the claims of Christ. Finally the well-to-do man reached for his memo pad and scribbled this note: "I am so deeply moved that I cannot speak." The minister was the first person in years to challenge this giant to confess Christ. He became a member of his church and was an effective Christian.

To Continue

Captain Harold E. Stahlman, United States Army, was a prisoner in Korea for thirty months. How well I remember the day his lovely wife came to my study, brokenhearted, with word of her husband's presumed death. Weeks stretched into months, and months into more than two years.

All the while, this beautiful young mother cared for her baby, assumed responsibilities for her missionary circle, and gave more than a tenth of her income to the church. She continued to write letters to a husband reported dead. By and by, pictures of Korean War prisoners appeared in the newspapers. One day Mrs. Stahlman recognized her husband in one of the photographs. Later she received a scrap of a letter from him. She notified the Defense Department that her husband was alive.

What a profile of courage!

To Save

A plane crashed and burned on a runway in Philadelphia. The hostess was Mary Frances Hausley. She stood at the door assisting passengers to safety. When she thought all were safe, she heard a woman screaming, "My baby, my baby!" With this prompting she returned to the flaming plane, never to be seen again. When the burned wreckage was unsnarled, Miss Hausley's body was found draped over the child she tried to save. The caption of *Time's* story read, "She Could Have Jumped."

To Vote

The courage and vote of Edmund G. Ross, obscure freshman Republican senator from Kansas, saved President Andrew Johnson from impeachment May 16, 1868.

What Courage!

Beethoven, the immortal German composer of the early nineteenth century, wrote much of his greatest music when he was deaf. He was once heard to say, "I shall hear in heaven."

In September 1857, David Livingstone, a gaunt and tired man, stood in the presence of a distinguished audience at Glasgow University to receive a well-earned honorary degree. His body was diseased and one arm was limp from an encounter with a lion. He was stooped, but not broken.

The Cross

Mark 8:34; John 12:32; John 19:17,22; Galatians 6:14

Four words destroyed slavery, "For whom Christ died."
—T. R. Glover

The Cross was the new power that was to shake the world—and redeem it!
—E. Stanley Jones

Beat On Your Heart

In 1580, a Dutch Protestant leader named Klaes was arrested and condemned as a heretic. Eventually he was burned at the stake. When the tragedy was over, his dear wife took their small son by the hand and walked through the back streets of town to the hill where their loved one had perished as a Christian martyr. At the place of execution, the bereaved widow gathered up a few of the ashes, placed them in her satchel, and hung it around her boy's neck, saying,

Son, I place these ashes on your heart, and on the heart of every son of these Netherlands in all eternity. Whenever and wherever in this world there is an injustice or wrong committed, these ashes will beat on your heart and you will speak out without fear, even at the fear of death.[1]

Beyond Humiliation

In his book, *The Scandal of Lent,* Robert Kysar declared that the cross forces us to examine our understanding of the love of God.

"On the Tree"

The late prince of the pulpit, Robert G. Lee, wrote:

Thus we see that the Cross was substitutionary. On the Cross, where the history of human guilt culminated, He was wounded for our transgressions. On the Cross, where purposes of divine love are made intelligible, He was bruised for our iniquities. As our substitute on the Cross, where the majesty of the law is fulfilled, He bore the penalty of our transgressions and iniquities. "Who his own self bare our sins in his own body on the tree" (1 Pet. 2:24). Only as our substitute could he have borne them. As Abraham offered the ram instead of Isaac his son, so Christ was offered once to bear the sins of man.

Christianity

Sören Kierkegaard, the Danish philosopher and theologian, declared that in removing from Christianity its ability to shock, it is altogether destroyed. It becomes a superficial thing, incapable of inflicting deep wounds or of healing them.

Comments

Calvary is a telescope through which we look into the long vista of eternity, and see the love of God breaking forth into time.
—Martin Luther King, Jr.

Christ is always closest when the cross is heaviest.
—E. Stanley Jones

Constraining Love

Deric Washburn wrote the screenplay for the film *The Deer Hunter*. It depicts the support and affection existing among prisoners of the Viet Cong. One unfortunate soul, Nick, could not free himself of the horror of being compelled to play Russian roulette. Even after his release he remains in Saigon playing this dangerous game with gamblers and derelicts. Nick's friend, Michael, is so concerned he returns to Saigon, hoping to rescue the deranged buddy. Finding him, he tries in vain to shake his psychotic state. Finally, Michael exhibits his love by demonstrating his willingness to put a bullet through his own head if it takes that to restore Nick's sanity.

Not as dramatically, perhaps, but Christians are challenged to enthrone love; to run the risk of being foolish, of losing status, in order to be faithful. "Greater love has no man than this, that a man lay down his life for his friends" (John 15:13). There are many ways to lay down one's life—and still live!

An Extra Cross?

I have a friend in Alabama, a humble pastor, who has a fascinating hobby. He is a whittler. Although he is not in the class, perhaps, with German woodcarvers—especially those of Oberammergau—he is very good. His specialty is whittling crosses from cedar. He has literally made thousands. Many of the youths in the local high school wear his crosses. He always carries some in his pocket. While eating in a restaurant one night, he gave me a beautiful cedar cross. The waiter was interested in our conversation and politely asked, "If you have an extra cross, I would like one."

The Fourth Temptation

In his novel, *The Chain,* Paul Wellman shared a scintillating story attributed to "Southern Negroes." It is known as the "fourth temptation." According to this beautiful legend, after Jesus had emerged victoriously from His wilderness temptations; after living courageously and triumphantly throughout His ministry; after His apostles failed, enemies and friends conspired in crime; then, while Jesus was hanging in excruciating pain on the cross, the devil returned and whispered in His ear, "They aren't worth it, Lord." It was then, according to the story, that the Master was heard to say, "Father, forgive them; for they know not what they do" (Luke 23:34).

God's Sign of Love

There had to be a cross—some meaningful dramatization of God's will and way for persons in this world. Without the cross there would be no gospel. It is understandable why the cross was a stumbling block to the Jews and foolishness to the Greeks; neither had a gospel—no recent word from God, no good news following their dark Fridays!

God's Voluntary Cloak

A Flemish sculptor was extremely poor. He frequently went without food and worked in a clammy studio. It was bitter cold the night he finished his masterpiece. The thoughtful and meticulous artist was concerned lest the firm, fresh clay of his creation should freeze and crack. He had too much of himself in the design to run the risk of its being ruined, so he wrapped it in his warmest coat.

The sculptor died from exposure during the night. His cherished statuette was found unharmed. The warmth of sacrifice had saved it. In some such thoughtful way, beyond our ability to conceive or comprehend, the cross is God's voluntary cloak of sacrifice draped in mercy over His creation.

Only the Cross

Through the centuries many schemes have been propounded for uplifting mankind and "bringing in the kingdom of God." These grand-sounding schemes have failed because they ignore the greatest power of all—the regenerating power of Jesus Christ in human hearts.

Many years ago, Dr. Lyman Abbott, prominent pastor in Brooklyn, New York, resigned his church. He stated in his letter of resignation: "I see that what I had once hoped might be done for my fellows through schemes of social reform and philanthropy can only be done by the influence of Jesus Christ. There is no dynamo in reform save the Cross of Jesus Christ!"

I, Not You!

The scholarly Scotsman William Barclay shared the story of a missionary who went to an Indian village to tell the story of Jesus. Following his talk, the Christian showed slide presentations of Jesus, using a whitewashed wall for the screen. When the picture of Christ on the cross appeared, a man sprang to his feet exclaiming, "Come down from that cross, Son of God. I, not You, should be hanging there!"

Is It Nothing to You?

The rope dangled in the breeze. It hung from the limb of a giant oak tree. A curious crowd enveloped the country store. The people had come, not to barter nor to buy, but to witness a heinous crime. A black man, accused of murdering a storekeeper, had been apprehended and hanged. His lifeless body lay in the store of that small Virginia community. Remembrances of that scene remain as grotesque as when first I viewed it as a boy.

As we drove home, my father said, "Son, today you have seen what madmen will do. The first murder was bad enough without adding another. I hope you will never be party to any such thing." His manner and words greatly impressed me. In my heart I wished we had arrived earlier. Perhaps my strong father and others like him could have thwarted the tragedy.

However horrible this memory, it is not to be compared with what happened on a hill outside Jerusalem. There, not an alleged criminal, but the Christ; not an accused murderer, but the Lamb of God was slain.

"Is it nothing to you, all you who pass by?" (Lam. 1:12).

Keep an Eye On the Cross

An English writer once said that every man struggling to succeed in the literary world should write with an eye on the far-off island where Robert Louis Stevenson lived. So, through the continuing centuries, all who have sought salvation have kept their minds and hearts focused on Calvary. There is more here than we can comprehend, but we can understand enough to know that we have been bought with a price.

The Linkage

In *The Modern Revival of Christian Faith,* Georgia Harkness said, "The cross is God's way of uniting suffering and love."

Over Oberammergau

A cross towers high above the Bavarian village of Oberammergau, where the Passion Play is presented each decade. No person can sit through the eight-hour drama without feeling the accusations of the cross and without finding himself in the crucifixion party. The cross means many things to many people. Whatever theology one embraces, Calvary is where God and mankind met, and God won!

Revamping the Cross

An unusual cross used to hang over the holy table in the chapel of Christ Church Cathedral, Saint Louis. It was a contemporary interpretation of the Missionary Cross. The Missionary Cross is, of course, a Greek Cross, with each of the four arms being the same length. It was originally known as the Jerusalem Cross, and at the time of the Crusades was adopted as the Crusaders' Cross.

The use of this contemporary cross provoked considerable comment. The designers attempted to picture the work to be done in the community by the church. The cross seeks to say that Christ lives or dies in the trades, vocations, and professions of a community.

In the center panel, for instance, was a family, the basic social and spiritual unit of society. On the arms were depicted the fur trade—doubtless Saint Louis's first business—the arts, the Municipal Opera, architecture, law, commerce, and the two major universities. The Saint Louis Cardinals, the newspapers, the shoe industry, and the breweries were also included. This vivid interpretation reminds us that when the cross of Christ runs horizontally through a community, it precipitates controversy.

In this case, it became necessary to revamp the cross!

The Symbol of Reconciliation

As a young minister, I frequently preached at road camps, commonly referred to as "chain gangs." Once, while speaking on the necessity of forgiveness, I noticed that tears filled the eyes of a burly man. Later, the guard told me this man desired a conference. When it was granted, the conversation ran something like this:

"I thought you said that whatever the sin, God would forgive. Is that right?"

"Yes," I replied, "if you satisfactorily meet the requirements of forgiveness and then demonstrate the new life in Christ."

"Well, I killed a man. I can't get him off my mind."

He began to weep. He told me the whole story. I suggested certain passages of Scripture, and daily disciplines. We prayed together during which time he reiterated his guilt to God.

Some weeks later, after the service, the guard told me the man wanted to know if I would eat dinner with him. This prisoner was one of the chefs. He prepared a good meal, and I complimented him on his culinary skills. To which he replied, "Thank you for telling me the story of forgiveness."

Watching Others Die

I once heard Martin D. Niemöller tell of his incarceration at Dachau. His cell was in plain view of the gallows. Day after day he watched men and women go to their deaths. He could hear their cries, curses, and prayers. He declared that the gallows became his best teacher. Through that horrible experience he was haunted by two questions: "What will happen on the day they lead you there and put you to the test? When they put that rope around your neck, what will be your last words? Will they be, 'Father, forgive them,' or will they be 'Criminals! Scum?' "

Niemöller said that if Jesus had cried out in vengeance, there would have been no New Testament, no church, and no Christian history.

A Witness to Faith

In the eyes of the world it (the cross) was a failure. But the cross on which He died has become the symbol of a faith which has sustained millions. This is not to say that every cross will be a success in the achievement of an external goal. Many of the crucified have simply disappeared. The cross is not a club to overcome an opponent by an appeal to human sympathy. It is a witness to faith and may or may not have a social impact.[2]

Death

Romans 8:35-39; 2 Corinthians 4:7-12; 2 Timothy 1:8-10;
Hebrews 2:14-18

In death, in the abyss, and in doubt we should remind ourselves, I have the word that I shall live no matter how hard death may press me.

—Martin Luther

Are You Prepared?

Joseph Addison went to Oxford in the seventeenth century and applied for admission at Magdalen College. He was ushered into a room draped in black and lighted by a single taper. When the president of the college—a gloomy Puritan—appeared, the candidate's examination related not to Latin, Greek, or literature, as he had thought, but to his personal faith. Suddenly the young man was asked, "Are you prepared for death?" Whereupon Addison fled, never to return.

Beyond the Sunset

One day Saint Francis was hoeing in his garden when a friend said, "What would you do if you knew you would die at sunset?" He replied, "I would finish hoeing my garden."

Comforting Hymns

It was no accident that during the painful illness of the former secretary of state, John Foster Dulles, he desired to hear the hymns of the church. He listened to the recordings of such offerings as "The Spacious Firmament on High," "When Morning Gilds the Skies," and "Through the Night of Doubt and Sorrow." The waning spirit of John Foster Dulles was rekindled night after night by listening to the great hymns of Christian faith.

Comments

Christians never say goodbye!
            —C. S. Lewis

We owe God a death.
            —Shakespeare

Don't bother me, can't you see I am busy dying?
            —H. G. Wells

Continue to Sing

The television movie, *The Thorn Birds,* reminded us of the Celtic legend which says the only time the thorn bird sings is at its death when it impales itself on a thorn; it continues to sing while dying.

Die Right

John Davis, known as "Uncle John," was 105 years old in 1981. He is South Carolina's only "AAA-rated trusty." He has been in prison since 1922. His crime? Burglary! He broke into a house and took a watch and five dollars. Burglary was a capital crime for black persons in Dillon County in the 1920s. Davis was sentenced to life. After escaping twice, he settled down, found Christ, and in 1940 became head cook at the Central Correctional Institution. He is free to leave, but he has nowhere to go. "Getting out here would be like digging my own grave. I got no living kin left, and who is going to take care of me, and pay for my medicine and my food and my clothes?"

Among other remarks, he said on his one-hundred-fifth birthday: "Since then [his escapes] I've met enough people to know right from wrong, and I've learned the best thing to do is to live right and pray right and treat other people right so I can die right."[1]

Don't Forget God!

In *Stay of Execution*, Stewart Alsop discussed what it was like to live with incurable leukemia. The disease was temporarily arrested. During this time, the not-too-active Episcopalian and noted journalist discussed a number of variables with his physician. Finally Alsop said, "There is one variable you keep leaving out."

"What's that?"

"God," he said.

The doctor and patient smiled. Alsop continued, "I don't really believe in God, or at least I don't think I do, and I doubt if my doctor does; but I think we both had in the back of our minds the irrational notion that God might have something to do with what happened all the same."

Face It Clean

Among the celebrated professors at Lynchburg College, Lynchburg, Virginia, is Sheldon Vanauken, author of the powerful book, *A Severe Mercy*. In it he told of his courtship and marriage to Jean Davis, and their days together at Oxford where they met C. S. Lewis, whose influence led them to Christian commitment. They were so in love and happy in the faith.

Subsequently, his bride fell victim to a mysterious disease. She was a patient at the Virginia Baptist Hospital for months. At last, at three o'clock in the morning, a telephone call brought word that Mrs. Vanauken was dying.

"How long?" the professor asked.

"They thought several hours," he was told.

Although time was of the essence, the weary and anxious man bathed and shaved before going to the hospital. "But I had to come to her—I had to face what must be faced—clean." He found her lucid.

Following a tender greeting, she said she was thirsty. "And I gave her a cup of water in the night—our old symbol of courtesy. Then I prayed one of the prayers we always prayed: 'Lighten our darkness, we beseech thee, O Lord; and by thy great mercy defend us from all perils and dangers of this night; for the love of Thy only Son, our Saviour, Jesus Christ. Amen.' "

In a day of frightening health care costs and carefully calibrated hospital profit structures, it is refreshing to note that Virginia Baptist Hospital, Lynchburg, Virginia, would not accept "a penny for all their care of her over months, not even for the meals they occasionally brought me."

The hospital's simple explanation was, she "had done more for them, for their nurses and other patients, than they had ever been able to do for her."[2]

Facing It

Death is the shadow that hangs over human life. It is the judgment. It is God's evaluation of your life and mine. Though impossible to do so, we are constantly attempting to escape the fact of death. The late William Randolph Hearst forbade anyone to use the word *death* in his presence. What a contrast to Philip II, King of Macedon and father of Alexander the Great, who commissioned a servant to come into his presence daily and solemnly announce, "Remember, Philip, thou must die."

Have Me Decently Buried

When dying, George Washington said to his physician friend, Dr. James Craik, "I feel myself going. I thank you for your attention. You had better not take any more trouble about me; but let me go off quietly; I cannot last long." Two days after his conversation with Craik he said to his secretary, "I am just going. Have me decently buried, and do not let my body be put into the vault in less than two days after I am dead. . . . 'Tis well."[3]

How Many Sundays?

The late Leslie Weatherhead told of being called to see a dying man who was afraid to die. As London's great preacher visited with the stranger about God, the church, Christ, and things of the Spirit, the man replied, "I have been too busy for these things. I have never had time." Weatherhead concluded his story by saying, "The man had been permitted to live four thousand Sundays!"

Spiritual Center for Life

A spiritual center for life gives meaning to every area of life. When despair and trouble come, the Christian must have the courage to exercise his faith on the evidence of what God has done in the past. One must remember Job's confidence:

"Though he slay me, yet will I trust him" (13:15). We must recognize that the hope we treasure is the gift of God and is our only valid response to the knowledge that He will be with us through the valley.[4]

The Mortality Rate—100 Percent

A brazen preacher told the congregation, "Someday every member of this parish will die!" The congregation was stunned, all except one man who laughingly said, "I don't belong to this parish." Small comfort! Despite medical miracles, the mortality rate remains at precisely 100 percent.

Nothing Wasted, Even Grief

To read Eugenia Price's *The Beloved Invader* is to be reminded that life has shocking ways of turning honeymoons into funerals. Ellen Gould died in the arms of Anson Dodge while honeymooning in India. The young minister and his charming wife had been guests of a British precinct officer in Allahabad.

After eating some grapes, Ellen became desperately ill. All night Anson and Dr. Hayworth struggled to keep her alive. With the coming of dawn, she whispered, "Anson, don't leave me." Her features changed. She was dead. In anguish the young minister cried, "No, God! No."

The Right Reverend Edward Ralph Johnson, bishop of Calcutta, conducted the service of memory. Reflecting on the funeral, all the confused husband could recall was the paraphrasing of Jesus' words, ". . . though she were dead, yet shall she live."

It was a long, sad voyage from Allahabad to Saint Simons Island, Georgia. During the weeks of heartbreaking travel, the young rector kept rehearsing Bishop Johnson's comment, "It is God's way not to waste anything. Even grief."

Friends at Saint Simons shared his crushing grief. Following another memorial service, Anson Dodge began the long, tedious task of recasting his life. Like the Indian lover, Shah Jehan, who erected the Taj Mahal, he with the cooperation of his congregation built a church in memory of Ellen—Christ's church! This cruciform structure of white pine, paneled in cedar, with delicate stained-glass windows, not only memorializes the devotion of a people to Almighty God, but also the growing faith of their shepherd and his mature love for Ellen Dodge whose body was eventually laid to rest under its altar.

His grief is reminiscent of the bereavement of Naomi who, bereft of husband and sons, said, "I went away full, and the Lord has brought me back empty" (Ruth 1:21).

Sad, Very Sad

Americans were saddened to hear of the demise of Arthur Godfrey, Wednesday, March 16, 1983. He was seventy-nine. With dogged determination, a gravelly voice, and a ukulele, he eventually cracked the entertainment world. It is claimed that at the height of his popularity as an entertainer, he had a daily audience of eighty million and received twenty-five thousand letters a day. It was not what he said that made him special, but the way he said it. Yet, according to Andy Rooney, who once worked for the "redhead," he did not have many friends. Godfrey did not want a funeral—and there wasn't one. "Sad," said Rooney, "very sad."

Contrast in Death

The French nurse who was present at the deathbed of Voltaire, being urged to attend an Englishman who was critically ill, asked: "Is the man a Christian?" "Yes," came the reply, "He is a man who lives in the fear of God, but why do you ask?"

"Sir," she answered, "I was the nurse who attended Voltaire in his last illness, and for all the wealth of Europe, I would never see another infidel die!"

The Ultimate in Courage and Love

Death is the shadow that hangs over humankind. To some it is a fearful thing, while to others it is a challenge. Louis XV, King of France, foolishly ordered that death was never to be spoken of in his presence. He sought to avoid every suggestion of death. Whatever camouflage or psychological facade is employed, death still comes. It startles us. Bishop Angus Dun said it well, "Death measures the ultimate in courage and in love."

Under Trivia

I could not believe my ears. I was shocked, even angry, when rising early Thursday, March 24, 1983, I heard a radio announcer flippantly remark: "Under trivia, Barney Clark is dead."

The casual spokesman made no reference to Clark's identity, or his heroic and sacrificial spirit. No appreciation was voiced for the team of extraordinary physicians who were participating in a daring experiment to save life; no family linkage; no mention that the principal inventor of the artificial heart, Robert Jarvik, "cried a little"; no admiration for this pioneer who desperately wanted to live, yet was willing to undergo stress and pain to be a breathing laboratory that physicians might learn to assist others. Clark said in one of his few interviews: "All in all, it has been a pleasure to be able to help people." For 112 days he demonstrated incredible courage and faith.

"Under trivia, Barney Clark is dead." No indeed! He has been removed from our sight, yes, but never from our memory and gratitude. He is no longer fettered to life-support systems, but free to rejoin his Creator.

I shall try to forget the inappropriate and irresponsible comment of the glib announcer and cherish all the more the assuring words of Jesus: "Greater love has no man than this, that a man lay down his life for his friends" (John 15:13).

Whether Life or Death

Immanuel Kant declared that no one had the right to talk about immortality until he worked so hard at being mortal that he longed for the immortal. Is not this the message of the apostle Paul? After a long and devoted career as an ambassador for Christ, he was arrested and thrown into prison. Not knowing what the future held for him, that is, on his captors' terms, he had the one hope that Christ would be honored in his body, whether by life or death.

"A White Soul"

When the poet Henry Wadsworth Longfellow lay in the dignity of death, his friend, Ralph Waldo Emerson, whose memory was failing, came to pay his respects. Standing by the casket, unable to identify him, Emerson, speaking slowly and calmly, said, "I don't remember this gentleman's name, but he was a white soul."

Easter

Ezekiel 37:1-3, 11-14; Matthew 28:1-10; John 5:25; John 11:25-27

> Christ the Lord is risen to-day, Alleluia!
> Sons of men and angels say, Alleluia!
> Raise your joys and triumphs high, Alleluia!
> Sing, ye heav'ns, and earth, reply, Alleluia!
> —Charles Wesley

Are You Ready?

When Dr. Cary Grayson told Woodrow Wilson the gravity of his condition, the President replied, "I am ready."

Comments

The resurrection is the land where great mists lie, but it is the land where the great rivers spring.

—David Cairns

H. G. Wells was once asked by a friend if he believed in another life. He replied, "One life is quite enough for little H. G."

Confirmation of Easter

He looked as old as the Judean hills and just as ugly. A short, stocky man draped in soiled robes stood at the entrance to Lazarus's tomb. Beneath his weathered face was a contagious smile. His clear, piercing eyes flashed the confirmation of Easter. Proudly he spoke of Bethany. With deep feeling, he described the sadness that claimed the community when Lazarus died. Gently he pointed to the tombs, saying, "Jesus came here and raised Lazarus. This is the place where the Master said, 'I am the resurrection and the life' " (John 11:25ff). So spoke the guide on one visit to Bethany.

Do You Know God?

In a splendid sermon (*Pulpit Digest,* March-April 1983), Lewis A. Drummond of The Southern Baptist Theological Seminary said: "When everything else is over and said and done, only one thing ultimately matters: Do you know God? Can you face eternity with Him?"

Facing Death

One of the penetrating churchmen of the past generation was Reverend James Gordon Gilkey. While living in Portland, Oregon, he was told by his physician that he had an incurable disease. Death could not be averted, nor long delayed. What did he do? Here is his own story:

I walked out to my home five miles from the center of the city. There

I looked at the river and the mountain which I love, and then—as the twilight deepened—at the stars glimmering in the sky. Then I said to them, "I may not see you many times more. But River, I shall be alive when you have ceased running to the sea. Mountain, I shall be alive when you have sunk down into the plain. Stars, I shall be alive when you have fallen in the ultimate disintegration of the universe."[1]

The Gift of Life

While a patient at Groote Schuur Hospital, Cape Town, South Africa, Philip Blaiberg told of the night when Christiaan Barnard, gowned and muzzled, walked into his sterile room carrying in his hand a plastic box. It contained his old heart. The eminent surgeon said: "Dr. Blaiberg, do you realize that you are the first man in the history of mankind to be able to sit as you are now, and look at his own, dead heart?"

What a dramatic moment! What a miracle! Second unto it was when the courageous patient met for the first time the woman who had given him life, namely, permission for surgeons to remove the heart of her dead husband. Blaiberg asked, "What does one say in such circumstances? She had lost a life, I had gained one."

This is precisely the gift of the revolutionary Christ: "I came that they may have life, and have it abundantly" (John 10:10).

Holy Week

May Holy Week be holy with ministries of unselfishness.
May Holy Week be holy with acts of forgiveness.
May Holy Week be holy with demonstrations of faith.
And may we keep it holy with love.

House Of Life

Death is no stranger. Much is made over it; sometimes funeral displays far exceed demonstrations of Christian discipleship. Extravagant sentimentality frequently prevails. The mortuary is a house of death; the church is a house of life.

If We Live the Eternal

The late and marvelous preacher, Ralph W. Sockman, while writing an Easter sermon one year, received word that a friend had died. He was a scholar, a doctor of philosophy from Columbia University, a distinguished missionary to China for forty years. A daily prayer of this remarkable servant included: "Oh, God our Father, I accept Thy gift of love; help me to pass it on for Jesus' sake." On the morning of the missionary's death, at age ninety-two, Lacey Sites said to those near his bedside: "If we live the eternal life now, we will always."

Not Yet Dead

At least once Samuel L. Clemens, better known as "Mark Twain," was listed as dead while being physically alive. This type of erroneous obituary has occurred all too often in the newspapers of our nation.

On one such embarrassing occasion, a man whose obit was printed in the paper rushed to the editor. The "corpse" lodged his protest: "How dare you print my obituary in the paper! I'm alive. See me. Here I am." "I sure am sorry," the editor answered, "And it's too late to do anything about it. The best thing I can do for you is to put you in the 'Birth Column' tomorrow morning and give you a fresh start!"

Lent

Fast from criticism, and feast on praise.
Fast from self-pity, and feast on joy.
Fast from ill-temper, and feast on peace.
Fast from resentment, and feast on contentment.
Fast from jealousy, and feast on love.
Fast from pride, and feast on humility.
Fast from selfishness, and feast on service.
Fast from fear, and feast on faith.[2]

More Beyond

For centuries Portugal's motto was "Nothing More Beyond." Their world was limited to the familiar dimensions of the area around the Mediterranean Sea. They believed that to sail beyond the horizon, their border, would be to drop off the edge of the world. Eventually, voyagers discovered worlds beyond and brought back evidence to substantiate their claims. Decision makers were compelled to alter their motto to read, "More Beyond."

Easter assures us there is more beyond the grave. We do not have a chart to guide us, save Jesus Christ; details are sketchy, but our destination is certain.

The Mystery and the Promise

Toward the end of his monumental work, *A Stillness at Appomattox, the War in Virginia*, Bruce Catton described the sober moments preceding General Lee's surrender.

> It was Palm Sunday, and they (the soldiers) would like to see Easter, and with the guns quieted it might be easier to comprehend the mystery and the promise of that day. Yet the fact of peace and no more killing and an open road home seems to have been too big to grasp, right at the moment, and in the enormous silence that lay upon the field men remembered that they had marched far and were very tired, and they wondered when the wagon trains would come up with rations.[3]

Never Mind the Crucifixion

John Sutherland Bonnell shares this experience from World War II. A soldier lay wounded on the battlefield. He had been given up for dead. As life slowly and painfully returned, he thirsted for water. No one answered his cries. No one attended his wounds. Mercifully, he slipped into unconsciousness. When he awoke, a chaplain was bending over him. "You say, my boy, that you were wounded on Good Friday, and that you have been lying on the battlefield ever since? Do you know that this is Easter morning?"

The lad answered, "How wonderful! For me, too, it is like a resurrection. Out there on the field I died a thousand deaths, but somehow we do not mind the crucifixion when we are sure of the resurrection."[4]

Palm Sunday

Henry Alford, English clergyman, was born in Somersetshire, October 7, 1810, to a family that had given England five generations of clergymen. He graduated from Trinity College, Cambridge, in 1832. Being a writer, as well as a theologian, he published and served smaller parishes before becoming dean of Canterbury Cathedral in 1856, a position he held until his death on June 12, 1871. He is buried at Canterbury. His epitaph reads: "The inn of a traveler on his way to Jerusalem."

See You in the Morning!

I shall long remember the homegoing of my father. He had been ill for some months. One Saturday morning, the Inner Voice told me I should visit him. He lived seventy-five miles up-country from Richmond, Virginia. Although the Sunday sermon had not been completely refined, I obeyed the prompting of the Spirit and made the journey.

Upon arriving, the nurse told me father had hoped I would come. She cleared the room and we had a wonderful visit. Death was imminent, but he was calm and lucid. After giving me several business directives, he declared he would soon be going. "Give my love to mother," I added. Then, with animation and joy he shared with me a moving dream from the previous night. They visited; mother was awaiting his arrival. I kissed him good-bye, and as I turned to leave he said, "Curt, I'll see you in the morning!" He died during my sermon that Sunday.

But I'll see him and mother in the morning!

Sharing the Faith

The Moravians refer to their common cemetery as "God's Acre." Members are buried beneath simple flat, white stones, all alike, to dramatize the democracy of death. During Holy Week, parishioners scrub clean those identifying stones. On Holy Saturday these loving people bring flowers for each grave. Then, before dawn on Easter morning, the community of believers meet at the church, and to the beat of a muted band, march into the cemetery to celebrate the resurrection of Jesus from the dead.

What We Least Understand

In *A Grief Observed* (Seabury, 1961), C. S. Lewis said: "There is also, whatever it means, the resurrection of the body. We cannot understand. The best is perhaps what we understand least."

Words Worth Hearing

In London during World War II, placards hung over broadcasting booths that read, "Is What You Are Saying Worth a Man's Risking His Life to Hear?" Jesus not only risked His life, indeed, He gave it for the privilege of authenticating the declaration: "I am the resurrection and the life; he who believes in me, though he die, yet shall he live, and whoever lives and believes in me shall never die" (John 11:25-26).

You Will Find Love and Welcome

John Todd was born in Vermont in 1801. Shortly afterwards his family moved to Killingsworth, Connecticut. Before John was six years old he was orphaned. He, his brothers, and sisters were parceled out among the relatives. John was assigned to a kindhearted aunt who lived ten miles away. She became father and mother to the homeless lad and saw him through Yale and into his chosen profession.

There came a time when the aunt was taken seriously ill. She knew that death was close at hand. She was afraid and uncertain about the future. In her anxiety she wrote John. Since he could not be at her bedside at the moment, he wrote her this letter:

It is now nearly thirty-five years since I, a little boy of six, was left quite alone in the world. . . . I have never forgotten the day when I made the long journey to your house in North Killingsworth. I still recall my disappointment when instead of coming for me yourself you sent your hired man Caesar to fetch me. And I can still remember my tears and anxiety, as perched on your horse and clinging tightly to Caesar, I started out for my new home. As we rode along, I became more and more afraid and finally said anxiously to Caesar, "Do you think she will go to bed before we get there?" "Oh, no," he answered reassuringly, "she'll sure stay up for you. When we get out of these here woods, you will see her candle shining in the window."

Presently we did ride out into a clearing, and there, sure enough, was your candle. I remember you were waiting at the door, that you put your arms around me, that you lifted me down from the horse. There was a fire on your hearth, a warm supper on your stove. After supper, you took me up to bed, heard my prayers, and then sat beside me until I dropped asleep.

You undoubtedly realize why I am recalling all these things. . . . Some day soon God may send for you, to take you to a new home. Don't fear the summons, the strange journey, the dark messenger of death. At the end of the road you will find love and a welcome; you will be safe there as here, in God's love and care. Surely He can be trusted to be as kind to you as you were years ago to me![5]

Education

Proverbs 3:13-16; Matthew 5:2; Romans 15:1-6; 1 Timothy 4:11

There are two kinds of education—one teaches us how to make a living and the other teaches us how to live.
—William Barclay

Life is always a race between education and catastrophe.
—H. G. Wells

Academic Island

In referring to the university community, John Gunther, using Chicago as an illustration, maintains that it has its own nationalism, its own special tang, color, and flavor quite independent of the state wherein it is located.

Aspiring to Do Good

Mark Hopkins, educator, ordained minister in the Congregational Church, and president of Williams College from 1836 to 1872, is quoted as having said to a graduating class:

If the only option available to Williams were to graduate men with the highest learning but without any interest in the welfare of mankind, or to graduate men with less mental capacity but possessing an aspiration to do good, I would choose the latter for Williams because it would render a more essential service.

Anthems for Humanity?

Norman Cousins says, "The great failure of education—not just in the United States but throughout most of the world—is that is has made people tribe-conscious rather than species-conscious. It has put limited identification ahead of ultimate identification. It has attached value to the things man does but not to what man is. Man's institutions are celebrated but not man himself. Man's power is heralded but the preciousness of life is unsung. There are national anthems but no anthems for humanity."[1]

The Bell Still Tolls

There is a moving story concerning the College of William and Mary, chartered in 1693. With buildings severely damaged, the institution was temporarily closed during the Civil

War. Afterwards, it reopened, only to face another suspension due largely to inadequate funds. The desertion lasted seven years. However, we are advised that during this anxious interim, its strong president, Benjamin Stoddert Ewell, rang the chapel bell every morning. There were no students, the faculty had disappeared, and buildings stood ghostlike against the sky.

Get the picture: a graduate of West Point, professor of mathematics, president of a colonial college nurtured by the Church of England, who also had served as chief of staff to General Joseph E. Johnston, personally assumed responsibility for a deserted college! Imagine, if you can, the discipline and dedication required of an educator to ring the familiar bell every morning. President Ewell demonstrated the synthesis between faith and learning so desperately needed today. His act eloquently declared: The educational life of this community will return. Buildings will be restored. Our faith will find fulfillment.

Challenging Voices

In his inaugural address in 1978, A. Bartlett Giamatti, the nineteenth president of Yale, said,

> Everyone in this hall can recall certain voices, the voices of teachers who changed the way we live our lives. I am concerned, at last, with the next generation of voices. I wish them to be as strong and confident and effective in what they do as those who came before. And they will be, if we recall our nature and our purpose and engage each other to fashion our future together.[2]

Start Them Early

After a lecture by the late Chicago educator, Francis Wayland Parker, a woman asked:

"How early can I begin the education of my child?"

"When will your child be born?" asked Parker.

"Born?" she replied. "Why, he is already five years old!" "My goodness, woman," he cried, "don't stand here talking to me—hurry home; already you have lost the best five years!"

Church-Related Colleges

The concern for Christian higher education was so very much a part of the life of our forefathers that of the first 270 colleges established in America, 180—two thirds—were church related. By the time of the Civil War there were five-hundred colleges in sixteen states and the majority of them were affiliated with some Protestant denomination.

Comments

Education is too important to be left solely with the educators.
—Francis Keppel, former U. S.
Commissioner of Education

Education is a controlling grace to the young, consolation to the old, wealth to the poor, and ornament to the rich.
—Diogenes Laertius

Continuing Growth

The late H. G. Wells wrote that his mother went to a finishing school, and at the age of nineteen she was finished. Ideas, he said, rattled around in her head like bullets in an empty container. You could hear the hard little bullets rattling around, ideas that were shaped thirty years ago.

Deny, Doubt, Declare!

Pascal said one should be able to deny well, to doubt well, and to believe well. Education should help persons do all three.

An Ill-Educated Man

In referring to the disastrous reign of King Edward VIII, Alistair Cooke wrote,

Edward comes out of it all as one of the least enlightened of British monarchs—a charming, spoiled, woefully ill-educated man, painfully simpleminded and ferociously acquisitive. He is more to be pitied than abused in that the worlds of art, literature, music, politics, science, religion, philosophy—the whole life of the mind—were closed to him.[3]

The Joy of Learning

Newspapers across America, on June 12, 1983, carried two contrasting, but equally unique, graduation stories: Isaac Dworetsky, sixty-four, a World War II bomber pilot, graduated from Bronx Community College, New York, as class valedictorian. He had a straight A average while working two jobs.

Isaiah Wexler, age thirty, received his fifth academic degree, M.D., from New York University. Wexler had earned a bachelor of arts degree from Yeshiva University in 1974; a master's in Jewish philosophy from the same school in 1978; a rabbinical degree that year, and was ordained; and a doctorate in political philosophy from Fordham in 1978. He studied at Fordham and New York Universities concurrently. Oh, yes, he was also an active rabbi!

Largest Class

Media reported there were 1,378,400 graduating from America's colleges and universities in 1983, the largest class in our history.

Nation's Report Card

America's schools are getting better according to an article in *Time*, October 10, 1983. A number of community schools were cited, as well as comments from prominent educators. Ernest Boyer, former U. S. Commissioner of Education under President Carter, and currently president of the Carnegie Foundation, is quoted as saying:

School is in a very real sense a mirror of its community. Time and time again, we saw that community support or community conditions were shaping the school. So, in a very real sense, the report card on the school is a report card on the nation.

Proliferation of Graduates

In 1982 American colleges and universities graduated the largest number in history: 945,000 bachelor's degrees, 303,000 doctorates, and an all-time high of 73,600 first professional degrees. . . . This class, almost evenly divided between male and female graduates, has great demographic diversity, with many older students and minorities.[4]

A Proud Parade

At the two-hundred-fiftieth anniversary of the founding of Harvard, students marched in a torchlight procession. The most provocative group was the freshman class, one month old, carrying a huge banner which read, "The University has been waiting 250 years for us!"

Psychological Preparedness

The following letter has been passed around from administrator to administrator among colleges and universities. It ran something like this:

Dear Mom and Dad:

I thought I should write before you receive the bill from the hospital so you will not be too alarmed. Let me say first that I did manage to escape with only minor burns and a few fractures when my dormitory burned to the ground last week. And having nowhere to live, I know you will understand why I am rooming with this very attractive and interesting student who so generously offered his quarters to me. While he is not exactly a communist (I'd call him more of a practicing Marxist) and is from one of the more rebellious and underdeveloped nations, I know that you won't be too bothered about these facts, remembering those perfectly splendid liberal views of yours on politics and human relations. Yet I must face the possibility that it may upset you to hear that by the time I come home for the holidays I will have become a mother.

Love,
Betsy

P.S. None of these things happened. But I did get a D-minus in political science and I flunked math, and I just want you to see those grades in proper perspective!

Vision for a University

In speaking to Littleton W. Tazewell concerning his plans for the University of Virginia, Thomas Jefferson said: "All 'sciences'—that is, all branches of learning—would fall within the province of this university, and the subjects should be taught in the highest degree to which the human mind has carried them."[5]

We're Flunking

Despite our nation spending $96 billion on elementary and secondary schools in 1980, The National Commission on Excellence in Education reported in April of 1983 that: "The educational foundations of our society are presently being eroded by a rising tide of mediocrity." SAT scores have plummeted in the last few years, too high a percentage of high school graduates are poorly educated, and the quality of new teachers has deteriorated. There are 23 million adults in America who are "functionally illiterate."

Winsome Victory!

Horace Mann will long be remembered for his prophetic contributions to education in America, especially public school education. He worked to broaden the basis of learning and to enrich the teaching experience. He often found himself out of step with the times. In his final address at Antioch College he said: "When I think of these things, I wish for another warfare on behalf of right. I would enlist for another fifty-year campaign." Later in that memorable speech the noted educator challenged the graduating class: "Be ashamed to die 'til you have won some victory for mankind."

Evangelism

Matthew 4:18-19; Matthew 28:18-20; John 1:41; 2 Timothy 4:5

You must be born again (John 3:7, NASB).
—Jesus Christ

Evangelism is the struggle for the salvation of this world.
—D. T. Niles

The Burning Fire

In referring to the evangelistic work of passengers when their vessel went aground and their voyage was temporarily interrupted, the seventeenth-century Quaker ship's captain, Robert Fowler, wrote in his log: "They gathered sticks, and kindled a fire, and left it burning."

Called to Serve

The late William Temple is believed by many to have been the greatest Archbishop of Canterbury for centuries. While still in his thirties he was called to London to assume responsibility for a famous parish. One cold, winter night three Episcopalian colleagues appeared at his home challenging him to become their leader in launching a New Life movement in England. They declared it was time to go to the people with the gospel of Jesus. "And, Temple, we think you are the man to lead it. We can only offer you half the salary you are getting. It might be all a mistake. We think you are the man to lead it. Will you accept?"

For days William Temple wrestled with the challenge. At last he picked up the telephone and called: "I am ready. When do you want me to start?"

The world knows the answer. William Temple took the plunge for God and the Lord made him a great man.

Conversion at Midnight

In the sixteenth chapter of Acts, we read of the imprisonment of Paul and Silas in Philippi. They were not discouraged because of the phony charges that placed them behind bars. The record declares that about midnight Paul and Silas were praying and singing hymns to God. The prisoners listened.

Suddenly there was an earthquake that shook the building and loosened its doors. The opening of the doors awakened the keeper of the prison, who drew his sword to take his life, when Paul cried out, "Do not harm yourself, for we are all here." The jailer called for lights and, with fear, fell down before these missionaries asking, "Men, what must I do to be saved?"

They said, "Believe in the Lord Jesus, and you will be saved, you and your household" (Acts 16:28,30-31).

Dramatic Conversion

On a sultry day in July, 1505, a lonely traveler was trudging along a dry road on the outskirts of Stotternheim, a village in the German region of Saxony. He was short of stature and wore the garb of a university student. Suddenly there was a shower, then a crashing storm. A bolt of lightning knocked the young man to the ground. Struggling to rise, he cried out in terror, "St. Anne, help me! I will become a monk."

The man who thus committed himself to being a monk later repudiated the system. A loyal son of the Catholic Church, he later shattered the structure. A devoted servant of the Pope, he was later to identify the Pope with the Antichrist. The young man was Martin Luther.

An Evangelist

The term "evangelist" comes from the Greek and means "one who announces good news." The word *evangelist* occurs only three times in the New Testament: (1) Philip is called an evangelist in Acts 21:8; (2) Among God's gifts to the churches were evangelists (Eph. 4:11); (3) Timothy is urged to "do the work of an evangelist" (2 Tim. 4:5).

Finding the Lost We Have Lost

I met an interesting man who is active in one of the great churches in Washington, D. C. I asked him what he did in his congregation. Enthusiastically, he said he was responsible for coordinating the calling of the officers of the church on inactive and homebound members. Each officer in this large, metropolitan church is expected to make three calls a week, or twelve a month. What a specific implementation of the Lord's parable of the lost sheep (Matt. 18:20).

Growth and Decline of Christianity

In 1900, two thirds of Christians lived in Europe and Russia; by 2000, three fifths of them will live in Africa, Asia, and Latin America. While Westerners cease to be practicing Christians at a rate of seventy-six hundred per day, Africa is gaining four thousand Christians per day through conversion from other religions, and three times that many through the birth rate.[1]

Hope for Nobodys

A little boy heard the noted American preacher, Howard Thurman, preach in India. One night after he and Mrs. Thurman had gone to bed, there was a knock at the door. Opening it, there stood a lad whose clothing marked him as an untouchable. In broken, but polite, English he said: "I stood outside the building and listened to your lecture, Sahib Doctor. Tell me, please, can you give some hope to a nobody?" Whereupon the

Indian boy dropped to his knees in admiration and reverence as the compassionate black Christian attempted to communicate the meaning of Christ's invitation: "Please come, everything is now ready" (Luke 14:17, NEB).

More Than the Mind

Writing on Dante's *Divine Comedy*, John Freccero of Cornell University reminds us that Dante's journey began where ancient allegories left off and that the frustrations of the pilgrim dramatize the insufficiency of a purely intellectual conversion. Knowledge and virtue to Socrates were synonymous; not so with Dante.

Personal Challenge

Dr. John Branscomb once related a conversation that led to the conversion of the late Dr. Paul Quillian. While Quillian was working in a bottling plant in Pine Bluff, Arkansas, he received his minister, who confronted him with the question, "How old are you?"

"About thirty," was the answer.

The conversation centered around a man, his work, and his witness. Then the preacher said to Quillian, "When you stand finally before the Lord God, what will you tell him you did on earth—made red soda water?"

The young man snapped back, "And what is wrong with red soda water?"

"Nothing, my son, except you happen to be endowed with great talents and abilities which I cherish for God and the Christian ministry."

Consequently, the young man went back to school and prepared for the preaching ministry. He itinerated in Arkansas. Finally this wonderful leader was called to the First Methodist Church of Houston, Texas, then a church of twenty-five hundred souls. After fifteen years of labor and love, the congregation numbered six thousand.[2]

A Place at the Table

Malcolm Muggeridge, with a Fabian Socialist upbringing, once an atheist, a career journalist, at one time hearty drinker and womanizer, at age seventy-nine surrendered his will to the Lord. This gadfly of British letters, an eloquent peddler of words, gathered up his contradictions and beliefs in November 1982, marched down to a small chapel in Hurst Green, Sussex, and, with his wife, became a member of the Roman Catholic Church. His decision to convert was inspired in part by the life and witness of Mother Teresa. Commenting on the experience, the mellowed old iconoclast said there was "a sense of home-coming, of picking up the threads of a lost life, of responding to a bell that has long been ringing, of finding a place at a table that has long been left vacant."[3]

Postponed

There is a moving scene in Augustine's *Confessions* where he seems ripe and ready for conversion. There is one man whom he wanted to talk to above all others, Bishop Ambrose. Again and again Augustine walked hopefully past the open doors of the cathedral library where Ambrose was deep in study. Ambrose was present for Augustine, but Augustine was not able to see Ambrose. Knowing how busy the bishop was, Augustine was reluctant to disturb him, so his conversion was delayed. We, too, become so enamored with self-interests, employment, that we sometimes fail to see those about us or to take the initiative in a conversation. There must be honest attempts at encounter and conversion.

A Quarter Before Nine

On May 24, 1738, Wesley had his morning devotions, dropped into Saint Paul's Cathedral, and was greatly moved by the music. That evening he reluctantly attended a prayer meeting in Aldersgate Street where a man—name not given—was reading Luther's Preface to the Epistle of the Romans. He reports, "A quarter before nine, I felt my heart strangely warmed. I felt I would trust in Christ, Christ alone for salvation; an assurance was given me that he had taken away my sin." It was an amazing day, a day that laid the foundation for the next fifty years of Wesley's remarkable life.

Redundant Churches?

The Wall Street Journal of June 21, 1983, carried a disturbing article on vacant church buildings in Britain. The delicate debate as to what should be done with idle structures intensified when the rector of a parish down the road from All Saints Church "took the bells down from the tower." He proposed to melt them. Many citizens from Saltfleetby, England, were incensed, especially Mrs. Aegerter, who lives next door to All Saints and who sweeps and cleans the church regularly.

This thirteenth-century stone structure is said to be one of 186 old buildings the Church of England has "mothballed." They have created a "Redundant Church Fund," apparently waiting for a revival, a miracle, or a demographic shift in population.

Their contemporary poet, Philip Larkin, asked: "When churches fall completely out of use, what shall we turn them into?" He continues. Shall we keep "a few chronically on show . . . and let the rest rent-free to rain and sheep?"

Since 1969, church authorities have indicated that 908 churches are no longer needed; 247 of them have already been demolished, and another 475 buildings have been "converted" to other purposes.

When is a church redundant? Is it not possible for a so-called active congregation to be spiritually empty?

The Revealing Book

The late E. Stanley Jones told the story of a missionary in India who labored for months trying to convert a man to Christianity. All the while the prospect was observing the teacher. He came for conferences many, many times. At last the humble man exclaimed, "I have found you out. You are not as good as your Book."

The Starting Point

After one of Dwight L. Moody's meetings, a locomotive engineer came forward and said he had decided to become a missionary to a foreign country. Moody asked him if his fireman were a Christian. "I don't know," was the reply, "I've never asked him." "Well," said Moody, "why don't you start with your fireman?"

Taking a Chance

Saint Columba, a sixth-century Irish missionary, was sent to evangelize northern Scotland. The adventure was hazardous because of the Picts who occupied the area. Columba and twelve men sailed to the nearby island of Iona. The first thing they did was to burn their boat. They were afraid to trust themselves with a seaworthy craft which might tempt them to leave. Thus, a boatload of men brought Christ to Scotland.

Tell the Story

In Archibald MacLeish's play *J. B.*, there is a provocative scene wherein the family is seated around the Thanksgiving table. As J. B. carves the turkey, the children begin urging their father to tell the story. They, of course, know the story. They had been brought up on how J. B. had become a shining knight in the business world. But tradition and expectation demanded a recapitulation of the saga on a day of celebration.

All of us have a story. Families hand down stories, and they are often repeated at festive occasions. Individuals have stories to tell, and so do congregations. Professing Christians are commissioned to tell the story of the promised Messiah, His life, death, and resurrection (Matt. 28:16-20).

Win a Few

A news item written by a brilliant space engineer from a previous church caught my eye. As he and his traveling companion were waiting in Chicago's crowded O'Hare Airport, a little woman, humbly dressed, approached and asked, "Are you saved?" They answered in the affirmative. As they talked together, my friend remarked, "I admire your courage and your faith. I suspect you are criticized and frequently embarrassed." "Yes," she replied, "but it is worth it all to win a few."

Your Platform

Alvin Dark, ardent Baptist, an all-American in football and a star baseball player at Louisiana State University, has teamed with John Underwood to write a delightful and disturbing account of his life under the arresting title: *When in Doubt, Fire the Manager.* The reader will gain new insights into the game inappropriately called, "The Nation's Pastime."

After years of solid performance with the Boston Braves and the New York Giants, where he was captain, he became a manager. Alvin guided the San Francisco Giants, the Kansas City Athletics, the Cleveland Indians, and the Oakland Athletics to a World Series championship. He also managed the San Diego Padres.

Despite his up-and-down career professionally and personally, this warm, open, born-again Christian says toward the end of his book:

> Baseball is the platform God gave me. I think without a doubt I serve Him best in that field, just as others might as postmen or doctors ("gifts differing according to the grace given to us," Paul wrote in his letter to the Romans).

Faith

Matthew 4:18-19; Mark 5:34; Hebrews 10:37-39;11:1-39; 1 John 5:4

In matters of faith every generation has to begin again.
—Sören Kierkegaard

Blind Trust

This amazing story of animal affinity came from Edmond, Oklahoma, and was reported by United Press International Telephoto November 25, 1982: Marie, a blind pony, was adopted by Ralph, her "seeing-eye" sheep, who leads her where she needs to go.

Comments

Faith is an act and an affirmation of that act that bids eternal truth to be present fact.
—Jack R. Taylor

The opposite of joy is not sorrow. It is unbelief.
—Leslie Weatherhead

Confidence

There is a supportive story in 2 Kings. Samaria, where Elisha and his servant lived, was unexpectedly surrounded by the enemy. Ben-hadad besieged the city by night. When the servant of the prophet saw the army round about the city the following morning, he exclaimed: "Alas, my master! What shall we do?" Elisha answered: "Fear not, for those who are with us are more than those who are with them" (6:15-16).

Faith and Fact

Faith is not credulity. It is not believing in something you know is not true. Neither is faith a substitute for knowledge.

Christian faith operates in the realm of meaning, not in the realm of fact. Faith recognizes fact but it is not out to obtain, contradict, or prove facts. Saint Augustine knew this when he said, "I believe in order that I may understand."

Faith in Afterlife?

In an interview with Dotson Rader (*Parade,* March 6, 1983), Bette Davis declared:

> I keep wondering how it will all end. I keep making bets about how I will finally go. I'm curious whether it will be in an airplane or somewhere else. I don't want to miss anything, that's why I would hate to die. I'm very religious, though I've never been a big churchgoer. Being a working woman, I decided God would allow me Sundays off. I also have a deep belief that most truly religious people aren't found in church. I don't believe in an afterlife. No, I believe we have our heaven and hell here, and then it's over.[1]

Faith Is: Hearing with the Heart

An American missionary in Africa wanted to translate the English word *faith* into the local dialect. He could not find its equivalent. So he went to an old sage, who was himself a fine Christian, for help in rendering the needed word into understandable language. The guru studied it, and finally said, "Does it not mean to hear with the heart?"

Faith Is the Victory

A nationwide poll was taken in the United States on religious questions. When asked whether they believed in God, 95 percent of those polled answered "yes." When asked whether religion in any way affected their politics and their business, 54 percent said "no." They had a belief, but they did not have a directing faith. Faith is action. Faith encompasses the entire spectrum of life's encounters and experiences.

From Ashes to Dreams

One needs to see the creative role of the church in this complex, corrupt, and challenging society. In the prologue to *From the Ashes of Christianity,* Mary Jean Irion tells of visiting a friend whose country home had been destroyed by fire. With dramatic delicacy she relates what it was like to move through the rubble of once beautiful furnishings now consumed and charred. Her friend, managing a smile, said, "Everything's gone, but they were only things. When we think about almost losing Mark. . . ." Then she told the terrifying experience of rescuing her child at midnight.

As they walked amid destruction, her companion announced they would build again, that the foundations were solid. "We have already named the new house 'Phoenix.' Isn't that a wonderful name?" That, of course, is the bird of Egyptian fable that soars above ashes and defies death.

God Calling!

Because of unexpected and unbelievable developments, I felt the only honorable decision was to resign from the church. It was difficult because I had a wife and three small boys. So, before a surprised congregation, I announced my resignation at the morning service. At approximately two o'clock that afternoon, the telephone rang. It was long distance. The chairman of the pulpit committee—a thousand miles away—was calling to invite me to become minister of a church in transition. It was a historic church, once a powerful witness. Attrition had taken its toll; it was dying with dignity. Cramped in the lungs of the city, the congregation decided to move out. After a prolonged conversation, I accepted over the telephone. There was no interview; no trial sermon; the telephone call was it! And I never had a more fruitful, happy ministry anywhere.

In the Future

On January 8, 1970, Enju Utake, age sixty-eight, opened a bank account payable in a thousand years. The article declared that the mayor of Hachioji, a suburb of Tokyo, had deposited ten thousand yen (about twenty-eight dollars) in a local bank so his direct descendants could collect a fortune on New Year's Day, 2970.

In the Struggles of Life

Adolf Hitler could not silence pastor Martin Niemöller, and kept him imprisoned for seven-and-a-half years. His ministry during and after incarceration was courageous and constructive. Having read many of his books and heard him during frequent trips to America, I was pleased that he granted me an interview in the Ecumenical Center in Frankfurt. He was warm and outgoing, repeating frequently, "We are responsible for mankind."

Toward the end of our visit he said: "Christianity is not an ethic, nor is it a system of dogmatics, but a living thing. One cannot deal with God in solitude or in remoteness only, but in the struggles of life."

Keeping Appointments

An unforgettable experience occurred in Tripoli, North Africa. Though plans for my visit to Wheelus Air Base had been made a year in advance, due to many factors I had been unable to communicate with my host for the past few weeks. After a hard flight from "Palestine," I landed at the commercial airfield about ten o'clock Saturday night. I wondered if the chaplains had remembered. This was the weekend of the Berlin Wall crisis in 1961. What should and could I say to our personnel? When I approached the airport, it was a genuine relief to see a smiling American colonel wave to me. After customs, the wing chaplain's assistant, a major, turned and said: "This is

Christian faith in people. We have never seen you before. You have never seen us, but we kept our appointment with each other."

Learning from Children

Martin Luther found great comfort in and inspiration from his children. Disturbed and depressed by his enemies, one day he noticed little Martin nursing in his mother's arms and remarked, "Child, your enemies are the Pope, the Bishops, Duke George, Ferdinand, and the devil. And there you are . . . unconcerned." Even as he noticed his child's complete trust, he realized his own anxiety was unwarranted; God had promised to protect him.

On another occasion Luther came upon Anasthasia, his four-year-old, prattling away about Christ, angels, and heaven. Whereupon the noted churchman said, "My dear child, if only one could hold fast to this faith." Quickly she replied, "Why, Papa, don't you believe it?" Luther was shocked and later wrote, "Christ has made the children our teachers."

National Faith

The author of the eleventh chapter of Hebrews reminded us that we are surrounded by "a cloud of witnesses" (12:1). Indeed! And so, we are, likewise, aware of the heroes of our national heritage. With reverence and thanksgiving, we would paraphrase portions of this noble chapter in Hebrews, as applied to emerging America, to read:

By faith, the *Susan Constant,* the *Godspeed,* and the *Discovery* found their way to the shores of Virginia. By faith, the Founders commenced a way of life that left its lasting mark in history.

By faith, the voyaging *Mayflower* found harbor in Plymouth Bay. By faith, these pathfinders dedicated to God, vowed to do his will on earth as it would be done in heaven.

By faith, Thomas Jefferson and his colleagues dared to draft a document of political independence that gave vision to new concepts and procedures in government.

By faith, George Washington left his spacious mansion and espoused the cause of the tax-burdened colonists. By faith, he forsook ease and comfort to be with his men amid the rigors of Valley Forge.

By faith, Alexander Hamilton established the financial credit of the nation, and thus revived the economic life of the young country.

By faith, James Madison gave generously of his brilliant mind to frame the Federal Constitution.

By faith, Andrew Jackson fought the battle of the impoverished and the underprivileged.

By faith, Abraham Lincoln saved the Compact of the Pilgrim fathers.

By faith, Woodrow Wilson saw the land of peace, saw the promise, but was never privileged to enjoy it.

And what more shall I say? For space would fail me to tell of the Hoovers, the Roosevelts, the Trumans, the Eisenhowers, the Kennedys, the Johnsons, the Nixons, the Fords, the Carters, and the Reagans, and those from every station and vocation who have contributed to our culture and to our faith; and of the uncounted and unsung throng of hardworking and devoted citizens who through generations have believed in honest toil, moral integrity, equality of opportunity, necessity of education, inescapable responsibility, and devotion to God. Such was the faith of our fathers.

Perpetual Praise

Persistence is a key to the door of reality and satisfaction. "Go again seven times (1 Kings 18:43, KJV). These words were spoken by Elijah to his servant. For three years, people in parched Israel had turned their dusty eyes and pleading faces to a cloudless sky. Men and beasts famished. Beyond the mooing of cattle, rustling of dried grass, and other complaints,

Elijah could hear the sound of rain! The prophet sent his servant to a vantage point to look for a rain cloud while he prayed. The servant returned saying, "There is nothing." Six times the prophet ordered him to go to the top of the hill and look, and six times the servant reported: "There is nothing." But on the seventh trip the weary servant saw something and joyfully exclaimed: "There ariseth a little cloud out of the sea, like a man's hand" (v. 44, KJV). The king was informed, the rains came, and the people rejoiced and praised God.

Persistence

In his autobiography, William Allen White related the story of a boyhood playmate, Temple Friend, who was kidnapped by the Indians when he was quite young. Ironically, Temple's grandfather was a missionary to the Indians. The Lord's servant persisted in believing his grandson was alive. He continued to love and serve the church. He never allowed Indian conduct to sour his spirit. When visiting an Indian village, the old man would line up the boys who would be about the age of his missing grandson, and whisper, "Temple, Temple," quietly in the ear of each boy, so as not to excite them or the community. He followed this procedure day in and day out. Finally, he found about twelve boys the age of his grandson in one district—all eight to ten years old—and he started the same procedure. At the middle of the line a little boy's face lighted up, and he responded, "Me Temple!"

Personal Faith

Leonard Griffith, minister of Deer Park United Church, Toronto, and who was from 1960 to 1966 minister of famed City Temple in London, says that when he was ten years old he went to a summer camp where the chief leader and counselor was a remarkable young man who made a lasting impression on him. Twenty years later, in the city where he was serving as minister, he discovered why the counselor had made such a tremendous impression on hundreds of boys. The man was a committed Christian.

One day he was told that the "Chief" was in the hospital, seriously ill. He went to see him. He was but a shadow of his former self. His teenage children were at the bedside. It was difficult for Mr. Griffith to be his strong self. He muttered some words of comfort. Smilingly, the patient said: "I am not going to get better. I have cancer and I am going to die—perhaps tomorrow." Then he turned to his children and said, "But we are not afraid. We know that everything will be all right."

This is the spirit and faith of a Christian.

To Believe

Martin Luther once said, "Miracles take place not because they are performed but because they are believed." Simon Lake believed in the possibilities of a submarine long before it was perfected. The Wright brothers believed in air transportation years before their daring flight at Kitty Hawk, North Carolina.

To Fly

One evening a young Air Force captain at Wheelus Air Base, Tripoli, came striding into the Protestant Men's banquet, very late. We were all but finished with the meal. He was still in his flying gear, and his face bore the marks of weariness and strain. He was president of the Protestant Men. He walked to the front of the room and rapped for attention. After thanking everyone for coming, he apologized for being late.

Then, in a voice laden with emotion, he said, "Men, it has been a hard day. Flying out of Turkey, I had difficulty with the radio, and I finally lost it altogether. Then, when I approached the landing field here, the gear would not go down. I circled and circled and circled, but still the gear would not go down. As I contemplated what I should do, something told me to circle the field once more. I did and the landing gear came clear. God was in the cockpit with me tonight." The strength of this man caused me to appreciate even more fully the words of the Air Force song always sung at the close of a chapel service: "Lord, guard and guide the men who fly."

Why Worry?

Dale Carnegie wrote of interviewing Henry Ford when Ford was seventy-eight years of age. He had expected to find a gaunt, nervous old man. When asked if he worried, Ford replied, "No. I believe God is managing affairs and He doesn't need any advice from me. With God in charge, I believe that everything will work out for the best in the end. So what is there to worry about?"[2]

Family

Joshua 24:15; Psalm 68:6; Mark 3:25; Ephesians 3:15

It is the quality of the couple's relationship that sets the stage for giving birth to a healthy family.

—Dr. Jerry M. Lewis,
Chief Psychiatrist,
Timberlawn Hospital, Dallas

Children, Remember

One of the great churchmen of our generation was the late Bishop Edwin Holt Hughes of the Methodist Episcopal Church. He declared that in his more active days it concerned him that he could not give more time to his children. Before leaving on extended itineraries he would assemble the family for conference and prayer, always admonishing them to remember who their father was. At last came the day when the bishop presided over the conference for the last time, prior to his retirement. Upon reaching the podium, he found a telegram awaiting him. It read: "Don't forget who your children are."

Compatible Concepts

Roland Bainton, in his book *What Christianity Says About Sex, Love and Marriage,* reminds us of the three views of marriage: the sacramental, which was elaborated by the early church and again in the Middle Ages; the romantic concept, which developed outside of marriage in the courts of love in the eleventh and twelfth centuries; and the view of marriage as companionship, convenience, and refinement of sex. The eminent scholar concluded by saying that the sacramental, romantic, and compatible concepts of marriage can be combined in a union which commences in mutual love and loyalty to God and continues in fidelity and common witness.

Contagion

President Hesberg of Notre Dame says: "The most important thing a father can do for his children is love their mother."

Guests with Cash

Marriages are a $17 billion business in Japan. It is said that three-quarters-of-a-million Japanese weddings take place in the fall. November is a popular month. Tokyo's three-hundred ceremonial halls are booked solid, with a service approximately every twenty minutes. The estimated cost is a phenomenal twenty-two thousand dollars per couple—six times that of a typical American wedding. One-hundred guests and more are invited, and gifts are expected. Cash is the most welcome gift—one-hundred dollars for a single guest, one-hundred-fifty dollars for a couple. This helps to defray expenses![1]

The High Cost of Children

Parenthood is emotionally and financially more draining than ever. Costs continue to escalate. Uncommon discipline, maturity, and unselfishness are prerequisites for parents who would rear wholesome, well-rounded, well-educated children.

Estimates vary, but one family analysis claims a two-parent family with an income of $29,500 can anticipate spending $226,000 in 1982 dollars or $28.12 a day, to raise and educate a son born in 1980 to age twenty-two. This projection includes four years of college at a private school. Two other interesting discoveries: Girls are about 10 percent more expensive to support than boys, and approximately one-third of total costs comes during the last four years of school.[2]

The Home Front

When John Foster Dulles was secretary of state, he called General Douglas MacArthur's home one day. Mistaking Dulles's voice for that of an aide, Mrs. MacArthur snapped, "MacArthur is not here. MacArthur is where MacArthur always is—down at that office!" With this she hung up abruptly. Within minutes the general received a call from John Foster Dulles saying, "Go home at once, boy. Your home front is crumbling."

Is This What We Are Coming to?

In *Brave New World,* Aldous Huxley referred to the alarming number of divorces in America. He predicted that some day marriage licenses would be sold like dog licenses—good for a period of twelve months with no lawsuit against changing dogs or keeping more than one animal at a time.

Latchkey Children

In the early nineteenth century, when children were left on their own, they wore their house keys on a chain around their necks. The theory being it provided the child with access to the house and security in the absence of parents. Emerging from that practice, but for different reasons, we have in our society today what is commonly referred to as "a latchkey child." This is one "who is unsupervised by an adult between the time he or she comes home from school until a parent arrives home from work, or in the mornings before school starts." Statistics suggest that there may be as many as ten million latchkey children in the United States. Consider their vulnerability!

Love and Marriage

A critic of Mark Twain declared that the author's most effective writing centered around the glory and love of marriage. Twain once imagined Adam standing at the graveside of Eve, reflecting on their sins, accomplishments, and joys. Finally Adam says: "Where she was, there was Eden."

A Mother's Love

Thomas Wolfe, noted author, told of George Webber, a huge man from North Carolina who wanted to be a writer above all else and came to New York in search of a career. Webber found the going very hard. He discovered how difficult it is to write and publish. Rejection slips, rejection slips! When things got unbearable, George would take a train and ride all night in a coach back to North Carolina. Arriving, he would walk from the station to their humble home where his mother was invariably waiting. The giant six-foot-ten-inch man would kneel before his mother, his aching head in her lap, and he would weep like a child. His mother's reply was always the same: "Son, I don't know what's wrong but whatever it is, it will be all right."

Obedience

A grandfather was visiting his six-year-old grandson when his mother called, "Tommy, it's time for your shower!" Grandfather asked, "Do you use the shower downstairs or the one upstairs?" Tommy replied, "Momma says that I can't take a shower upstairs, and when Momma says no, we'd better do no!"

Returning to Roots

It occurred during my senior year in seminary. I was home for Christmas. Father suggested that we drive upcountry to visit the place of his birth in Lunenburg County, Virginia. We drove as far as possible, then parked the car and walked to the site of the old homestead. Weeds and grass claimed the place. Although leaves carpeted the ground, father seemed perfectly at home as he described the scene of his childhood. I sensed a tenderness in his voice, pride in his heart. At last he said, "I would like to drink from the old spring." Finding a trace of the footpath, we followed it to the spring branch. Kneeling, he brushed the leaves aside and drank from the hallowed stream. Then I followed.

Father wept a little—as I did—for, in turning back to the old place, he not only led me over ancestral ground but also relived a happy childhood. He shared information on our relatives I needed to know. In looking back with my father, I gained a new perspective and appreciation for our family.

Shocking Graphics

Allan C. Carlson, Lutheran historian, and others like him invite us to reflect on U. S. Census Bureau statistics. The number of divorced persons per 1,000 climbed from 35 in 1960 to 100 in 1980; among blacks the increase was from 78 to 257. The number of men presumably living alone jumped 100 percent in the decade of the 1970s, and totaled 7.2 million in 1981. Estimated unmarried couples living together tripled in the same period, totaling 1.5 million in 1981. Marital fertility plummeted by about 50 percent. In 1980, approximately 19.7 percent of American children lived with one parent. These are shocking graphics and point to the possible social decomposition of our society.

Sound of Music

Motion-picture engineers classify the most dramatic sounds in the movies to include: a baby's cry, the blast of a siren, screeching automobile tires, the roar of a forest fire, a fog horn, the slow drip of water, galloping horses, a distant train whistle, the howl of a dog, and the sound of the wedding march. These experts claim that one sound above all others creates more charisma, arouses more expectancy, than all the rest. It is the sound of the wedding march! It suggests that a family is being started.

Take Time for the Kids

Consider Susanna Wesley, mother of John and Charles Wesley. She bore nineteen children in twenty-one years. She lost ten of them. Her neighbors marveled at her ability to organize the home. A modern home, so we are told, has some ninety labor-saving devices. Susanna had very few. Moreover, she taught her children until they were five years old. Every afternoon she took one child into the privacy of her room and there shared with the child the finer things of the Christian faith. Little wonder that from this home, suffused with faith and love, came the dynamic founders and leaders of the Methodist Church.

Three Rules

In his autobiography, *A Time to Heal,* Gerald R. Ford said his parents had three rules: "Tell the truth, work hard, and come to dinner on time—and woe unto any of us who violated those rules."

Togetherness

It was my privilege to live with an Australian family for ten days. The husband and father was an orchardist—an exporter of fine fruit. The home was immaculate. Their four children

were married, doing well, and living in the same general vicini-
ty. I was impressed by their togetherness. Practically every
night the family assembled at one home or another to visit. On
Thursday afternoons the father and his three sons played golf.
Sunday mornings they went to church together; they sang in
the choir. I left saying to myself, "If more Americans could see
how this family lives!"

Trading Places

Crime frequently erupts in unexpected places. Violence is
not the normal reflex of any race, culture, or person. The trou-
ble-prone psyche is vulnerable to pressures and frustrations.
Individuals react differently to circumstances. The John W.
Hinckley family is a sad case in point.

Jack and Jo Ann Hinckley are said to have been good parents,
loving, providing, and sharing with their three children. Despite the father's prosperous business, a neighbor reported,
"He wasn't one of those absentee fathers by any means." Yet
John, Jr. apparently continued to withdraw into his world
while other members of the family progressed. Although the
Hinckleys found solace in their religion and openly answered
to becoming "born-again" Christians, something apparently
went wrong in the family. Young John became a drifter, caught
up in fantasy. Yet, when he faced trial for the ultimate crime
in American society, his father, a Colorado oil millionaire who
had "kicked his son out" of the house the year before, wept
aloud: "I wish to God I could trade places with him right now."

Violence

Among others, a study by the University of Rhode Island
discovered the American home to be one of the most dangerous places to live outside of riots and war. Statistics differ but
indicate the extreme escalation of violence in the home. Some
30 percent of American couples experience some form of
domestic violence during their marriage. It is claimed that 20

percent of all police officers killed in line of duty are killed while answering calls involving domestic quarrels. It is also estimated that from six to fifteen million American women are battered each year. As if this were not enough to destroy the home, it does not include the staggering problem of child abuse.

Willingness to Listen

Joseph E. Persico shared an intriguing experience in his biography of Nelson A. Rockefeller. He and courtly staffers had flown down from Albany, New York, to the governor's home at Pocantico on a cold Saturday morning to review drafts of a budget message to be delivered to the state legislature. Addressing a servant in French, Rockefeller ordered hot coffee and tea for his chilled colleagues before plunging into work. T. Norman Hurd, budget director, was explaining a passage when a tow-headed boy bounced into the room. Little Mark began talking. The governor listened, not to Dr. Hurd, but to his son. "Yes, that's right, Marky. That's a two. And that number is a nine. See, we're on page twenty-nine."

Persico thought of how he was rearing his children. Like most of us, he did not appreciate interruptions. "Nelson Rockefeller was passing along an unspoken lesson absorbed from his own father—'These people work for us. Never mind their age, their position, they defer to you.' Thus are young princes bred. I was doing it all wrong."[3]

God

Genesis 1; Isaiah 64:4; John 4:24; Romans 8:28

God became man that man might become like God.
—Augustine

If the majesty of God is his royal authority to reign, and if the dominion of God is the providence of his reign, then the power of God is his royal ability to reign.

—Bill R. Austin

All but God is changing day by day.

—Charles Kingsley

Absorbed in the Sunset

A mother had called her five-year-old son to dinner five times. He was slow responding. Impatiently, she declared, "This is the fifth time I have called Billy to dinner. I will have to see about this, and I will spank him and teach him a lesson." Running from the dining room towards the front porch, she found her son standing there, absorbed in contemplation. "Young man, why don't you come to dinner? I have called you five times." "But Mother," he replied, "I only heard you three times, and, besides, I am watching God put the world to bed."

Any Late Gospel?

Roy L. Smith concluded his book, *The Future Is Upon Us*, with this experience from a pastorate in Minnesota. One lovely spring morning, as the preacher parked his car by the church, he greeted the friendly custodian, who cheerily replied, "Any late news from God this morning?"

Depression

John Wesley came down for breakfast in a melancholy mood. He was miserable. Sensing the situation, Mrs. Wesley went upstairs, dressed in black, and came down to join him. "Who is dead?" Wesley asked. "God," she replied. "Oh, no!" he said. Mrs. Wesley responded, "I thought so, from your countenance and conduct."

The Empirical Ego Must Go

In interpreting the marvelous life of Thomas Merton, Monica Furlong wrote:

> The task of the religious man is, rather, a self-emptying—a quieting and ordering of his life by prayer and self-denial and goodness so that God can take possession of him. To this end, the exterior self, the empirical ego, the fascination with ourselves as objects of reflection, must go, and a terrifying emptiness must be faced, an utter aloneness in order to reach the next stage. This is a passing out of the self, a surrender of the private little bubble of being, and only at this point of complete emptiness and nakedness is the soul free to be filled with the presence of God.[1]

Finding and Loving Him

In *A Twentieth-Century Testimony*, Malcolm Muggeridge wrote: "The true purpose of our existence in this world, which is, quite simply, to look for God, and, in looking, to find Him, and, having found Him, to love Him, thereby establishing a harmonious relationship with His purposes for His creation."[2]

Giving in to God

Significantly enough, the celebrated and much-read C. S. Lewis entitled his autobiography *Surprised by Joy*. In characteristic brilliance and artistic attractiveness, he shared the intimacies of his life, his desire to discover faith, and his difficulties in finding it. He spoke frankly of his mother's death; study and snobbery at Oxford; World War I; his father's death; and his rediscovery of self. At last, in his room at Oxford in 1929, he wrote: "I gave in, and admitted that God was God, and knelt and prayed: perhaps, that night, the most dejected and reluctant convert in all England. . . . The Prodigal Son at least walked home on his own feet."[3]

God, Always Present

She was a gifted speaker, a queenly soul from a distant land. Her message was challenging and compassionate. In dealing with the turbulence of the times, she focused on God's guidance and support. Toward the close of her address, she shared a dream. In the dream she was running from danger, and in the coastal sands she observed her tracks and those she thought were God's. He was ever so close and protective. Having survived many threatening experiences, at last sorrow struck while on her spiritual pilgrimage. The trauma moved her to talk boldly with God, saying, "You were with me through danger and disappointment. I could see Your tracks as You accompanied me. But when death came to the family, You seemed to have disappeared. Where were You?"

"My child," God gently replied, "you saw only one set of tracks because I was carrying you!"

God for Today

Bishop Gerald Kennedy of California related the experience of a colleague, Bishop Trice Taylor, who while visiting a tribe in Liberia was greeted by the old chief who said: "Bishop, we believe in God. But sometimes He is so far away. You be God for us today."

God Works Every Day

God gets up in the morning
And says, "Another day?"
God goes to work every day
   at regular hours
God is no gentleman for God
   puts on overalls and gets
dirty running the universe we
   know about and several other
      universes
Nobody knows about but Him.[4]

Hands Too Full

Saint Augustine declared: "God wants to give us something, but cannot, because our hands are full—there's nowhere for Him to put it."

How God Communicates

C. S. Lewis said God whispers to us in our pleasures, speaks to us in our consciousness, and shouts to us in our pain.

Individual Responsibility

More than 130 years ago, a group of twenty distinguished Americans met in the Astor House in New York City during the presidency of Millard Fillmore. Among the dinner guests was Secretary of State Daniel Webster, who had been unusually quiet. In an effort to engage him in conversation, a colleague asked, "Mr. Webster, will you tell me what was the most important thought you ever had?" Following a brief silence, he confidently replied, "The most serious thought that ever occupied my mind was that of my individual responsibility to God."

Please Be There

In the autobiographical novel, *The Late Liz*, the reader glimpses the sins of skid row; not poverty-stricken skid row, but the skid row of silken sheets and soft furs. Accordingly, Elizabeth Burns had had too much money, too much booze, and too many men for too long. After thirty years of hangovers, and going wrong, she came face to face with herself and with God. After experiencing new life, she knew there was something she had to do. It was most difficult. It involved asking for forgiveness from one she had wronged. She trembled as she thought of it. Standing by a table before entering the room, she prayed, "Father, I am going through with this, but I am not going to like it. I guess this is some of what it means to be a Christian, not all gravy, not all light and joy. I don't quite see why I have to do it, so Father, please be around, please be there."

Reliability

James Russell Lowell suggested that God never would have allowed man to get at the matchbox of the world had he not known that the world was fireproof and foolproof.

Three Dollars' Worth, Please

I would like to buy three dollars' worth of God, please, not enough to explode my soul or disturb my sleep but just enough to equal a cup of warm milk or a snooze in the sunshine. I don't want enough of Him to make me love a black man or pick beets with a migrant. I want ecstasy, not transformation; I want the warmth of the womb, not a new birth. I want a pound of the Eternal in a paper sack. I would like to buy three dollars' worth worth of God, please.[5]

The Trinity

In his book *The Joyful Christian,* C. S. Lewis wrote: "I said . . . that God is a Being which contains three persons while remaining one Being, just as a cube contains six squares while remaining one body."[6]

Trust Him

The story is told of William Quayle, the Methodist bishop of Kansas, who lived a century ago. Having a fitful night, he awoke at four o'clock. Suddenly there was a great voice. "William, this is God. You may go to sleep now. I am awake."

God's Patience

When Robert Ingersoll, the famous atheist, was lecturing, he once took out his watch and declared, "I will give God five minutes to strike me dead for the things I have said." The minutes ticked off as he held the watch and waited. In about four-and-a-half minutes, some women began fainting, but nothing happened. When the five minutes were up, Ingersoll put the watch into his pocket. When that incident reached the ears of a certain preacher, Joseph Parker, he asked, "And did the gentleman think he could exhaust the patience of the Eternal God in five minutes?"

What Would You Have Me Do Today?

The Danish novelist, Arker Larsen, said God entered his life from the farm workers he knew as a boy. Larsen declared he comes to God every morning asking: "What orders have you for me today?"

Where Was God?

During World War II, following word that an only son had been killed in action, a priest was called to the home of grief-stricken parents. The father, pacing the floor, weeping, in anger demanded, "Where was God when my son was being killed?" Silence prevailed. Then the ministering priest replied, "I guess where He was when His Son was being killed." The calm, profound answer impacted the father, for it brought God out of remoteness into the circle of real life.

Heaven

2 Kings 2:1-3; Matthew 22:2; John 14:1-7; Romans 8:28-39;
Revelation 21:1-4

Hello, Central! Give me heaven,
For my Mama's there.
—Charles K. Harris

Earth has no sorrow that heaven cannot heal.
—Thomas Moore

Earth Recedes—Heaven Opens

Shortly before Dwight L. Moody died, he spoke these words: "Earth recedes; heaven opens before me." This statement has become famous around the world.

Moody's son, William L. who was with his father, testified that the evangelist continued: "No, this is no dream, Will. It is beautiful. It is like a trance. If this is death, it is sweet. There is no valley here. God is calling me, and I must go." Soon the rest of the family was assembled. Only recently, the evangelist and the family had lost two of the grandchildren, Dwight and Irene.

Moody's face suddenly lit up, and he exclaimed: "Dwight! Irene! I see the children's faces!" There is a blessedness of meeting our loved ones over there!

Comments

Where imperfection ceaseth, heaven begins.
                    —P. J. Bailey

Earth breaks up, time drops away,
In flows heaven, with its new day.
                    —Robert Browning

In heaven the Son will furnish the light.

As much of heaven is visible as we have eyes to see.
                    —William Winter

Continuous Challenge

Billy Graham said in his book *World Aflame:*

Heaven will be more modern and up-to-date than any of the present-day constructions of man. Heaven will be a place to challenge the creative genius of the unfettered mind of redeemed man. Heaven will be a place made supremely attractive by the presence of Christ.

Coronation Day

While on his deathbed, D. L. Moody cried out: "This is my Coronation Day. Don't try to call me back." Charles Haddon Spurgeon, when facing death, implored: "Can this be death? Why, it is better than living!"

Grave Not the End

Many times Billy Graham has declared: "For the Christian, the grave is not the end; nor is death a calamity, for he has a glorious hope—the hope of Heaven."

Do You Know Him?

It is reported that a fellow minister once remarked to Horace Bushnell, "When Christ sees you nearing the gate, Dr. Bushnell, I am sure He will say, 'There comes a man I know.'" Quickly, but humbly, the great Christian replied, "And I shall be able to say I know Him."

The First Million Years

When looking through the Churchill Memorial in Fulton, Missouri, I was attracted to a section in the pictorial display that featured Sir Winston's own paintings. Beneath an excellent likeness of the former Prime Minister was penned this personal note: "When I get to heaven, I mean to spend a considerable portion of my first million years in painting and so get to the bottom of the subject."

Heaven—a Place

Heaven is a place (John 14:2), but the Bible does not locate it. However, it is where God and Christ are, and that will be heaven enough. It is a place of glory. Gold and precious stones (Rev. 21:18*ff.*) suggest moral values; white robes (Rev. 6:11) imply purity; there will be leaves for healing (Rev. 22:2) and crowns for victory (Rev. 4:10). The unclean will not be there (Rev. 21:27).

—Herschel H. Hobbs

Go Straight

When an old bishop was asked the way to heaven, he replied, "Take the first turn to the right, and go straight forward."

He's Been Everywhere

Lowell Thomas, the Renaissance man who was a premier newscaster for decades, died in his sleep, Saturday, August 29, 1981. He was eighty-nine, and a world celebrity.

A reporter for Universal Press International wrote: "He was the first man to broadcast from a ship, from an airplane, from a coal mine and from a submarine. His reporting work took him to both poles and almost everywhere in between." In this same release was a beautiful comment written by a celebrated reporter in 1958 which read: "The day will come when a compact man, with piercing blue eyes, wavy salt-and-pepper hair, a thin mustache and a voice like an organ will stride briskly toward the Pearly Gates. The guardian angel will recognize him at once. 'Here comes Lowell Thomas. He's been everywhere else.' "[1]

The Master Is There

The late John Baillie told the story of an old man, very ill, who asked his doctor what heaven would be like. Just then the listening physician heard his dog, which had followed him, barking and scratching at the door. Turning to the patient, the doctor declared the noise was his dog, who did not know what was happening in the room but wanted to be with his master. "Is it not the same with you?" the doctor continued. "You do not know what lies behind the door called death, but you know your Master is there."

May There Be Work to Do

When President Harper of the University of Chicago was dying, he called in some of his close colleagues and friends and asked them to pray. "Now let us talk with God, let us not be formal; let us be simple." The noted administrator/educator concluded the circle of prayer with these inspiring words: "And may there be work to do, tasks to accomplish; and this I ask for Jesus' sake."

My Holy Land

Years ago, W. J. Dawson visited the renowned English preacher, Dr. Joseph Parker. Dawson found his friend, Parker, in the garden. Telling him of his coming visit to the Holy Land, Parker, waving his hand at the blue sky above, exclaimed, "My holy land is there!"

Not a Monastery

"Heaven," declared Ian Maclaren, "is not a Trappist monastery. Neither is it retirement on pension. No, it is a land of continual progress."

This World Is Not My Home

For years the late Charles E. Fuller conducted "The Old-Fashioned Revival Hour" on radio. One of the favorite selections of the revival hour quartet was "This World Is Not My Home." Yes, Christians are in the world, but they are not of the world. The Word of God describes the believer in Christ as a pilgrim, a stranger, a traveler. The Christian in this life does experience "a foretaste of glory divine," but the ultimate glory awaits him. He longs for the "city whose Builder and Maker is God." And he yearns to behold Jesus face to face.

Soul Aloft

The French author, Gustave Flaubert, once said, "The principal thing in this world is to keep one's soul aloft."

Watch the Sharp Corners!

Perhaps you remember the movie, *Heavens Above*, starring Peter Sellers. It was the story of a minister appointed to a fashionable church in England by mistake. He took the teachings of Jesus so seriously that before long his people were up in arms, leveling charges and countercharges, but all the while asking themselves, "Are we such steamheated, upholstered, well-lighted Christians that we have planed down the sharp corners of responsibility?"

The Way

Students of history are forever searching for additional information concerning the possible lost continent of Atlantis.

Persons tend to speculate about heaven in much the same way: where is it, what is it like, and how does one get to heaven. No one can supply adequate answers, no one, that is, but Jesus, who said: "I am the way, and the truth, and the life; no one comes to the Father, but by me" (John 14:6).

Being with Jesus, in this life and the one to come, is heaven both here and there.

Will You Be Surprised?

We win God's approval when we win others to Christ and to His church. A medieval monk said when one gets to heaven one will be surprised by three things: first, to see many whom one did not expect had a chance to make it; second, one will be surprised that some who thought they had it made won't be there; and third, one is surprised if one makes it.

Your Invitation

Near the close of the poem, *The Hound of Heaven,* Francis Thompson, nineteenth-century English poet, wrote:

Save Me, save only Me?
All which I took from thee I did but take,
    Not for thy harms,
But just that thou might'st seek it in My arms.
All which thy child's mistake
Fancies as lost, I have stored for thee at home:
Rise, clasp My hand, and come![3]

Hell

Matthew 10:26-28; Mark 9:43-45; Luke 16:19-31; 1 John 3:13-14

That's the greatest torture souls feel in hell: in hell, that they must live and cannot die.
                                            —John Webster

The devil can cite Scripture for his purpose.
                                            —William Shakespeare

Avoiding Hell

Not everyone is as fortunate as Alfred Nobel who in 1888 read his own obituary in a French newspaper. One of his brothers had died, but a careless reporter had used a statement prepared for the wrong man. Alfred, principal inventor of dynamite, was disappointed with the published account. He was described as a "merchant of death" who had made a fortune from explosives and human exploitation. This haunting image caused him to reevaluate his life and revamp his will. Consequently, his money has made possible the famous Nobel Peace Prizes.

One Has a Choice

Many years ago two Massachusetts state senators wound up in an angry debate, in which one told the other he could "go to _____." The man thus consigned protested to Governor Coolidge and asked him to intervene over the outrage. To which Coolidge replied: "I've looked up the law, Senator, and you don't have to go there."

Comments

Hell is the wrath of God—His hate of sin.

—P. J. Bailey

In hell there will be no love, for all creatures there will be incapable of loving.

—Arthur E. Travis

If one is determined to go to hell, he must climb there.

—Anonymous

Hell is paved with good intentions, not with bad ones.

—George Bernard Shaw

Devil, you're getting a black eye tonight!

—Jimmy Lee Swaggart

Fourteen Minutes' Worth

According to reports, John Louis Evans, III, convicted murderer, was executed in Atmore, Alabama, April 22, 1983. It required three powerful jolts of electricity over a period of fourteen minutes to kill him.

Hell Enough

These lines from Frank L. Stanton are pertinent:

It doesn't matter what they preach,
   Of high or low degree;

The old Hell of the Bible
   Is Hell enough for me.

What About Hell?

Several years ago, Dr. Arthur E. Travis wrote a provocative book, *Where on Earth Is Heaven?* In it the retired Southern Baptist author-professor-pastor-counselor included a chapter on "What Is Hell?" He began the chapter by admitting the controversy of the subject: "Man's natural mind loathes the idea of hell and prefers to believe either that death is the end of existence, or that somehow all human beings will eventually go to heaven. The argument is used, often by theologians, that any idea of hell as a place of eternal punishment is contrary to the concept of a God of love."

Later in the chapter, Travis continued:

> If he [man] chooses to relate rightly with God, then he becomes a child of God, and God is able to give Himself to man with all the joys of a happy life on earth and the blessedness of eternity in heaven. When a free human being uses his freedom to reject the truth of God, and to refuse to relate rightly with him, then there is no alternative except to allow him to do so. In making this choice, man becomes responsible for the results of separation from God. He lives his life in this world without God, and when he dies, God will not pick him up against his will and drag him into a place so drastically different from the kind of person he has chosen to become. . . . My personal belief is that if an unregenerated human should should be taken into heaven when he dies, it would be worse for him than hell would be.[1]

The Reality of Hell

The rich man of Luke 16 became painfully aware of hell and its stark reality, as will every person who rejects the love of the Savior. As one old preacher expressed it, "After you've been in hell five seconds, you'll believe in it!"

A Living Hell: Bitterness

His father and I were good friends. The man whom I shall call John died suddenly, leaving a devastating shock. Years later, John, Jr., moved to the city where we were located. Hearing I was serving a church in the community, he looked us up, and eventually affiliated with our congregation. I was delighted to think he wanted to be part of our fellowship. Like his father, I assumed he, too, was a commendable churchman. I soon learned, however, that he was bitter over his father's death, was blaming God, and trying to punish Him for taking his father in the prime of life. When Victory Sunday arrived—the day we underwrite the program needs of the church—young John wrote a big "0" on his pledge card.

This bright, attractive, articulate man with a splendid business connection had permitted bitterness to consume his potential, distort his personality, and sour his soul. The antidote to bitterness is acceptance and forgiveness. What if God had retaliated for the crucifixion of His son? The cross would be just another death marker; there would be no church, no salvation!

Making Our Own

My old homiletics professor, Halford E. Luccock, used to tell the story of a man who was a chronic complainer. He was always behind in his chores, his work, and his desk was usually cluttered with unanswered mail.

One night as he slept, he dreamed he had caught up in his work and in his correspondence. Through the window he noticed that his lawn was beautifully manicured. What a relief to have everything shipshape!

There remained a haunting question: "What do I do now?"

Presently the happy postman came whistling down the street. He carried no mail, just out for a stroll. In his dream the frustrated owner of the house hailed the postman to ask, "Please tell me, what place is this?"

Politely he replied, "Don't you know this is hell?"

The Devil's Chapel

Wherever God erects a house of prayer,
The devil always builds a chapel there;
And 'twill be found upon examination,
The latter has the largest congregation.

—Daniel Defoe

Repentance

When Lorenzo de Medici, dictator of Florence, lay dying, he sent for the noted priest-reformer, Girolamo Savonarola. "Sire," said Savonarola, standing by the bedside of the dying tyrant, "God is good, God is merciful, but for His forgiveness, three things on your part are necessary."

"What are they?" whispered Lorenzo.

"You must have a sure and lively faith in the mercy of God." "I have that," said Lorenzo.

"Then," said Savonarola, "you must restore all your ill-gotten wealth, or at least charge your sons to restore it in your name." The dictator hesitated, but reluctantly nodded in the affirmative. "Finally, you must restore the liberties of Florence." With this, Lorenzo bristled, his eyes flashing with anger. He turned his face to the wall as if to say he would sooner go to hell than do that.

Damned to the Uttermost

"Any man who hears the gospel and persistently refuses to believe and receive it shall be damned. All anyone needs to do to be saved, saved to the uttermost, is to believe on the Lord Jesus. It is not necessary in order to be damned that one be what the world calls a wicked person . . . Refusing to believe on Jesus Christ is in itself a damnable sin, and reveals a damnable state of heart."

—R. A. Torrey

Wings to Flee

Art thou a mourner? Rouse thee from thy spell;
   Art thou a sinner? Sins may be forgiven;
Each morning gives thee wings to flee from hell,
   Each night a star to guide thy feet to Heaven.
—Walter Malone

The Subtlety of Satan

Among the great number of books authored by C. S. Lewis is the highly provocative *The Screwtape Letters.* In it the profound Englishman had the devil brief his nephew, Wormwood, on the subleties and techniques of tempting people. The goal, he counsels, is not wickedness but indifference. Satan cautions his nephew to keep the prospect, the patient, comfortable at all costs. If he should become concerned about anything of importance, encourage him to think about his luncheon plans; not to worry, it could induce indigestion. And then this definitive job description: "I, the devil, will always see to it that there are bad people. Your job, my dear Wormwood, is to provide me with people who do not care."

Those Who Don't Expect to Go

Harry Leon Wilson wrote in *The Spenders:* "Hell is given up so reluctantly by those who don't expect to go there."

Watch the Ego!

The late Bishop Fulton J. Sheen used to say: "Hell is the ego, sated with its own satisfied wishes, having to consume itself forever with no hope of release."

What Have You Done?

In *Gone with the Wind,* its author, Margaret Mitchell, has Rhett Butler ask Scarlett O'Hara, "What have you done to make hell yawn before you?"

Exposition of Future Punishment

Henry Ward Beecher once mused: "I do not accept the doctrine of eternal punishment because I delight in it. I would cast in doubts, if I could, till I had filled hell up to the brim. I would destroy all faith in it, but that would do me no good; I could not destroy the thing. I cannot alter the stern fact. The exposition of future punishment in God's Word is not to be regarded as a threat, but as a merciful declaration. If, in the ocean of life, over which we are bound to eternity, there are these rocks and shoals, it is no cruelty to chart them down; it is an eminent and prominent mercy."

When the Heart Turns Gray

I am reminded of Lord Byron's lines in *The Countess of Blessington:*

> I am ashes where once I was fire,
>   And the soul in my bosom is dead;
> What I loved I now merely admire,
>   And my heart is as gray as my head.

The Holy Spirit

Genesis 1:1-2; John 16:5-7; Acts 2:1-4; 5:3-4; 20:30;
1 Corinthians 12:3; Ephesians 4:30

I am content to think of the Spirit and of the Risen Lord as one at least in action.

—William Barclay

And equal adoration be,
Eternal Paraclete, to Thee!
—John Dryden

Ask to Be Shaken

One day Theodore Roosevelt had been speaking sternly to his son, Kermit, and in desperation finally reached down to shake him. Whereupon Ethel, Kermit's sister, touched her father's arm and cried out, "Shake me, Father, shake me!"

The church that wants spiritual power must ask to be shaken.

Asking for Help

The early church asked for the Spirit. They acknowledged His power and His way. Sensitive souls have always turned to the Spirit for help. The Spirit does not add qualities of life we do not possess. Those qualities are not something poured into us from the outside. They are inside humans and respond to the Spirit, developing every potential to its fullest.

John Milton asked the Spirit to aid him as he began his epic poem, *Paradise Lost.* But it would have been of little help had he not possessed the genius of a poet.

John Wesley declared that the success of his work was due to the Spirit, but we must remember that Wesley was a born leader. The Spirit used him. There was something in Wesley that responded to the Spirit.

Comments

"The early Christian communities," said Bishop Martin Dibelius, German theologian, "were witnesses to the Holy Spirit."

"Breathe on me, Breath of God," prayed Edwin Hatch.

Billy Graham says that throughout the Bible it is clear the Holy Spirit is God Himself.

Dr. Ernest F. Scott said in his book, *I Believe In the Holy Spirit,* that the title of the Book of Acts could be called *The Acts of the Spirit,* for the whole purpose of the author is to show what happened to the apostles when they were filled with the Spirit —"Humble men became powerful leaders."

The Life-giving Spirit

The pearl diver lives at the bottom of the ocean by means of the pure air conveyed to him from above. His life is entirely dependent on the breath from above him. We are down here, like the diver, to gather pearls for our Master's crown. The source of our life comes from the life-giving Spirit.

—Henry Drummond

The Cornerstone of Theology

The late Archbishop Temple of Canterbury, a knowledgeable leader and a scholar in his own right, declared that a fundamental principle in theology is that "God is Spirit." God has and continues to reveal Himself throughout time in many ways, but in human history He acted (and does act) to make Himself uniquely and fully known in Jesus Christ.

Do It Again!

William Booth, founder of the Salvation Army, is said to have been converted in Wesleyan Chapel, Nottingham, England. A plaque marks the site of his spiritual baptism. As a consequence, leaders of this noble army periodically journey to the Wesleyan Chapel, the shrine of their movement, in hopes of recapturing the spirit of their illustrious founder.

One day, years ago, an elderly black man, dressed in the simple uniform of a street preacher, was found in the historic chapel. Not knowing the white minister's attitude, he asked, "Can a man say his prayers in here?"

"Of course you can."

Whereupon the humble man, dropping to his knees near the

sacred spot, head erect and eyes closed, was heard to say: "Dear God, do it again!"

Don't Blaspheme the Spirit

In Matthew's Gospel (12:31-32), Jesus declared that all sins would be forgiven except those "against the Spirit." As a young man, John Bunyan lived in horror and despair because once, in a rash moment, he had spoken what he thought was a blasphemy against the Holy Spirit.

Ethereal Communication

On the day Major Gordon Cooper orbited the earth for the twenty-second time, his wife, Trudie, set her alarm clock for 4:30 AM. She reports that she awoke at 4:00 and immediately turned on the television, only to hear the announcer say that Gordon had just awakened. Though literally worlds apart, and without any visible means of communication, the affinity between husband and wife, their concern and love were so strong they awakened at almost precisely the same time. This is the miracle of the Spirit.

Something even more startling happened around AD 33, soon after Jesus had ascended. While on earth, He had admonished His disciples to tarry in Jerusalem until they received power. Half-frightened, half-dubious, half-believing, they remained. And behold, as they were together in one place, "A sound came from heaven, like the rush of a mighty wind, and it filled all the house where they were sitting" (Acts 2:2).

The Heavenly Dove

When Nansen started on his Arctic Expedition he took a carrier pigeon. After two years of desolation in the Arctic regions, he wrote a message, tied it to the pigeon's wing, and let it loose to travel two thousand miles to Norway. Imagine it— one tiny bird making a journey of two thousand miles. Finally, the bird flew into the lap of Nansen's wife in Norway. She knew, by the arrival of the bird, that all was well in the dark night of the North. So, with the coming of the Holy Spirit, the Heavenly Dove, the disciples knew that Christ was alive, for the Spirit's coming and manifestation of power were proofs of that fact.

Fruit of the Spirit

"But the fruit of the Spirit is love, joy, peace, patience, kindness, goodness, faithfulness, gentleness, self-control; against such there is no law" (Gal. 5:22-23).

Gifts of the Spirit

Having gifts that differ according to the grace given to us, let us use them: if prophecy, in proportion to our faith; if service, in our serving; he who teaches, in his teaching; he who exhorts, in his exhortation; he who contributes, in liberality; he who gives aid, with zeal; he who does acts of mercy, with cheerfulness (Rom. 12:6-8).

To each is given the manifestation of the Spirit for the common good. To one is given through the Spirit the utterance of wisdom, and to another the utterance of knowledge according to the same Spirit, to another faith by the same Spirit, to another gifts of healing by the one Spirit, to another the working of miracles, to another prophecy, to another the ability to distinguish between spirits, to another various kinds of tongues, to another the interpretation of tongues. All these are inspired by one and the same Spirit, who apportions to each one individually as he wills (1 Cor. 12:7-11).

And his gifts were that some should be apostles, some prophets, some evangelists, some pastors and teachers, to equip the saints for the work of ministry, for building up the body of Christ, until we all attain to the unity of the faith and of the knowledge of the Son of God, to mature manhood, to the measure of the stature of the fulness of Christ (Eph. 4:11-13).

Whoever speaks, as one who utters oracles of God; whoever renders service, as one who renders it by the strength which God supplies; in order that in everything God may be glorified through Jesus Christ. To him belong glory and dominion for ever and ever. Amen (1 Pet. 4:11).

A Guiding Presence

The great Quaker, Rufus Jones, observed that what happened at Pentecost was not that the early Christians were empowered to speak foreign languages, but that they were imbued with the power to pass over a tangible to an invisible, guiding Presence.

Inconceivable Power

The Holy Spirit has transforming power, uplifting power. That power makes us more than we are and fills us with energy. He makes a home for God in our hearts. He gives us purpose, direction, and stability. A person without the Spirit is a phlegmatic, pathetic soul.

In one of his essays, Robert Louis Stevenson wrote that as a young man he sailed out into the ocean to see the founding of a lighthouse. Nothing would satisfy him until he put on a diving suit and went down where the men were working. When they stood on the floor of the sea, his companions signaled for him to spring up on a great rock which towered above his head. Young Stevenson thought they were joking, but again they repeated the signal. He obeyed and, to his surprise, he landed on top of the rock. He had forgotten that the water was buoyant and that the force of the ocean would support his body.

Just so, the Holy Spirit supports and enlarges our feeble efforts.

Renewing Spirit

We sometimes say that a person is not what he used to be; and, physiologically speaking, it is an accurate statement. Every minute, five million cells in the human body are destroyed and replaced. The physical miracle of renewal takes place without personal awareness. But spiritual renewal requires constant vigil and desire. "It is the Spirit that gives life" (John 6:63).

The Spirit Binds

Clare Boothe Luce once declared, "The portrait of a saint is only a fragment of a great and still uncompleted mosaic—the portrait of Christ."

A quality stained-glass window is made up of hundreds of tiny pieces of glass held together with lead. Each saint is a beautifully colored window through which the glory of Christ shines.

That which binds saints together is the Holy Spirit.

Spirit of God

Ancient persons were awakened only by what was contrary to the normal course of events. Religion had its beginnings with a sense of awe and power outside the visible world. The Spirit came to Samson and he demonstrated miraculous strength. The Spirit enabled Joseph to interpret puzzling dreams and to withstand the hostility of his brothers and sensual temptations in Egypt. The prophets declared the Spirit as righteousness and felt the Spirit within them. The Spirit enabled David to conquer one crisis after another. The Spirit of God devastated Saul of Tarsus and later cleansed and commissioned him to proclaim the gospel. Sustained by the Holy Spirit in the wilderness, Jesus came to His hometown of Nazareth and, standing up in the familiar synagogue, declared: "The Spirit of the Lord is upon me, because he has anointed me to preach" (Luke 4:18).

The Spirit Transcends

An American father, a government employee, was away on a prolonged assignment. His little son missed him dreadfully and, while looking at his father's picture one day, said to his mother, "I wish Daddy would come out of that frame."

If we accept Jesus Christ as the portrait of the Father, the Holy Spirit has the power which enables the likeness to come out of the frame of the gospel story.

Spiritual Power

There is a pertinent dialogue in the sixteenth chapter of Judges. Delilah says to Samson: "Please tell me wherein your great strength lies" (v. 6). After three unsuccessful attempts to discover the source of Samson's strength, Delilah renews her efforts. Finally Samson succumbs and declares his power is in his hair. You remember the rest of the story. He not only lost his hair, but he lost his strength.

When we consider Christian ministry of all believers, irrespective of station or training, we must inevitably ask, where does the strength come from? First and foremost, it comes from God! "God did not give us a spirit of timidity but a spirit of power and love and self-control" (2 Tim. 1:7).

Temples of the Spirit

Shortly before his death, Timothy Richards, missionary statesman to China, told of this experience. He was in Shantung visiting with a Chinese philanthropist who voiced unashamedly that he had read the New Testament through three times. Whereupon Richards asked what were his impressions and what ideas were generated. Reflectively he replied, "I think that the most marvelous thing that impressed me was this—that it is possible for us men to become temples of the Holy Ghost."

What Must We Do?

On the Day of Pentecost the confused and frightened multitude asked, "What shall we do to be saved?" Boldly, Peter replied: "Repent, and be baptized every one of you in the name of Jesus Christ for the forgiveness of your sins; and you shall receive the gift of the Holy Spirit" (Acts 2:38).

Winds of the Spirit!

It would seem that those who experienced the first Pentecost were acutely aware of the winds of the Spirit (Acts 2:2). Scholars remind us that Pentecost is the most ancient religious festival we celebrate. In the early Jewish calendar, Pentecost, or the Feast of Weeks, was dedicated to gratitude, acknowledging God's gift in Noah, the covenant, and the regularity of physical seasons that produced seedtime and harvest. Later, Pentecost was associated with the giving of the law to Moses at Mount Sinai. While most Jewish festivals were provincial, centering on a given cause and community, Pentecost paid a great deal of attention to others. The stranger, those of other faiths, or those who happened to be in the community or in one's home at the time of the festival, were included.

Hope

Psalm 42:5; Psalm 146:5-7; Proverbs 13:12; Romans 5:1-5;
1 Corinthians 15:19

Hope keeps the heart whole.
—Anthony Brewer

And Now: Faith, Hope, and Love

The late Roy L. Smith of the United Methodist Church told a powerful story of a dear, aging couple who lived in the Great Lakes area of America. There were no close neighbors, and the Smiths agonized over their situation. During a family conference, it was decided to invite the isolated couple to come and live out their days with them. The Smiths went by boat to the little island where the couple lived. Following pleasantries, Dr. Smith adroitly reviewed their concern, and extended a gracious invitation.

Addressing his wife, the old man said, "Of course we cannot accept the invitation, can we, dear?"

Smith rephrased and reiterated their desire to afford them more security. Whereupon the couple, arm in arm, led the Smiths down a narrow but neat path that led to a beautifully tended little plot of green grass. There was a mound and a white cross. From the depth of his soul, the husband, putting his arm around his wife, said, "We can't leave our island home, for you see we lost a son here."

Whatever life may bring, God will not leave us on this floating island called Earth, because He, too, lost a Son here! (See Jer. 29:4-14; John 14:18).

Articulated Hope

Mrs. Rose Fitzgerald Kennedy, who was ninety-three years old on July 22, 1983, applauded and admired by millions, was quoted by many before and during her celebration. Knowing the sorrow she has gracefully borne, I was challenged by words that appeared in *Parade* magazine addressed to and about her grandchildren:

> I hope they will have the strength to bear the inevitable difficulties and disappointments and griefs of life. Bear them with dignity and without self-pity. Knowing that tragedies befall everyone, and that, although one may seem singled out for special sorrows, worse things have happened many times to others in the world, and it is not tears, but determination that makes pain bearable.[1]

Broken Branches

Archibald Rutledge told of seeing a bird build its nest, and then a storm came at night and destroyed it. Next morning as Rutledge lamented the loss, he heard a buzzing and twittering overhead. Stepping back into the bush, he observed the glimmering birds beginning a new home on the broken tip of the same branch on which the old one had rested.

We glimpse similar courage by victims of disasters in places like Galveston, Mexico City, and all over the world.

Comments

The end of birth is death; the end of death is birth: this is ordained!
—Edwin Arnold

Hope is a commitment, not a hilarious celebration. No army can march on a retreating mind.
—David Lloyd-George

Dedicated Individuals

One of the remarkable men of our century was, of course, Albert Einstein. He lived simply. He could have been an extremely wealthy man had he been willing to sell his talents on the platform or to the media. Einstein did not believe that wealth made people better. He believed that dedicated individuals were our hope.

The stewardship of self demands that we be generous with our talents, realizing our debts to God and humankind.

Fresh Hope

A blind sailor by the name of Hank Dekker navigated his twenty-five-foot sloop alone from San Francisco to Hawaii. Midway in the 2,376-mile voyage, he encountered a storm which caused his craft, *Dark Star,* to capsize. Other than floundering for a couple of days while Dekker reorganized the boat, no serious damage resulted; he drifted only twenty miles off course. Using Braille charts and compass and a computerized navigation system that read his position aloud, the brave man covered the distance in twenty-three days. "I've got a twenty-four-hour night," he says, "and they've [others] got a twelve-hour night."

This extraordinary feat not only gave the sailor tremendous

satisfaction, but it also offers fresh hope for the sightless and the seeing alike.

God's Banner

Every known civilization and religion has its version of the episode known as "the Flood." This story has persisted because of its profound moral and spiritual implications. It has apparently convinced mankind that destruction, darkness, and thunder do not speak God's last words. As the late Joseph Sizoo once said, "Floods are affairs of earth, but the rainbow is God's banner of hope."

Hoping to Find Him

James A. Pike died in 1969. His death was dramatic and tragic. During his turbulent lifetime this controversial person turned from the practice of law to the Christian ministry, from the Roman Catholic Church to Protestantism, from bishop to a church dropout, from alcoholism and chain-smoking to abstention.

Ironically, death came to this brilliant man while he was researching a new book on the historical Jesus. Wishing to rummage through old bookstalls in Jerusalem and to walk again where Jesus walked, Dr. and Mrs. Pike had gone to the Holy Land in search of information and inspiration. While driving in the desert on a hot August afternoon, they became lost. Following grueling experiences, Mrs. Pike finally secured help. It was too late. Her fifty-six-year-old husband was dead.

A writer for *Time* reported on the irony of the fact that the Right Reverend James A. Pike, once again on the brink of something new, "Should perish in the wilderness of the Judean desert, looking for Jesus." A friend, reacting to the sad story, commented, "Yes, and to think he could have found Him in California!"

I Hope . . .

When his friend Arthur Hallam died, Tennyson was crushed. He went into seclusion with his Bible, books on theology and philosophy, and out of that experience came the poem, "Crossing the Bar." The revealing and concluding lines are:

> I hope to see my Pilot face to face
> When I have crost the bar.

It Is Available

A strange case was heard before the Court of Special Sessions in Brooklyn, New York. Harry G. Purvis, local businessman, was charged with violating a community ordinance. He had placed a large sign on his building calling for peace through world federation. The neighbors objected to the sign and hauled him into court, charging that under a certain ordinance nothing could be advertised that could not be obtained on the premises. Peace, the petition contended, could not be packaged and sold.

Among the witnesses for the defense was the distinguished journalist, Norman Cousins, who said that in his opinion the product being advertised was available. And the product was hope!

Knot Your Thread

The noted Charles Haddon Spurgeon told the story of a famous tailor who was on his deathbed. His associates asked him to tell them the secret of his success in business. In a solemn voice he said: "Always put a knot in your thread."

A New Heart

On Sunday, December 3, 1967, Dr. Christiaan Barnard of Cape Town, South Africa, and a surgical team of thirty shocked the world by performing the first successful heart transplant. Louis Washkansky, fifty-five, received a new heart from Dennis Darvall, who had been killed in a car accident. This long and costly medical miracle triggered controversy as well as a proliferation of transplant operations.

New Hope!

The visit of Pope John Paul II to distraught Poland, his native land, in June, 1983, where he touched millions with his gentle, yet courageous, demeanor, will long be remembered. Beyond the enormous throngs of worshipers, the dramatic meeting with the one person the Polish government would like forgotten—Lech Walesa—was the face-to-face confrontation between General Jaruzelski and Pope John Paul. Like a humorless statue, the general stood wearing colored glasses, suited out in a green uniform, awkwardly and nervously read a statement. The Pope, dressed in "angelic white," standing a few paces away, listened with bowed head. Then, in kind, but devastating, language, the Pope lectured the cowed general on the problems of his homeland.

Watching on television, a Warsaw professor said: "The general is actually trembling. Look at that. The whole trip is worth this moment."

It is believed that the Pope's official visit to Poland, at least for a season, transformed the country from one of fear and bad memories to one of fresh hopes!

Not an Island, but Hope

Easter Island is a small spot of volcanic ground in the South Pacific about thirteen miles long and seven miles wide. It is approximately two thousand miles west of Chile. The little island is so named because it was discovered by the Dutch navigator, Roggeueen, on Easter, 1722.

Considerable speculation surrounds its original occupants. Archeologists, however, appreciate its gigantic statues and tablets which are mysteriously inscribed. The stones lay silent, as if ancient artisans had been disturbed and suddenly left their work incomplete.

To view the eerie landscape is to experience awe and gratitude.

I heard the eloquent preacher of First Baptist Church, Richmond, Virginia, Peter James Flamming, tell the story of the history of Easter Island to introduce a sermon which he called, "Easter Is Not an Island." He stressed that we are tempted to look back on Easter as if it were an ancient happening. But to early Christians Easter was the confirmation of the continuing revelation of God's grace and power. Using Philippians 3:10 as his text, he declared that first-century Christians believed in the power of the resurrection. It was the centerpiece of their faith and hope.

Personal Witness

When our son, Paul, was playing varsity football at Yale, my wife and I were fortunate to acquire an apartment at Yale Divinity School, where I had attended years before. As I left the apartment one day to observe practice, I was accosted by two black women, neatly dressed and wearing disarming smiles. Quickly and politely they introduced themselves saying, "We are from Jehovah's Witnesses and would like to visit with you."

Apparently they had observed there were new occupants in Curtis Hall, and of all the unlikely places for Jehovah's Witnesses to appear in the role of evangelists would be Yale Divinity School! But there they were, "witnessing" to their own brand of religion. Many members of cults put us "evangelicals"—Baptists, Methodists, Presbyterians, Pentecostals, Disciples, and so forth—to shame. We ought to be confronting men and women, boys and girls with the claims of Christian discipleship.

Prayer as Hope

One of the great shaping personalities of Protestantism was Martin Luther. We sometimes have the impression that all this brilliant monk did was nail a list of protests on the church door in Wittenberg. Nothing could be further from the truth. He worked as an inspired man, preaching, lecturing, and writing daily. The complete edition of his papers runs into thousands of pages. He worked inconceivably hard, and yet in spite of all this, Luther managed to pray for an hour or two every day. He said he prayed because he had so much to accomplish. We are recipients of this hope, and in a world that is so corrupt and needy, we also need to pray.

Ready for Responsibility

When John Rockefeller, IV, was born, he was not given the middle initial "D" but told when he felt he was able and ready to assume the responsibilities it suggested, the initial would be bestowed. After schooling at Harvard and Yale, teaching in Japan, serving in the Job Corps, though still restless and uncertain of his future, he wrote his father that he wanted "the name and the responsibility." He subsequently served successfully as a college president and was elected governor of West Virginia.

Rescue

On May 23, 1939, the submarine *Squalus*, a five-million-dollar vessel, sank off Portsmouth, New Hampshire. The famed McCann rescue bell was used for the first time. Through this bell-shaped valve, men were able to reach and to rescue the thirty-three men trapped inside. When the rescue squad reached the stricken submarine, they tapped with metal on the hull in an effort to locate the sailors. The imprisoned men, answering in similar fashion, asked in the language of the Morse code, "Is there any hope?"

Student Prayer

I hope that I will always be for each person what he needs me to be.

I hope that each person's death will always diminish me, but that fear of my own will never diminish my joy of life.

I hope that my love for those whom I like will never lessen my love for those whom I do not.

I hope that another person's love for me will never be a measure of my love for him.

I hope that every person will accept me as I am, but that I never will.

I hope that I will always ask for forgiveness from others, but will never need to be asked for my own.

I hope that I will find a person to love, but that I will never seek one.

I hope that I will always recognize my limitations, but that I will construct none.

I hope that loving will always be my goal, but that love will never be my idol.

I hope that every man and woman will always have hope.[2]

Symbols of Hope

A widely-circulated query from a British missionary society to one of its congregations in Uganda during dreadful days asked, "What can we send you people? You are being persecuted. Your archbishop has been martyred. What can we send you?"

The reply: "Not food, not medicine, but two-hundred-fifty clerical collars." The communique continued: "You must understand, when our people are being rounded up to be shot, they must be able to see their priests."

Humor

Genesis 18:9-15; Psalm 52:6-7; Matthew 6:16; Luke 7:31-35

Everything is funny as long as it is happening to somebody else.
—Will Rogers

O Lord, make my enemies ridiculous.
—Voltaire

At What Age Does Stewardship Start?

As the offering plates were being passed during worship, a little boy seated with his father whispered loudly: "Don't pay for me, daddy. I'm under five."

Bulletin Blooper

The first communion service of the new year will be held Sunday. Why not start the new year tight?

Bury the Baptist

A Methodist minister wired his bishop to ask if it would be all right for him to conduct the funeral of a Baptist. The bishop wired back, "Bury all the Baptists you can."

Don't You Like Our Colors?

A none-too-alert motorist sat motionless behind the wheel of his car. The traffic signal changed from green to yellow to red and back to green again. Still he sat staring ahead. Whereupon a police officer approached the absentminded man and demanded: "Mister, don't we have any colors you like?"

Invisible Luggage

There is a charming story concerning the noble statesman, William Ewart Gladstone. Crossing the frontier between

France and Belgium, he was interrogated by an officious customs officer: "Have you anything to declare?"

"Only a bunch of grapes," replied the Englishman.

The officer countered, "You cannot pass with those grapes, sir. They are dutiable."

"I will pay no duty," replied Gladstone.

"Then you must leave the grapes behind," said the customs examiner.

"No, I shall pass, grapes and all," insisted Gladstone. Whereupon he started slowly eating the grapes until they disappeared. "Now," he said with a smile, "I shall pass, grapes and all."

This is how we may go through the tediums of experience, carrying with us God's grace.

It Has to Be Ralph

The Sunday School class was studying that phenomenal Old Testament character, Samson. The articulate teacher began to enumerate the exploits of this physical giant: the killing of a lion with his bare hands; slaughtering a thousand Philistines with the jawbone of an ass; and turning loose three-hundred foxes with their flaming tails tied together in a Philistine cornfield.

Not being able to constrain himself any longer, Johnny interrupted. "Mr. Brown, wasn't his first name Ralph?"

Kind of Lonesome

A man in Portland, Maine, notified the Bureau of Missing Persons of the absence of his wife. He said she had been missing for fifteen years. The chief was shocked and asked why he had waited so long to report it. "Well," he said, "I just got kind of lonesome."

Laughing at Your Pains

A lady who lives alone reported: "I don't get lonely because I have some men friends who keep me company. I wake up with Charlie Horse, eat meals with Will Power, spend my days with Arthur Itis, and go to bed with Ben Gay."

Moving Heaven and Earth

"I'd move heaven and earth to break 100," an aspiring golfer remarked. His exasperated partner retorted, "You better concentrate on heaven, you've dug up enough earth for one day."

Nice to Show Up

On Monday night, January 17, 1983, friends of George Burns gathered to celebrate his eighty years in show business. "It's nice to have an eightieth anniversary," the eighty-seven-year-old comedian told two-hundred admirers at a Hollywood restaurant. "It is even nicer to show up for it."

Not Here to Pray

Major football games in Texas are not authentic unless someone of "the cloth" invokes the blessings of God on the contest. It is reported that before a University of Texas-Texas A & M game, a Baptist minister shocked the huge throng by including in his petition this sentence, "Lord, we are not here to pray, we are here to beat the dickens out of those guys from Texas A & M. Amen."

Not to Be Outdone

A Maine potato farmer and a Texas rancher were engaged in conversation at a political rally. The man from the Lone Star State asked, "How much land do you tend?"

"About a hundred acres."

"I farm about six thousand myself."

The man from Maine was not overly impressed, so the

Texan continued, "There's a much bigger ranch down near San Antone. To give you an idea of its size, the owner can start off in the morning in his car, and he ain't barely crossed his place by noon."

"I had a car like that myself once," the man from Maine said.

One Liners

Following the wedding a father commented, "I lost a daughter but gained a telephone."

A man reported that his wife was so religious that her contact lenses were made of cathedral glass.

Permission to Shoot

Herbert Hoover once said that any President should have the right to shoot at least two people a year without explanation.[1]

Return to Sender

The late Carlyle Marney told a delightful story of a young wife who could not put up with her spoiled husband any longer. Here is the note she pinned to his coat as she sent him back home:

Dear Mother-in-law:

Attached to this note find your infant son. I have tried to help him grow up, but you beat me to him, and you are all he needs. So I send him back to you just like I got him.

Faithfully yours,
Would-be wife

P.S. He eats most anything, provided it's like you fix it![2]

Timely Humor

Just prior to undergoing surgery following his attempted assassination, President Reagan is said to have remarked to medical personnel, "I hope you are all Republicans!" Afterwards, his first comment was inspired by W. C. Fields's epitaph, "All in all, I'd rather be in Philadelphia."

Try to Remember

When Frederick C. Howe, lawyer and political scientist, finished the first draft of his autobiography, he submitted it to his wife for review. After reading it, she laughingly asked: "But Fred, weren't you ever married?"

He stammered in embarrassment: "I am sorry. I guess I forgot that. I'll put it in now."

Unintentional

During an interim pastorate in a small-town church, a college commitment necessitated my absence one Sunday. The worship committee secured a former preacher, now employed at a funeral home. The dear brother sent me his sermon topic for the bulletin: "Does God Have a Plan for Your Life?" (Rom. 8:28 32).

Not bad! I thought. The information, however, was submitted on a note pad from his mortuary with a picture of a casket at the top, advertising a popular type of vault. Among other pleasant reminders were: "Fast Dependable Service . . . twelve, ten, and seven gauge air seal—bolted end-seal porcelain—stainless steel."

When Silence Speaks

Being challenged by his articulate priest, a bright, sensitive young man decided he wanted to become a monk. He discussed it many times during high school days with the pastor of his parish. Seeing he could not discourage the aspirant but warning him of the rugged discipline required, the pastor finally recommended the lad to the proper authorities.

The superior in charge of the desired order told the candidate he would be allowed to speak but two words for the first ten years. At the end of that exhausting period, he was asked, "Do you have any comment?"

"Food cold."

Another decade of dedication was endured. The monk's confessor asked, "Do you have anything to say?"

"Bed hard."

At last the third decade of silence passed. Again the candidate for the chosen order was asked to comment.

"I quit."

"Good," replied the superior, "you've done nothing but complain for the last thirty years."

Without Thinking

While discussing the several abilities of their parishioners, one member volunteered, "There's a man who says what he thinks—without thinking."

Influence

1 Samuel 10:24; Luke 8:46; Galatians 5:9; James 2:1-7; 1 Peter 2:16-17

We must have your name. There will be more efficacy in it than in many an army.

—John Adams, letter to George
Washington, 1798

Give me a man who is weak, and I will help him become strong, through letting him talk and through talking with him.

—Benjamin Disraeli

Blessed influence of one true, loving human soul on another.

—George Eliot

"You Have Blessed My Life"

Years ago when William Burt, a Methodist bishop, retired, he received a bound book of autographed tributes from those who had served with him on a certain board of the denomination. The following letter is a tribute concerning his Christian influence:

Dear Bishop Burt:

Your years have passed like sunlight. They were beautiful, and filled with service in the old world and in the new. God has been with you, and you have been with God.

Would you might live a hundred years to bless mankind, but wherever you are, in earth or heaven, you will like the place. You make it good to live where you are around.

You have blessed my life, and I want to live with you forever in the skies.

Your brother everywhere,
William A. Quayle

A Commanding Hero

When Robert Burns, the eighteenth-century Scottish poet, was at the height of his literary popularity, he observed the admiration of a small boy who followed him around. One day he turned and said to the lad, "Walter, what do you want?" The boy answered that some day he, too, wanted to be a writer. Whereupon Burns laid his hand on the lad's head and said, "You can be a great writer some day, Walter, and you will be." The boy became the enviable and prolific novelist, Sir Walter Scott.

Contagion of a Loving Heart

One day Saint Francis of Assisi encountered Brother Juniper, an incredibly stupid man. He had been known to cook rabbits without drawing or skinning them. To this ignorant human being the happy saint said, "Cheer up, Brother Juniper! Don't you know you possess the greatest gift of all—a loving heart!"

Conversion

In 1871 the *New York Herald* sent Henry Stanley to Africa in search of the missionary, David Livingstone, who was long overdue. After unbelievable hardships, the journalist found the explorer in central Africa, where he spent four months with him. Stanley went to Africa a conceited and confirmed atheist, but Livingstone's influence, gentleness, genuineness, goodness, and zeal won Stanley. Stanley became a Christian, saying, "I was converted by him, although he had not tried to do it."

Enduring Proof

Beyond his phenomenal talents and disciplines, biographers declare that the essence of Albert Schweitzer was the man himself, a symbol of the good life. One is not only overwhelmed by the comprehensiveness of his ministry, but also by what others were able to accomplish because of his contagious example. He animated countless millions of souls by his philosophy and practice of "reverence for life." The scholar once said: "If affirmation for life is genuine, it will demand from all that they should sacrifice a portion of their own lives for others."

A Father's Counsel

John Wooden, UCLA's legendary basketball mentor, born in Hall, Indiana, knew the rigors and compensations of agrarian living. His father, a rural mail carrier and farmer, made a lasting impression on young John. Upon graduating from the county school in Centerton, Indiana, Joshua Hugh Wooden gave his son this written creed: "Be true to yourself; make each day your masterpiece; help others; drink deeply from good books, especially the Bible; make friendship a fine art; build a shelter against a rainy day; pray for guidance, count, and give thanks for your blessings every day."

From Guerrilla to Communist Party Chairman

Back in the 1930s, a Chinese guerilla named Mao Tse-tung often spoke from a rock outside a village in South China. The armies of Chiang Kai-shek forced him to retreat further and further inland. Mao Tse-tung, however, took his ideas with him, teaching people as he went. The day came when nearly a billion people, almost a quarter of the population of the earth, looked to this evil man for leadership.

Make no mistake about it, one person always has and always will make the difference between success and failure—however measured—between good and evil.

Giving: an Opportunity to Serve

At a banquet honoring a highly successful fundraiser for colleges and universities, the person who presented him said, "Here is the greatest beggar in America!" Not pleased by the unintentional misconception of his host, the honored guest replied, "I am not a beggar. I have never begged from anyone. But I have given a lot of people opportunities to be of service to their fellows in this world."

Humble Contagion

In a large church we once served, one Sunday a peculiar-looking man walked down the aisle to place his membership. Soon I discovered Julius (not his real name) was a casualty of World War II. He was emotionally brittle; he could handle only menial tasks, but he was exceedingly loyal to the church. He would come by several times a week to speak to members of the staff, to bring the secretaries flowers, and more often than not, regardless of what I was doing, to speak with "the pastor."

Often when I went to the chapel or the sanctuary during the week to visualize the congregation and to pray, there would be

Julius in deep meditation. Every month or so he would come down the aisle to renew his faith.

On my last Sunday at this church, when I told Julius goodbye, he wept like a child.

At the time of his death, a friend wrote that a sizable congregation assembled to worship and to thank God for Julius. This humble man had had a great influence on a metropolitan church.

Pass It On

R. L. Middletown shared a scintillating story concerning a wealthy industrialist who stopped every morning at a certain shoeshine parlor. An Italian boy always shined his shoes. Tony liked Mr. Ward, and the feeling was mutual. One morning Ward asked his young friend, "If you could have one wish fulfilled, Tony, what would that wish be?"

The boy stopped, looked his friend in the eye, and replied, "I would like to study medicine. Above everything else in the world, I would like to be a doctor. . . . But I have to take care of my mother."

Deeply moved, the philanthropist retorted, "Tony, suppose I told you that I would give you—not lend you—enough money to see you through the university and medical school, what would you say?"

Smilingly the boy answered, "I would say you wouldn't do it."

"I will do it, Tony. You are shining your last pair of shoes."

The boy laid down the shine rag and kissed the shoes that were being bathed in tears.

Their friendship continued. Arduous years of schooling were completed. Time passed. Tony married. He enjoyed a lucrative practice. Then one day, a beautiful car stopped in front of Ward's office. The young doctor hurried up the familiar stair. The meeting of the men was very tender. Finally, Doctor Tony said, "This is a great day for me. Here's a check for all the money you have spent on my education, with interest."

Ward took the check, looked at it for a brief moment, slowly endorsed it, and handed it back, saying, "Tony, I never expect any returns from the investments I make in human life. Anyhow, God has credited me with it on His books, so it does not belong to me. Take it and find another boy that is worthy. Send him through school on it. Maybe someday he will hand it back to you."

The Power of One Person

In the 1920s, a sociology class at Johns Hopkins University made a study of children in deprived neighborhoods in Baltimore. They identified two-hundred children who appeared doomed to spend years in prison. After twenty-five years, another study was made to discover what had happened to those particular children. Surprisingly, only two were incarcerated. As these men and women were interviewed over and over again came the name of their teacher, "Aunt Hannah." The sociologists were correct in their predictions. By all indications the children would be dregs of society; but there was an intervention, Aunt Hannah, an elementary school teacher who loved them.

Roads to Remember

Roads are romantic. They are scrolls of memory. The road we walked to school, the country store, our grandparents, church—all suggest experiences we never tire of telling.

One cannot travel the Appian Way without sensing something of the proud culture of the Romans and their significant contributions to society. To drive the Freedom Road in Israel is to relive the conflict between Arabs and Jews which continues to this moment. One tingles with excitement as one travels along fast, open, beckoning highways to such cities as Paris, London, New York, Boston, and Los Angeles. Roads are filmstrips of life. They speak volumes, and so do biblical roads. Happenings along the roads to Damascus, Gaza, Jericho, and Emmaus all incite memory and gratitude (see Luke 24:32).

Safely Home

Louisa May Alcott told of a memorable night in 1854. Her father, Amos Bronson Alcott, an extravagant and visionary man, returned home unexpectedly from an unprofitable speaking junket. It was in cold February, and when the doorbell rang, Mrs. Alcott flew downstairs crying, "My husband!" Five white figures in long, flowing gowns trailed behind her. Louisa Alcott declared that her father was bedraggled, half-frozen, and hungry, and that they fed him and brooded over him. Everyone was anxious to know if he had made any money on the trip. Finally little May asked, "Well, did people pay you?" Then, with a weird look, he opened his pocketbook and showed one dollar, explaining that his overcoat had been stolen and that he had had to replace it with a shawl. Many people did not keep their promises, he declared, traveling was costly, but the stage was set for another year.

Then, said Louisa, she observed and would never forget how beautifully her mother answered him, though much had been built on his success; but with a beaming face she kissed him and said, "I call that doing very well. Since you are safely home, dear, we don't ask anything more."

"Anna and I choked down our tears, and took a little lesson in real love which we never forgot."

Saying Yes

In reviewing the life of the late Henry Fonda, Dan Sullivan, theater critic for *The Los Angeles Times,* shared this intriguing conclusion: "Something in Fonda said yes to men who said no."

Standing Tall

The former governor of Oregon, Tom McCall, died January 8, 1983, of cancer. Cecil Andrus, former Interior Secretary, said: "We all live in a better world because there was a tall man like Tom McCall."

Tell God "Thank You"

A preacher friend of mine, returning from a tour of Europe where he had visited his clergyman cousin, related this story: A London scrubwoman was taken ill. Friends sent her to the hospital. During her convalescence she visited along the corridor. She developed a fondness for a twelve-year-old, freckle-faced, red-haired boy in the room across from hers. They visited daily.

Early one morning she was awakened by confusion and conversation. Presently, the boy's mother, brokenhearted, ventured into the charwoman's room, exclaiming, "Doctors say Johnny has only ten minutes to live. Won't you say something to him?"

With the courage and conviction of a great Christian, the charwoman walked calmly into Johnny's room, sat on his bed, took his thin hands between her calloused palms, and said, "Listen, Johnny, God made you. God loves you. God sent His Son to save you. God wants you to come home with Him."

With great difficulty, the lad raised up on his elbows and entreated his friend, "Say it again."

Softly she repeated, "God made you. God loves you. God sent His Son to save you. God wants you to come home with Him."

Johnny looked into her benign face and said, "Tell God, 'Thank You!'"

Trust and Triumph

A beautifully touching story emanated from Phoenix, Arizona, a few years ago. It was the account of a seven-year-old boy who accidentally fell into a two-hundred-seventy-five-foot well. For forty-five minutes the lad was trapped in darkness, with multiple fractures.

"Daddy, get me out of here," he yelled.

"Don't worry, son, and don't be scared. We will get you out. Just push against the sides of the pipe so you don't sink."

Eventually, proper rescue equipment arrived. A rope was lowered into the well. Mr. Stage, the lad's father, gave specific instructions how to place the rope over his shoulders and beneath the arms, and to hold on. The boy obeyed, and was lifted to safety. The father commented: "He always did mind good." Irrespective of grammar, there existed a trustful relationship between father and son.

A similar rapport should exist between a Christian and God.

Untouchable

In writing about T. S. Eliot, Karl Shapiro made a revealing analysis of this remarkable man:

Eliot is untouchable; he is Modern Literature incarnate and an institution unto himself. One is permitted to disagree with him on a point here or a doctrine there, but no more. The enemy at Eliot's gate searches his citadel for an opening and cannot find one.

Were It Not for Christians

John Wesley declared that the world would be Christian were it not for the *Christians!*

World Citizens

Only three times in our history has the American flag flown at half-mast for persons other than citizens of the United States. These exceptional occasions honored Winston Churchill, Dag Hammarskjöld, and Anwar Sadat, men of universal stature and influence.

Integrity

Job 2:9; Proverbs 28:18; Matthew 5:37; Luke 8:15;

Why is it that men know what is good but do what is bad?
—Socrates

Modern man suffers from repression of conscience.
—Paul Tournier

Anxiety Whispers

The tragedy of Watergate for the whole country is that people at the heart of our government yielded to the anxiety that whispers so convincingly in all our hearts that achievement is more important than character. God help us out of this wreckage to learn anew that the highest value and most enduring power in human enterprise is character.[1]

Campus Conduct

A social eruption occurred on the campus of an American university. The nature of the case was so serious that it was necessary for the president of the institution and his council to handle it. In reply to a personal question, one of the top students snapped, "Sir, I'd wager that there are not ten men on the campus who wouldn't have done exactly what I did under the circumstances." Whereupon the president replied, "Young man, has it occurred to you that you might have been one of those ten?"

Challenging Example

In the February 26, 1963, issue of *Look*, C. P. Snow made this trenchant comment concerning Winston Churchill: "He has not only helped to save us from dying. He has shown us a pattern of how life can be lived."

Cheating on Tax Returns

Commissioner Roscoe L. Egger, Jr., of Internal Revenue Service reports cheating costs the federal government about $70 billion a year in taxes. "That means that of every five dollars that should go to IRS, only four dollars arrive." An accelerated effort is being made to catch cheats. It is believed that for every dollar spent in the search, twelve dollars could be realized in extra revenues.

Comments

What is morally wrong can never be politically right.
—Abraham Lincoln

I have to say that in the last years at ABC—say 1976—I felt pretty bad. I was wallowing in a lot of money and not enough self-respect.[2]
—Harry Reasoner

Deception

Abraham Lincoln spoke wisely: "You may fool all the people some of the time; you can even fool some the people all the time; but you can't fool all of the people all the time."

Depending on Perspective

Henry David Thoreau was thrown in prison for refusing to pay his taxes because a portion went to support the Mexican War. Ralph Waldo Emerson went to see him in jail and said: "Thoreau, what are you doing in there?" He replied: "Waldo, what are you doing out there?"

Honesty at Home

In his *London Journal,* Boswell reported that the literary giant Samuel Johnson, eighteenth-century English lexicographer and author, did not permit a servant to say he was not home when he was busy in his library for fear he might hurt the servant's idea of truth. Johnson said he might be able to explain it to a philosopher but not to a servant.

How Honest Can You Get?

During the 1983 National Spelling Bee held in Washington, D. C., thirteen-year-old Andrew Flosdorf of Fonda, New York, eliminated himself from the contest when he informed the judges he had misspelled "echolalia." The judges had failed to catch the error. When questioned as to why he turned himself in, he straightforwardly replied, "I didn't want to feel like a slime."

An Impeccable Character

In 1860 Robert E. Lee considered himself a failure. His friend, Joseph Johnston, had risen to the rank of brigadier general while Lee, past middle age, had required twenty-two years to advance from captain to lieutenant colonel. Yet, in one of the most unfortunate periods in American history, Lee, a man of impeccable character, was chosen to lead the soldiers of the South. Irrespective of sectionalism or prejudice, he remains one of the most honored of American heroes.

Living with Honor

Francis I, King of France, was defeated in the battle of Pavia, February 24, 1525, and taken captive to Madrid, the city of his conqueror, where Charles V imprisoned him. While in prison, he sent this dispatch to his people—"All has been lost save honor."

Not for Sale

Basil Miller reported that at the end of the American Civil War, General Lee was broke, as were many of his countrymen. Money was scarce. About that time a state lottery offered him ten thousand dollars a year for the use of his name. He replied, "Gentlemen, my name is all I have left, and that is not for sale."

Out of Sight, Out of Mind

In his dramatic critique of American culture, Philip Slater, in *The Pursuit of Loneliness,* reminds us we are living in the period of the "toilet assumption," namely, that when something disappears or is no longer visible, we think we are rid of it. This is true with the race situation, with the poor, with the environment. If somehow we can keep them out of sight, we feel that the battle is won.

Precisiveness

When Calvin Coolidge was President, some of his Vermont neighbors decided to recognize his devotion to the old family farm by giving him a handmade rake. The orator who presented the rake dwelt at length on the qualities of the hickory wood from which he believed it was made. "Hickory," he said, "like the President, is sturdy, strong, resilient, unbroken." Then he handed the rake to Coolidge, and the audience settled back for his speech of acknowledgment. Coolidge turned the rake over, looked at it carefully, and uttered one word, "Ash."

Put More In

H. G. Wells sensed the challenge of living with integrity when he declared that a "gentleman" is one who puts more into life than he takes out. What a viable test!

Too Close to Call

When John Newton was captain of a slave ship, he conducted worship twice every Sunday. Apparently he saw no conflict between slave trade and being a Christian. Be it said, however, this man who eventually wrote the wonderful hymn, "Glorious Things of Thee Are Spoken," when eighty-two, said, "My memory is nearly gone, but I remember two things—that I am a great sinner, and that Christ is a great Savior."

True to Self

In Shakespeare's *Hamlet,* Polonius says it well: "This above all: to thine own self be true,/And it must follow, as the night the day,/Thou canst not then be false to any man."

Truth Takes Its Toll

A few days after the birth of Isaac Watts, his father, a clothier, began a jail sentence in Southampton because he believed he had the right to worship in the fellowship led by the Reverend Nathaniel Robinson rather than in the established Church of England. The elder Mr. Watts's stand for truth did not disgrace or divide his family. Quite the opposite! Every day Mrs. Watts took tiny Isaac to the prison, and, seated on a horse block outside, fed him in sight of his incarcerated father. When Isaac was nine months old, his father began another six months' imprisonment for the same cause—religious freedom! Was it not love of truth, love of freedom, love of family, love of Christ, that impelled Watts to demonstrate such demanding integrity? Was young Isaac absorbing homilies of truth to be expressed later in his magnificent hymns?

Wise Enough to Cheat?

Cheating has become a way of life. We see it and read of it every day. A dramatic case in point is Janet Cooke, former reporter for *The Washington Post,* who won the Pulitzer Prize for feature writing in 1981. When her heroin-addicted Jimmy turned out to be a fictitious character and the whole story contrived, she was allowed to resign and the *Post* returned the Pulitzer Prize. Yet, after a few months of relative silence, she emerged a hero, sought after for interviews and by publishers.

Americans love celebrities regardless of the merits of their achievements. Stardom is a profitable commodity. Writing on the Janet Cooke case in his syndicated column of February 10, 1982, Bob Greene concluded:

> Had she done her journalistic job according to the ethics that reporters are supposed to follow, she would still have her Pulitzer Prize. And she would be relatively anonymous. Today she is a star, though, a marketable commodity, and she owes it all to the good fortune that she was wise enough to cheat.[3]

The Word Is Integrity

General William F. Dean was a prized prisoner of the Communists during the Korean struggle. One day, the General was advised that he had five minutes in which to write a letter to his family. It appeared to be the end. Calmly he accepted the order and proceeded to write. In the body of this now-historic letter appears a single line worthy of remembrance: "Tell Bill the word is integrity."

Jesus Christ

Matthew 1:20-21; Mark 1:9-11; Romans 1:1-7; 1 Timothy 2:8-9

Life with Christ is an endless hope, without Him a hopeless end.
—Anonymous

Jesus Christ is middle C on the Christian keyboard of life.
—Claude H. Rhea

Always Say a Good Word

In the 1890s, a book appeared entitled *Beside the Bonnie Briar Bush.* It was authored by John Watson, who wrote under the pen name of Ian Maclaren. In the volume is the story of a lad who decided to enter the ministry. Before finishing school, however, his saintly mother died and he went to live with an aunt. By and by, the young man completed seminary and was ready to take his first church, indeed to preach his first sermon as pastor. The bright boy labored long on his sermon, then proudly read it to his aunt. When he asked for criticism, his aunt expressed appreciation for its beauty but reminded him that many of his parishioners had had little schooling. It was then she shared his mother's words of admonition just before her death: "When you stand up to preach, always say a good word for Jesus Christ."

The Ascension

Following His resurrection, Jesus appeared and disappeared to an assortment of persons over a period of perhaps six weeks. J. B. Phillips, and others, claim this was necessary to convince His followers of His living presence. Thus He was teaching them to further believe and to grow. The ascension was not a media event, but the consummation of His visible ministry and the formal commissioning of His disciples (Matt. 28:16-20).

Luke's account of Jesus' departure is equally satisfying. "And they returned to Jerusalem with great joy, and were continually in the temple blessing God" (24:52).

Behold the Man!

He was born in an obscure village, the child of a peasant woman. He grew up in another village, where He worked in a carpenter shop until He was thirty. Then for three years He was an itinerant preacher. He never wrote a book. He never held an office. He never had a family or owned a home. He didn't go to college. He never visited a big city. He never traveled two-hundred miles from the place where He was born. He did none of the things that usually accompany greatness. He had no credentials but Himself. He was only thirty-three when the tide of public opinion turned against Him. His friends ran away. One of them denied Him. He was turned over to His enemies and went through the mockery of a trial. He was nailed to a cross between two thieves. While He was dying . . . his executioners gambled for his garments, the only property He had on earth. When He was dead, He was laid in a borrowed grave through the pity of a friend. Nineteen centuries have come and gone, and today He is the central figure of the human race. All the armies that ever marched, all the navies that ever sailed, all the parliaments that ever sat, all the kings that ever reigned, put together, have not affected the life of man on this earth as much as that one solitary life.[1]

Beyond Baby Jesus

It seems to me that one of the tragedies of Christmas is that we continue to worship Baby Jesus. In fact, too many of us are still in the nursery with rhyme and song. We are too often teddy-bear Christians. The greater message of Christmas is that this baby, who uniquely invaded the world, grew up to be the Savior of mankind. His devastating courage and contagious love compel us to visit Bethlehem, the starting place in the celestial journey, the Bethlehem of new birth.

Christ or Chaos

Long before Woodrow Wilson became President of the United States, he was a noted scholar-teacher. He once declared: "Nobody could defeat Alexander Hamilton; whether he was in office or not, he alone had the constructive program and they either had to submit to chaos or to follow Hamilton." In a far more graphic and final sense, persons must chose between chaos and Christ.

Discovering Jesus

I like this marvelous declaration by Albert Schweitzer:

> And to those who obey Him, whether they be wise or simple, He will reveal Himself in the toils, the conflict, the sufferings which they shall pass through in his fellowship, and, as an ineffable mystery, they shall learn in their own experience Who He is.[2]

Don't Look Dismal!

Elton Trueblood and others remind us that Jesus was not only a Man of sorrows and grief, but He was also a Man of joys. At times the Lord used blunt language (Matt. 3:7), and demonstrated blazing anger (Luke 19:45-46) to actualize truth. These and other passages reassure us of the Master's humanity.

Christ's use of irony and humorous parables tell us a great deal. Listen to Him: "And no one after drinking old wine desires new; for he says, 'The old is good' " (Luke 5:39). "Woe to you, scribes and Pharisees, hypocrites! For you are like whitewashed tombs, which outwardly appear beautiful, but within they are full of dead men's bones" (Matt. 23:27)—terribly strong language! Or consider this astonishing comment, "It is easier for a camel to go through the eye of a needle than for a rich man to enter the kingdom of God" (Matt. 19:24). "How can you say to your brother, 'Let me take the speck out of your eye,' when there is a log in your own eye" (Matt. 7:4).

Years ago when Trueblood read this last passage in family devotions, their four-year-old son began to laugh. It was then that the noted Quaker saw the ridiculousness of the comment and it formed the seedbed for his book entitled *The Humor of Christ.*

"And when you fast, do not look dismal, like the hypocrites" (Matt. 6:16).

Do You Know Him?

In *The Gift of Janice,* Max Wylie, novelist and playwright, declared he knew only a dozen people who consciously thought of Jesus and who tried to bring the simple truths of His teaching into all the affairs of their lives. The Christian churches, he said, have become so preoccupied with God, they have mislaid Jesus, the God-man.

Irresistible Impression

Mahatma Gandhi knew imprisonment and suffering as few persons, but his spirit soared above his surroundings. He meant it to be a great compliment to our Lord when he declared that the man who had impressed him most had never set foot on Indian soil, Jesus of Nazareth.

The Legacy of Christ

The legacy of Christ is not tension, but peace.
The legacy of Christ is not war, but peace.
The legacy of Christ is not advice about peace, it is peace!

Let Jesus In

Once I heard this story concerning King Edward VII of England. He and his queen were out walking late one afternoon when suddenly she stumbled and sprained an ankle. In great pain, and with considerable difficulty, she limped along, holding to her husband's shoulder. At dusk, they approached the home of a humble man. The king knocked on the door. "Who's there?" came the query.

"It is Edward. It is the king. Let me in."

The man on the inside shouted back, "Enough of your pranks now. Be off. . . ."

The king, not being accustomed to such language, was shocked. He hardly knew what to do, but he knocked a second time. The cottager inquired, "What do you want?"

"I tell you it is the king! It is Edward, your king. Let me in."

In anger the man shouted, "I'll teach you to torment an honest man trying to get his sleep." He threw open the door in disgust, only to see that indeed it was his king! With profuse apologies the laborer invited the royal visitors in and sent for help to attend his queen.

Years later, when the Britisher was too old to work, he would spend much time rocking on the porch and visiting with neighbors. He took great delight in reviewing that experience, always concluding with the same words: "And to think, to think, I almost didn't let him in! To think I almost didn't let him in!"

"Behold, I stand at the door and knock; if any one hears my voice and opens the door, I will come in to him and eat with him, and he with me" (Rev. 3:20).

Not until you open your heart and let Jesus in will you know what God is like.

Let Loose in the World

The English poet, John Masefield, in his moving play, *The Trial of Jesus,* has the wife of Pontius Pilate ask the centurion in charge at the crucifixion, "So you think He is dead?"

"No, lady, I don't."

"Then where is He?" she persists.

"Let loose in the world, lady, where none can stop His truth."

The Living Christ

The late and beloved scholar of the Christian Church (Disciples of Christ), W. E. Garrison, declared there were two high tides in the Christian year: the night of the nativity, and the morning of the resurrection. While they are events in time, they are also timeless, mysterious, and symbolic. No one can fully comprehend what happened in Bethlehem any more than one can understand what happened in Jerusalem. If one can accept history and common observation, these events shaped one's comprehension of life and continue to have a transforming potency.

Christmas and Easter proclaim the same essential message: Emmanuel, God with us; the living Christ!

Look at Mary's Child

There is an old legend which maintains that when Jesus was a baby growing up in Nazareth, the neighbors used to say when they were discouraged or depressed, "Let us go and see Mary's child." After looking upon the precious One, sunshine and peace returned and the distraught souls returned to their tasks with high heart.

Loving Jesus

Joseph Fort Newton, in his fascinating autobiography, *River of Years,* dramatically described the day when as a small lad he looked for the first time into an open grave. It was the burial of his father. Snow lay on the ground. A strong wind was blowing, and a fire was burning a few feet away. Though too small to fully comprehend what he saw and felt, young Joseph Newton knew in his heart something powerful had happened. He stood close to his mother, gripping her hand. With great sincerity, the old country minister read, "I am the resurrection and the life; he who believes in me, though he die, yet shall he live, and whoever lives and believes in me shall never die" (John 11:25-26).

Reflecting on the experience, Newton declared,

Never shall I forget the power of those words. It was as if a great, gentle Hand, stronger than the hand of man and more tender than the hand of any woman, had been put forth from the Unseen, to caress and heal my spirit—from that day to this, I have loved Jesus beyond the power of words to tell![3]

The Irresistible Cross

George Tyrell of England, a courageous exponent of truth, was expelled from the Jesuit order. In the midst of his troubles he said, "Again and again, I have been tempted to give up the struggle, but always that strange Man hanging on the cross sends me back to my tasks again."

Something for Christ

That incredible four-star general of the cross, Dr. Albert Schweitzer, returned to Europe on furlough from Africa when he was eighty years old. Not being able to comprehend why such a famous person would leave the comfort and security of Europe to live in Lamberene in the first place, let alone to return to the swamps of the dark continent at such an advanced age, a reporter asked the humble Christian for an explanation. Thoughtfully he replied, "You see, I had to do something for Christ."

Strangely Warmed

Fresh out of Oxford, John Wesley was perplexed over England's complicated social problems: slavery, economic uncertainties, corruption, drunkenness, gambling, and prostitution. This deeply religious, sensitive soul became a parish minister and, subsequently, a missionary to American Indians along the coast of Georgia. His ministries were far from successful. Disappointed and discouraged, he returned to Britain.

During the voyage, his ship was raked by a raging storm. Wesley was unashamedly frightened. In fact, the only calm persons aboard were Moravian missionaries. Noticing their behavior, Wesley asked if they were not afraid. "Why should I be afraid," one answered, "I know Christ." Then, with disarming directness, he asked, "Do you know Christ?" Wesley was uncomfortable, for in his heart he now realized he did not know Christ.

Back in London, on Wednesday evening, May 24, 1738, John Wesley attended a society meeting and worship at Aldersgate Street and listened to a reading of Martin Luther's preface to the Book of Romans. The rest is history. According to Wesley, "About a quarter before nine. . . . I felt my heart strangely warmed. I felt I did trust in Christ, Christ alone for my salvation."

Surrendering to Christ

The late E. Stanley Jones wrote in *Victory Through Surrender* that for fifty years his home was a suitcase. He never knew loneliness because long ago he surrendered his life to Christ.

To Bring Wholeness

In *When God was Man*, J. B. Phillips asserted that Jesus was "perfect wholeness coming into a world ridden with disease and deformity of body, mind and soul."

Leadership

Genesis 33:12-14; 1 Chronicles 13:1-4; Matthew 20:25-28;
Hebrews 13:7-8

And when we think we lead, we most are led.
—Lord Byron

Lead, follow, or get out of the way.
—Ted Turner

Born Leaders

Some years ago when I was in Southern Rhodesia—now Zimbabwe—I was privileged to visit a gold mine operation. Within a compound where recruited workers lived was a series of small, walled-in areas where testing occurred. These men could neither read nor write. The problem was to discover natural leaders. Each area contained the tools—barrels, ropes, picks, mine props, and so forth—to solve a particular problem. In small teams, competing units sought to solve the obstacles. They were timed. The men who proceeded logically and swiftly were chosen as team leaders in the mine. A top management person told me he never ceased to be amazed at the native intelligence of some of the illiterate men. Later, when I was two miles beneath the earth's surface, though frightened, I could appreciate the adeptness of the miners.

Brains, Bluster, Bravado

Time, March 21, 1983, in a cover story, used these terse words to describe Chrysler's Lee Iacocca:

> Without debating the pros and cons of government bailouts and economic problems, what has transpired at Chrysler Corporation since 1981 is phenomenal! A Gallup poll reported that small- and medium-size businesses found Mr. Iacocca the American business executive they respected most. His charisma, courage, confidence, and competitiveness distinguish him as an exceptional leader.

Called to Serve

In the second year after the Israelites had left Egypt, Moses felt that it was God's will for him to take a census of the people, all except the Levites. Members of this tribe, particularly the men, were put in charge of everything sacred, including the ark of the covenant. Normally belongings were packed in wagons and carts, as these nomads moved from place to place. The precious symbols of their faith, however, were carried by the Levites. The ark of the covenant was transported on a stretcher-type litter which the bearers usually carried on their shoulders. These men were especially selected to care for the symbols of their faith, and they were willing to carry the "Sanctuary" on their shoulders.

As leaders of the church, we have been carefully selected and screened for our loyalty, stewardship, and attendance. Our task is none other than to literally and spiritually carry this church and its causes on our shoulders and in our hearts.

Cost Samplings

The former commissioner of baseball, Bowie Kuhn, says it takes about five-hundred thousand dollars to prepare a prospective baseball player for the big leagues. We spend a small fraction of that sum on training and supporting church leaders.

CBS reported October 16, 1983, that each member of Congress costs American taxpayers $1,946 annually. Each garnered congressional vote costs thirteen dollars.

Incidentally, the cost of running Congress has increased 800 percent in the last twenty-two years.

Don't Forget the Bones!

There is an arresting story in the thirteenth chapter of Exodus. Following four-hundred agonizing years of slavery, years of hoping, years of praying, the Israelites were allowed to leave Egypt. The announcement of their departure was unexpected; preparations to leave were hurriedly made. The trek before them was long and threatening. The liberated souls could take only items necessary for survival. But we read that "Moses took the bones of Joseph with him" (v. 19). This remarkable leader realized that survival kits were incomplete without spiritual symbols of their heritage and hope. There would be little joy in the future if they forgot their past.

Free to Choose

In his book, *How Are You Programmed?*, J. Edward Barrett referred to mankind as the "presiding self." How do you think of people? Are we just animals who remember, who take out insurance, and become obese with age? Are people monkeys who are capable of doing mathematics?

Although mankind has more in common with the animal kingdom than we care to admit, we are nonetheless capable of presiding over both our genetic and historic programming. We are free to choose courses of action; to commit ourselves to objectives.

Great Military Leader

Born in Missouri to humble parents on Lincoln's birthday, 1893, Omar Nelson Bradley learned early the lessons of integrity and hard work. Following his father's death in 1908, he assisted his mother, who took in boarders. Despite hardships, or perhaps because of them, and memories of the studious habits of his father, a schoolteacher, Omar graduated from high school with an overall average grade of 91.4. Appointed as an alternate from his district to West Point, and because the principal candidate failed to qualify, young Bradley, who had passed, was selected.

This hardworking student, excellent athlete, and marksman, stood forty-fourth in a class of 164 when he graduated from West Point in 1915.

Standing five-feet, eleven-and-a-quarter inches tall and weighing 145 pounds, he, like his mother, became prematurely gray (he had some gray hairs at age eighteen), and who because of a teenage ice-skating accident had to wear dentures much earlier than most persons, he nevertheless quietly pursued excellence. Teaching thirteen of his twenty-three years of commissioned service, he developed competence and confidence.

After spending twelve long years as a major, he was promoted to lieutenant colonel. Yet this quiet, thorough man—who was never a full colonel—was first in his class to be made general, and ultimately chief of staff of the Army. This family man, an elder in his church, was highly respected and beloved.

Lacking MacArthur's brilliance and arrogance or Patton's harshness and obscenities, General Bradley is considered one of America's military giants. General Dwight D. Eisenhower once said to him:

In my opinion you are preeminent among the Commanders of battle units in this war. Your leadership, forcefulness, professional capacity, selflessness, high sense of duty and sympathetic understanding of human beings combine to stamp you as one of America's great leaders and soldiers.[1]

Instincts to Lead

Eight-hundred Rhodes Scholars and six-hundred spouses convened at Oxford University in the summer of 1983 to celebrate the eightieth anniversary of the trust that administers the fund left by the entrepreneur, Cecil John Rhodes. As an indication of his belief that Oxford was a civilizing place, and in the hope of developing leaders for world peace, Rhodes provided funds from a fortune of $20 million to make available scholarships for outstanding, well-rounded young men to attend Oxford.

Candidates were to be judged on their "literary and scholastic attainments, qualities of manhood (including) courage and kindliness, and instincts to lead, and on their fondness for or success in sports." This prestigious scholarship program has been referred to as "a talent hunt for an elite that will lead."

Commenting on the reunion of Rhodes Scholars, George Cawkwell, himself a winner from New Zealand in 1946, now vice-master of Oxford's University College, was quoted in *Time* (July 11, 1983,) as saying: "Many scholars are brilliant. Most are not. But the world is not run by brilliant people. It is run by good, sound individuals."

Keeping One's Cool

It was a symbolic ceremony. Britain's Prime Minister Edward Heath and the premiers of Ireland, Denmark, and Norway had gathered in Brussels to sign a Treaty of Accession to the European Common Market.

The principals had worked long and arduous months—eighteen, in fact—pursuing mutual need and agreement. The hour of consummation was at hand. As Prime Minister Heath approached the formal chambers, a woman identified as Karen Cooper stepped out of the crowd and hit the distinguished Englishman in the face with a canister of black ink. People were stunned. Mr. Heath quietly turned away, retired to his quarters, changed, and returned to the scene, immaculate and confident as ever.

The Leverage of Timing

Ray Wilbur used to say that when he presented a proposition to his faculty at Leland Stanford University and it received unanimous consent, he knew that he was ten years too late. Any original, significant, or expensive proposal will generate debate, if not opposition.

A Missing Element

Norman Cousins said that Adlai Stevenson had all the qualities that went with leadership—intelligence, energy, compassion, integrity, eloquence, charm—yet he was the last in any company to see himself in a leadership role. He loved to analyze problems but didn't want to arrogate to himself the job to go charging off after solutions.[2]

No Substitute for Experience

There is a wonderful story in the Book of Numbers. It has to do with the children of Israel marching toward the Promised Land. Moses said to his father-in-law, Hobab: "Come with us, and we will do you good; for the Lord has promised good to Israel" (10:29).

The old man was not greatly moved by the invitation and declined. Moses persisted: "Do not leave us, I pray you, for you

know how we are to encamp in the wilderness, and you will
serve as eyes for us" (v. 31). Whereupon Hobab gladly accepted because he felt needed; he could justify the investment of
his time. His son-in-law had said: "You will be our eyes." As
much as to say, you know your way around. We are depending
on your experience and leadership to get us through!

Christian Leadership

Dr. Lloyd C. Elder, prominent Southern Baptist leader, has
perceptively written: "The pastors of local churches have his-
torically wielded a vital leadership role not only in their own
congregations but often within the denomination. They have
done this through the pulpit, as well as other communications
media.

"For good or bad, pastors and other church staff members are
those most often elected to denominational places of responsibility. They make up the majority of messengers (representatives) at any Southern Baptist Convention. What the minister
says and does continues to have a pacesetting effect on Baptist
laypersons. The pastor's skill and spirit in the area of communication is important in a time of communication crises.

"As a rule, Baptist laypersons have their greatest leadership
role in the local church. There is a growing emphasis today on
recovering the gifts and ministry of laypersons. Many boards
and committees include lay membership, but few involve significant laywomen participation. Great concern has been expressed by many that not enough laypersons have been called
to serve in major denominational leadership posts. The mobili-
zation of the laity is absolutely imperative if Bold Mission
Thrust (Southern Baptist emphasis to reach the world for
Christ by AD 2000) is to be a reality. . . ." (from *Blueprints*,
Broadman Press, 1984).

Points of View

Sigmund Freud believed that psychological maturity excluded religious dimensions. To him life could be understood only in terms of motivational forces. While Carl Jung maintained that the "spiritual quest is essentially an attempt to become what we were meant to be."

The Servant Role

In *Journey to the East,* Hermann Hesse described the activities and relationships of explorers who were sent on a difficult mission by a certain order. A servant, Leo, cared for their every need: prepared the food, washed their clothes, and was at their beck and call. In terms of protocol, he was the lowest of the least. As the mission progressed, Leo's adaptability and spirit proved invaluable.

The servant's worth became more evident when their ship was wrecked and Leo was missing. Trying to proceed without him proved impossible. Eventually one member of the party made his way back to headquarters, where he met the leader. And, lo, it was none other than Leo! Though assuming the role of servant during the expedition, in reality he was their leader. Hesse was saying: real leadership has more to do with service than with status.

Some Secrets

In a magazine article called "Life at the Top . . . ," Randy Cohen warned against the temptation to be a well-rounded person. Neither Byron, he said, Einstein, nor Colonel Sanders was well-rounded, yet each reached the top in his field. "Remember," Cohen continued, "the successful don't have hobbies; they have servants."

Take Off the Blinders

In commenting on Governor Orval Faubus's stand in Little Rock, Arkansas, during the 1957 race riots, Harry S. Ashmore wrote in his book, *An Epitaph for Dixie:* "Perhaps the most charitable thing that could be said of the Arkansas governor was that he had misunderstood the past, miscalculated the present, and ignored the future."[3]

That Little Difference

Charles William Eliot, once president of Harvard University, is said to have collected this philosophical gem while in conversation with a campus laborer who said: "There is not much difference between men but the little difference there is makes all the difference in the world."

Word in Advance

Browne Barr told of a school teacher in Connecticut by the name of Libby Fisher who taught for fifty-five years. For more than half a century she had seen the "little monsters" come and go, day in and day out. She was familiar with their tricks and with their parents; yet life was never stale. She was described as someone who always looked as if something wonderful was about to happen and that she had private word in advance. This is the posture of a Christian.

Would You Agree?

In his book, *Beyond Easy Believism,* (Word Books, 1982), Garry R. Collins reminded us that it is claimed the two most influential men of this century are Elvis Presley and Hugh Hefner. "As leaders of a moral revolution they directed millions into a passive acceptance of self-centered hedonism."

Life

John 1:4; John 10:10; Mark 8:35; 1 John 3:14

Live your life. Don't let your life live you.
—Archibald MacLeish

Every person confronts three great questions: Where am I from? Whither am I going? And what must I do on the way?
—John Ruskin

Begin at once to live, and count each day as a separate life.
—Seneca

The Beginning

A priest, a minister, and a rabbi were discussing the controversial question: "When does life begin?" The priest said life begins at conception. The minister said it was at "quickening," or possibly even birth. The rabbi said life begins when the kids leave home and the family dog dies.

Disappointment

Dr. Helmut Thielicke, in his book, *Being a Christian When the Chips Are Down,* reports on a conversation with an eloquent man in his sixties, punctiliously dressed. The well-groomed gentleman confessed he had never really found himself. He wanted to be a musician. Instead, he was compelled to take over his father's business. He was not a businessman. "So my life ended up as a heap of ashes before it had ever really caught fire."

Good Counsel

Sarah Dale Mannakee, who was born during the presidency of Ulysses S. Grant, and once taught where the Hatfields and McCoys feuded—Williamson, West Virginia—started painting seriously at age eighty-four, had her first show when she was ninety-four. "I started out painting the things I knew and loved, like rivers, oceans, flowers and hillsides." Some of her secrets for longevity include "stay busy, sleep well, eat well . . . and don't be a sourpuss!"[1]

Has Your Life Spoken?

Governor Jay S. Hammond of Alaska declared May 23, 1982, as Rosa Parks Day, in honor of this courageous woman who dared to sit in the front of the bus during the Montgomery, Alabama, bus sit-in. With only nine thousand blacks scattered throughout this vast state (including military personnel), about seven hundred of them came to see and hear the sixty-nine-year-old lady speak. Observing her deep cold, her friend of many years, an attorney in Anchorage, Ashley Dickerson, said, "Rosa, you don't have to say anything. Your life has spoken."[2]

In Danger of Living

During the latter days of Robert Louis Stevenson's illness, a clergyman wrote expressing his willingness to come and talk with the noted novelist "as to one in danger of dying." The beloved Britisher replied he would be delighted to receive the minister and to talk to him, "as to one in the danger of living."

Irregular People

Life is filled with what Joyce Landorf calls "irregular people," people who have a knack of being awkward in their speech, in their social graces, adept at alienating persons, and who find it difficult to perceive of their wrong, let alone apologize. Mrs. Landorf tells of "an irregular mother-in-law" who flew thousands of miles to see her son and daughter-in-law's new house. Proudly, she was given the grand tour. Her only comment was: "It's too bad you don't have a stainless steel sink."[3]

Just for Today

Just for today, try to live through this day only and not to tackle your whole life's problems.

Just for today, try to be happy. This assumes that what Abraham Lincoln said is true—that "most folks are about as happy as they make up their minds to be." Happiness is within.

Just for today, try to adjust yourself to what *is* and do not try to adjust everything to your own desires.

Just for today, take good care of your body. Exercise it, care for it, nourish it so that it will be a perfect machine, lasting a long time and responsive to your every will.

Just for today, try to strengthen your mind. Study. Learn something useful. Do not be a mental loafer all day. Read just a few lines that require effort to understand, which necessitate thought.

Just for today, be agreeable. Look as well as you can, talk low but plainly and firm of voice; act courteously; criticize no one unjustly; and do not find unnecessary fault with things.

Just for today, have a program, a plan to do something. Write down what you expect to accomplish by the end of each hour. You may not be able to follow it exactly, but it will save you from two pests—hurry and indecision.

Just for today, have a quiet half hour all to yourself. Relax. Somewhere in it think of God and of the Universe, so as to get a little more perspective in your life.

Just for today, be unafraid. Be especially unafraid to be happy, to enjoy what is beautiful, to love and to be loved by those who believe in you. Be unafraid of the morrow, for then you may again repeat—*just for today.* [4]

Keep Sending Me Life

After thirty-six years and the appearance of 1,864 issues, *Life* published its last issue as a weekly newsmagazine on December 29, 1972. As would be expected under the circumstances, it was a swan-song format. However, that which caught my eye was the promotional card—so prominent in periodicals these days—attached between pages 72 and 73, reading, "Please start sending me *Life*."

This is more than a technical inaccuracy, too costly to eliminate. It is, in reality, everyone's prayer: "Dear God, please keep sending me life."

Little Things

Most of us
miss out
on life's
big prizes.
The Pulitzer.
The Nobel.
Oscars.
Tonys.
Emmys.
But we're
all eligible
for life's
small pleasures.
A pat
on the back.
A kiss
behind the ear.
A four-pound bass.
A full moon.
An empty
parking space.
A crackling fire.
A great meal
A glorious sunset.
Hot soup. . . .
Don't fret
about

copping life's
grand awards.
Enjoy its
tiny delights.
There are plenty
for all of us.[5]

The Miracle of Water

William Stidger once asked a Filipino what was the most useful thing America had done for his people. Immediately he replied, "Artesian wells. They have saved our babies. Many times have I thanked God for water, for deep, clear water. . . . The miracle of water is the miracle of life."

Nothing Is Momentous

In her book *Robert Frost and John Bartlett,* Margaret Bartlett Anderson shared this wisdom from her last visit with the snowcapped philosopher-poet: "And remember," he said, "nothing is momentous. We always think it is, but—nothing is momentous."

One Day at a Time

The nineteenth-century Scotsman, author Robert Louis Stevenson, is reputed to have said: "Anyone can carry his burden, however heavy, until nightfall. Anyone can do his work, however hard, for one day. Anyone can live sweetly, patiently, lovingly, purely till the sun goes down."

The Makeup of Life

Martin Buber described life as an "I-Thou" relationship. This is an upward and outward relationship with God and man. Our Christian faith magnifies the second aspect as well as the first. No person should think of himself as complete apart from other persons. Alfred Lord Tennyson said it like this, "I am a part of all that I have met."[6]

Responding to the Trumpet

The educator, lawyer, statesman, poet, Archibald Mac-Leish's life covered four decades plus nine. He died in the spring of 1982. He had authored some forty volumes of poetry and plays that had won him wide acclaim and a cluster of medals and honorary degrees. Writing in *Time,* May 3, 1982, Otto Friedrich said: "MacLeish lived in a time of desperate battles, and it must be said to his credit that when the trumpets sounded, the poet answered."

Rustproof Your Retirement

Retirement
doesn't have to be
a red light.
It can be
a green light.
Othmar Ammann
would agree.
After he "retired"
at age 60,
he designed,
among other things,
the Connecticut and
New Jersey Turnpikes;
the Pittsburgh Civic Arena;
Dulles Airport;
the Throgs Neck Bridge;
and the
Verrazano Narrows Bridge.
Paul Gauguin "retired"
as a successful stockbroker
and became
a world-famous artist.
Heinrich Schliemann
"retired" from business
to look for Homer's

legendary city of
Troy.
He found it.
After Churchill made his
mark as a world statesman,
he picked up
his pen and won the
Nobel Prize for Literature
at age seventy-nine.
Don't just go fishing
when you retire.
Go hunting.
Hunt for the chance
to do what
you've always
wanted to do.
Then go do it![7]

Serving God

For years Leo Tolstoy searched for an answer to the question, "What's the purpose of life?" He addressed it to many of his contemporaries. No one gave him a satisfactory answer. Then one day he met a peasant friend, who upon listening to the well-worn query, immediately replied, "To serve God." Whereupon the Russian literary genius declared it to be the highest wisdom he had ever encountered.

Life and Peace

A man has found himself when he has found his relation to the rest of the universe, and here is the book (the Bible) in which those relations are set forth. And so when you see a man going along the highways of life with his gaze lifted above the road, lifted to the sloping ways in front of him, then be careful of that man and get out of his way. He knows the kingdom for which he is bound. He has seen the revelation of himself and of relations to mankind. He has seen the revelation of his relation to God his Maker, and therefore he has seen his responsibility to the world. This is the revelation of life and of peace.

—Woodrow Wilson

Vindictiveness

It is said that when Otto Von Bismarck surrendered to resentment, he ate too much, drank too much, talked too much, and spent his nights rehearsing conflicts real and imaginary. He carried the bile of bitterness and the inner seethings of resentment. When he had no immediate cause for hate, he would dredge up a skeleton from the past and chew on it for awhile. One morning Bismarck proudly announced, "I have spent the whole night hating." So, the weight of resentment eventually broke his health. He grew a beard to hide the twitching muscles of his face. Jaundice, gastric ulcers, gallstones, and shingles wracked his body. After ascending to enviable prominence and power, he spent his sullen retirement in shameful vindictiveness. When a publisher offered him a large sum of money for his life's story, he began to write with a reckless disregard for truth, heaping hate on men and women long dead. Hatred was Bismarck's passion. He died at the age of eighty-three, an embittered, cynical, desperately lonely old man, miserable and self-consumed.

What Is It Worth?

The price of human life has been variously computed. The estimate—depending on the context and risk factors—ranges from twenty-eight thousand dollars to $33 billion. In referring to his book, *Valuing Life: Public Police Dilemmas*, Steven Rhoads of the University of Virginia cited a number of approaches to the problem, including: "high-risk jobs, the effects of regulation from federal agencies, the discount savings approach and how much people are willing to spend to save their lives." Rhoads suggested that in light of differences in pay between high-risk and low-risk jobs, and figuring in inflation and other variables, the value of a human life works out to be around four-hundred thousand dollars.[8]

Younger Every Day

Meister Eckhart, German mystic of the fourteenth century, said of himself:

> Today I am younger than I was yesterday, and tomorrow I will be younger than I am now. The reason is that every day I am born anew in Christ and every rebirth is a new beginning, another springtime.[9]

Love

Joshua 22:5; John 15:12-17; 1 Corinthians 13; 1 John 4:7-12

God loves you as if you were the only one to love!
—Augustine

The Contagion of Love

The early Latin writer, Tertullian of Carthage, declared that the one thing that converted him to Christianity was not the arguments they gave him, because he could find a counterpoint for every argument they would present. "But they demonstrated something I didn't have. The thing that converted me to Christianity was the way they loved each other."

Destroying What We Love

In *The Ballad of Reading Gaol,* Oscar Wilde described the restlessness of a prisoner awaiting penalty for the murder of his wife. He paced back and forth in his cell. The condemned man is pictured as miserable, frightened, not because of his inevitable doom, but because he had killed what he loved!

The Irish poet maintained:

> Yet each man kills the thing he loves,
>   By each let this be heard,
> Some do it with a bitter look,
>   Some with a flattering word,
> The coward does it with a kiss,
>   The brave man with a sword![1]

Eternal Love

Robert and Elizabeth Browning were blessed with one of the greatest marriages of history. It was completely sweet and spiritual, full of confidence and affection. Elizabeth, always hampered by poor health, was now on her deathbed. Do you remember what they did? They clasped their hands in a pledge of endless love and asked their son, a sculptor, to make a plaster cast of their hands. After Elizabeth's home going, Robert made it a habit of going to the church where they were married. There he would get down on his knees and kiss the steps where they once stood together and thank God for their love.

Family

Victor Hugo wrote: "A home is built of loving deeds that stand a thousand years."

Family Encouragement

A mother whom I baptized as a young girl, now married and living in Australia, mentioned that her grandmother in America would soon celebrate her ninetieth birthday. Whereupon her father-in-law suggested it was important for her to be with her blood family in Saint Louis and provided her with a round-trip plane ticket.

As time for her departure from Saint Louis approached, her grandmother inquired if she needed anything. Kathy replied that she had her limit in baggage and that she really did not need anything. Subsequently, the grandmother said she should be able to use a four-wheel-drive vehicle on the ranch in Australia and presented her with a check for the purchase.

For All to See

The New York Times reported that the wall of a public library in that city had been defaced. Apparently an energetic boy took it upon himself to draw a heart in chalk on the building. Inside the masterpiece he scrawled, "Billy Mayer loves everybody."

For One of the Least

During the fall of 1982 a frightened woman took refuge in the woods near the campus of the University of Maryland, gave birth to a baby, and abandoned it. Weeks later the decomposed body of the child was discovered by police.

When Sherry Frohlich, whose husband is a police officer, heard the body was that of a deserted infant, she was concerned. Learning that under Maryland law an abandoned body could only be released to a relative or friend, she determined to qualify. After clearing legal hurdles and fulfilling requirements of the medical examiner's office, she explained what she and her church—Landover Christian—hoped to do for the child for whom she qualified to receive as a friend.

An interesting scenario followed. The Frohlichs named the child Terry Lynn Frohlich, which would fit either gender. A burial plot was selected. A funeral home contributed its facilities and services, including the casket, without charge. Individuals bought an appropriate headstone. Pastor Joe Jones of the Landover church conducted the service. He concluded the worship with these words: "One day I think we'll all meet with the child. I think Terry Lynn will thank us for being here today and will be grateful that we cared."

This moving story of Christian concern brings into sharp focus the powerful words of Jesus: "As you did it to one of the least of these my brethren, you did it to me" (Matt. 25:40).

Greater Love

Russell Conwell was a captain in the Union Army during the American Civil War. One day, following a hasty retreat, the young captain left his sword at his previous station and sent his orderly, John Ring, to retrieve it. He never returned. Captain Conwell reported that when he looked on the lifeless body of John Ring and realized he had given his life for him, he vowed he would endeavor to live two lives, that of Ring and that of himself, and this is precisely what he did. He worked eight hours for himself and eight hours for John Ring.

He Saved My Life!

Love never counts the cost. This was dramatically demonstrated, as reported on the evening of December 27, 1982, when Jack Kelly (the late Princess Grace's brother) and his wife, Sandee, drove into a gasoline station in Fort Lauderdale, Florida, to make a telephone call. Nattily dressed, Kelly walked toward a phone booth to dial a friend for directions to a party, when a man came up from behind him, gun in hand, and asked for his money. "Get lost!" replied Mr. Kelly. The gunman said, "Your woman will be next if I don't get your cash!" Whereupon the former Olympic athlete went after the mugger, fearing he would drive off with his wife. The robber got away, but not before wounding Jack Kelly. As he was rolled into the Broward General Medical Center, sobbing Sandee pleaded, "You've got to save him! He saved my life!"

Ingredients

An anonymous soul has expressed it well:
Love is the spark that kindles the fires of compassion.
Compassion is the fire that flames the candle of service.
Service is the candle that ignites the torch of hope.
Hope is the torch that lights the beacon of faith.
Faith is the beacon that reflects the power of God.
God is the power that creates the miracle of love.

The Language of Love

In the closing paragraphs of *The Court Years,* William O. Douglas, the brilliant, controversial justice of our time who sat on the Supreme Court for thirty-six years, recited the influence of his mother on his illustrious career. She was a widow. She was proud of her son and frequently quoted from Sir Walter Scott: "And dar'st thou, then,/To beard the lion in his den,/ The Douglas in his hall?"

She also had a little speech which she would give occasionally, nominating Bill for the presidency of the United States. Her words and gestures greatly inspired her remarkable son.

Following graduation from Whitman College, he decided to pursue the study of law at Columbia University. At last the night came when young Douglas left Yakima, Washington, to hop a freight train that would take him to New York City. His mother walked with him to the alley where he would take a shortcut to the freight yards. Holding his head with both hands, she kissed him and quoted Scott's lines again, then added this admonition: "Go to it, son; you have the strength of ten because your heart is pure."

Love Conquers All

Leslie Weatherhead shared this story of a boy who lived in Leeds. Following his father's death, his mother was compelled to go to work. The boy was a problem, not too dependable. One day his mother warned him not to play near some new construction. He disobeyed, and was seriously injured. In the hospital, he heard an indiscreet nurse tell his mother he would never walk again. When the boy's mother entered his room, he plaintively asked, "Mother, do you love me?"

"Yes, of course, I love you."

"Then everything is all right. I know that I will never walk again for I heard the nurse, but if you forgive me and love me, I can stand the rest."

Love Keeps No Score

Jerry Banks of Henry County, Georgia, was hunting one day in 1974. He came across two bodies that had been shot. He made his way to the highway, flagged a motorist, and sent for the sheriff. Banks returned to the scene and stood guard over the strangers until authorities arrived. His reward? He was arrested and charged with double murder. Subsequently he was tried, found guilty, and sentenced to death. Eventually, the Supreme Court ordered a new trial. Again, he was found guilty and sentenced to death. All the while the accused continued to affirm his innocence. Meanwhile, new evidence emerged. Finally, after spending six years in prison, five of which were on death row, Jerry Banks was freed, December 22, 1980. The humble man is reported to have commented, "I just didn't believe God'll let 'em kill me for something I didn't do."

"Love keeps no score of wrongs; does not gloat over other men's sins, but delights in the truth" (1 Cor. 13:6, NEB).

Love of Christ

Legend has it that a wealthy merchant traveling through the Mediterranean world looking for the distinguished Pharisee, Paul, encountered Timothy, who arranged a visit. Paul was, at the time, a prisoner in Rome. Stepping inside the cell, the merchant was surprised to find a rather old man, physically frail, but whose serenity and magnetism challenged the visitor. They talked for hours. Finally the merchant left with Paul's blessing. Outside the prison, the concerned man inquired, "What is the secret of this man's power? I have never seen anything like it before."

"Did you not guess?" replied Timothy. "Paul is in love."

The merchant looked bewildered. "In love?"

"Yes," the missionary answered, "Paul is in love with Jesus Christ."

The merchant looked even more bewildered. "Is that all?"

Smiling, Timothy replied, "That is everything."

Love Transcending

Celeste Campbell, age fourteen, needed a kidney transplant. Every member of her large family offered to donate a kidney. But it came down to Gregory, her brother, a senior at Saint Paul's School in Garden City, New York, who had been accepted at Dartmouth. Robert Weiss, assistant director of the Children's Kidney Center of the Einstein Division of Montefiore Hospital in the Bronx, said of the forthcoming operation, it "is an excellent tissue match." When asked if this meant giving up a football career in the Ivy League, Gregory replied, "If I can't play, I can't play. It's a small sacrifice for what's going to happen to Celeste."[2]

Not in History, But News!

Linda Lavin, TV's "Alice," told what it was like when a fire swept through the hills where they live in California. She was in the kitchen preparing dinner for ten people when she and her husband, Kip Niven, realized that, should the wind shift, the fire would quickly destroy their home. The children were given boxes and told to pack up the things they really wanted to save. All the while Linda wondered what she would grab—clothes, a vase, a pillow? In that awful moment of decision, Linda discovered her roots were not in things, or the house, but in the family. So she took her "wedding pictures." Why? "Because all the rest is history, and that's still news!"

Standing By

The late Dr. Daniel A. Poling told of being in Boston when he received word that young Clark was desperately ill. He rushed home to discover his son needed surgery. The little fellow, quite young, was afraid. Finally, the wistful boy said, "Daddy, I will do it if you stay with me." Poling promised him he would. Clark was wheeled into the operating room. The doctors and nurses assured Poling his son would be all right, and for him to wait outside. They did not want him in the operating room. But he persisted and stayed. Later, as Clark roused from anesthesia, his first words were: "Daddy, did you stay by?"

"Dear Lord," added Poling, "suppose I hadn't?"

Three Daughters

The story is told of a king who desired to know how much his three daughters loved him. The first two declared they loved him more than all the gold and silver in the world. The third said: "I love you better than salt." The king was not exactly elated and attributed his youngest daughter's reply to her immaturity. The cook, overhearing, left salt out of the king's breakfast. Then the father awakened to his daughter's declaration: "I love you so much that nothing is good without you."

Unique Calling

The Richmond Times-Dispatch on June 23, 1982, carried an arresting story. It concerned a humble black woman, Dessaymore Scott. According to the report, she had no family; and she did not remember her parents. Although never married, she raised six children who had been abandoned by their parents. "I was given them," she said, "the family I didn't have." All of her adopted children had gone through high school, four through college and business schools. At the time of the story, Miss Scott was sixty-eight years old and had been the full-time sexton for Fourth Baptist Church in Richmond for twenty years. The newspaper said that she arrives at 7:30 in the morning and often remains at church until 9 o'clock at night.

She was described by friends as a flower:

There is a garden in her face,
Where roses and white lilies grow . . .
There is a song placed deep in her heart,
And its tune only a few would know.

What We Are

The dimensions of love came home to our family as never before on August 27, 1979, when we were en route to Florida. We had lost a wonderful son when he was thirty. Peter had been an athlete all his life. He was a hardworking, clean-living, highly disciplined person, but he died suddenly. Our friends across the country and around the world were wonderfully supportive. Among the pyramid of letters, messages, and telephone calls, I cite one from a friend of twenty-five years, a highly competent individual, extremely successful in his profession, and a dedicated elder in our denomination.

He was in Kentucky at the time. From his motel room, he wrote Sybil and me on a pocket note pad. The quintessence of his message was, "I have heard you say 'Everyone has a minister except the minister.' Now we want to minister to you."

This man is one of the busiest persons I know. He flies fifty thousand miles a year in his work, not to mention ground transportation. Yet he canceled all appointments and flew to Georgia, where he and his wife stood by us night and day, and eventually drove us on to Florida. All together, this was five days out of his week. This, I submit, is suffering, supportive love. Love is more than what we say and do; it is what we are.

Maturity

Deuteronomy 11:8-9; Proverbs 14:25-29; Matthew 13:53-58; Romans 12:14-21; 1 Corinthians 3:19-23

Watch not the ashes of the dying ember.
Kindle thy hope. Put all thy fears away—
Live day by day.
           —Julia Harris May

And, having gained truth, keep truth: that is all.
           —Robert Browning

Birth and Death

When George Papashvily was a small boy in the Caucasus region of Russia, he was taken to visit a revered old man who lived in the mountains. It was customary for each child to take the hermit a gift in return for which the little one received a proverb.

Although frightened, George timidly approached the stern-looking sage. The wise man asked the youngster what he wanted and where he wanted to go when he grew up. After exchanging questions, the centenarian whispered in the lad's ear, "This minute, too, is part of eternity." The truth, of course, eluded the boy for years, but later he realized, as do we all, that birth and death are not irreconcilable parts but form a harmonious whole.

Don't Ask God Why

One mark of spiritual maturity is the confident acceptance that God is in control, without understanding the whys and whens of happenings. "Woe to him who strives with his Maker,/an earthen vessel with the potter!/Does the clay say to him who fashions it, 'What are you making?' " (Isa. 45:9).

Don't Ask Too Many Questions

You will remember Ernest Hemingway's story, *For Whom the Bell Tolls,* based on John Donne's comment. It was the custom in a certain village to ring the church bell on the death of a citizen. People would come running when the bell tolled to ask who was dead. On one occasion, this was the response:

No man is an island, entire of itself; every man is a piece of a continent, a part of the main; if a clod be washed away by the sea, Europe is the less . . . any man's death diminishes me, because I am involved in mankind; and therefore, never send to know for whom the bell tolls; it tolls for thee.

Have You Chosen Your Epitaph?

When Congressman Claude Pepper of Florida was asked how he would like to be remembered, he replied: "He loved God and the people and he sought to serve both."

In Spite of Self—God!

At one point in his life, William Cowper, eighteenth-century English poet, became suicidal. Deciding to end it all, he took poison. It didn't work. Then he intended to throw himself into the Thames River; he was miraculously restrained on the bridge. Next day he fell on a knife, and the blade broke off! At last he resorted to hanging himself; he was rescued when unconscious and revived.

Following foiled suicide attempts, Cowper picked up a copy of the Bible and began reading the Book of Romans. He found himself, and the One who had sustained him through terrible days and fitful nights: God! It was this survivor who eventually wrote the hymn: "God Moves in a Mysterious Way," the first stanza of which reads:

> God moves in a mysterious way
> His wonders to perform;
> He plants His footsteps in the sea,
> And rides upon the storm.

Look Out for the Sharks

In his book, *The Old Man and the Sea,* Ernest Hemingway told the story of a Cuban fisherman who for eighty-four days went without a strike in the Gulf Stream, then late one afternoon he hooked a giant fish. So huge and powerful was the fish that it towed his skiff for two days before the exhausted old fisherman, mustering his last ounce of strength, finally harpooned the monster. It was lashed to the craft. The old man was happy.

He guessed it would weigh fifteen-hundred pounds—it would buy a lot! Alas, he had not reckoned with the sharks. When he arrived home, all he had left was the gigantic head and a skeleton picked lean and white.

It behooves us to contemplate the sharks of the soul lest we bypass the great prize.

Look Your Best

We mow our lawns and landscape to make our grounds more attractive. We pick our flowers and put them in a vase to make the house inside more full of color and beauty. Why shouldn't the person inside the house look attractive, too? Looks aren't everything. You don't have to be pretty to be very successful at marriage. But I still believe it helps to look as pretty as you can for your man as he rushes off to work, and as he returns to your arms at the end of the day. It isn't the requirement for love, but I think it nurtures it.[1]

No One Is Perfect

The well-known columnist, "Dear Abby," received a letter with this disclosure and request: "I'm single, I'm forty years old, I'd like to meet a man about the same age who has no bad habits." Abby replied, "So would I."

Perception

Mark Twain said when he was about twenty he considered his father as being ignorant and out-of-date. By the time the noted writer reached thirty, he saw improvement in his father; and when he reached forty, he declared that his father had "come quite a long ways." Like Mark Twain, we all must learn to appreciate intergenerational stages and growth. Growth is an unmistakable sign of life and is not confined to any age.

Personal Discipline

When Howard Thurman's mother was visiting him in Washington some years ago, he noticed one Friday that she was not eating. Adroitly he inquired about her health. Politely she evaded his questions. Finally she divulged that "for more than twenty years she had never eaten any food on Friday." The memory of what had happened on that day was so stupendous that she not only recalled the events and thanked God for His Son, but she used as much of each Friday as possible to deepen her spiritual life.

Personal Growth

Immanuel Kant declared that no one had the right to talk about immortality until he worked so hard at being mortal that he longed for the immortal. The apostle Paul is a magnificent example. After a long and devoted career as an ambassador for Christ, he was arrested and thrown into prison. Not knowing what the future held for him, that is, on his captors' terms, he had the one hope that Christ would be honored in his body, whether by life or death.

Personal Identity

In *In Search of Myself,* D. R. Davies says, "I found myself in finding God. What I was searching for was my own identity, and without knowing it my search was for God."

Rare Maturity

In *A Book of Americans,* Rosemary Benét visualized Nancy Hanks returning to earth seeking information on her son, Abraham Lincoln. Among other pensive queries, she asks:

> Where's my son?
> What's he done?
> Did he grow tall?

Did he learn to read?
Did he get to town?

It is a tenderly touching poem. Nancy Hanks never knew—
or did she?—that her son grew strong, as strong as justice and
as straight as a woodsman's wedge.

She never knew—or did she?—that he learned to read the
printed word and to courageously perform the correct deed.

Nancy Hanks never knew—or did she?—that the boy whom
she left at nine, went to town, the big town of Washington,
D. C., in the most crucial hours of his country's history, and
left a monument not only in marble but also in our memories
as the great watershed of justice, a giant of righteousness.

Abraham Lincoln reached a rare maturity.

Senior Partners

In 1982, at least fifty thousand Americans entered into marriage in which one partner was sixty-five or older. Demographers estimate that by the year 2025, every sixth person will
be sixty-five or older. Consequently, the number of eligible
marriage partners in their sixties and above is rapidly increasing.[2]

Small Enough to Sleep

The great naturalist, Charles William Beebe, recorded some
of his experiences with Colonel Theodore Roosevelt. Sometimes at night they would view the heavens together, identify
stars and galaxies, some three-quarters-of-a-million light-
years away. After feeding on the miracle of the stars for awhile,
Roosevelt would say, "Now I think we are small enough. Let's
go to bed." The conversation is reminiscent of the psalmist:
"This is the Lord's doing;/it is marvelous in our eyes" (118:23).

That's Me

Arthur Miller, noted playwright, says that in any successful drama there must be something in it which says, "Hey! That's *me!*"

What's Your Worry?

Thomas Carlyle was an anxious, serious, searching type of person. He had a soundproof room built in his London residence so he could work in unbroken peace. However, a neighbor had a cock that crowed rather vigorously during early morning. Carlyle complained to the owner about it. Whereupon the neighbor replied that the rooster crowed only three or four times at most. "But," answered Carlyle, "if you only knew what I suffer waiting for that cock to crow!" Like Carlyle, many harrassed and suffering people spend their days waiting for something dreadful to happen!

When the Inner Self Says—No!

During a melee on the ice, the coach of the Los Angeles Kings hockey team told a player on the bench to join in the brawl. Much to the coach's embarrassment, Paul Mulvey said "No!" Feeling the senselessness of the situation, he disobeyed the order. There are times when disobedience registers enviable courage, perception, and maturity.

Which Do You Feed?

Billy Graham told the story of an Eskimo fisherman who came to a village every Saturday. He always brought his dogs with him: one black, the other white. The dogs were trained to fight on command. One Saturday the white dog would win; the next Saturday the black would win. The Eskimo would take bets from the observers. He always won. When asked to explain the phenomenon, he replied: "I feed one dog and starve the other. The one I feed always wins because he's stronger."

There are two natures deep within each person: one good, the other evil. The one we feed, nurture, always wins!

Willingness to Help

Marshall Bennett of Ohio told me this true story: His father, suffering from heart problems that had not been satisfactorily diagnosed, went to Houston to consult with the famed cardiac surgeon, Michael Ellis DeBakey. Waiting in the reception room with her husband, Mrs. Bennett overheard two of DeBakey's assistants discussing their dilemma. "What shall we do?" they were saying. "The patient from Brazil speaks only German and Portuguese."

Mrs. Bennett volunteered, "I can speak German. May I be of assistance?" Subsequently, she interpreted for the physicians. After about ten minutes, Mrs. Bennett commented that perhaps she should return to her husband who was quite ill. Whereupon she was informed that a vascular surgeon had already been assigned to her husband and was sitting by his side in the waiting room.

What perception and supportiveness!

Ministry

Numbers 4:9-15; Hosea 12:10; Luke 4:16-21; Romans 12:6-8

I might have entered the ministry if certain clergymen I knew had not looked and acted so much like undertakers.
—Oliver Wendell Holmes

Anonymous Supporter

In his autobiography, *With Head and Heart,* Howard Thurman included a moving story from his segregated, impoverished background. There were only three public high schools for black children in Florida, but several private, church-related institutions. The nearest to his home in Daytona Beach was the Florida Baptist Academy in Jacksonville. Arrangements were made for young Howard to live with a cousin, doing chores in exchange for a room and one meal a day.

Following preparations—the packing of a borrowed trunk without handles—Howard said his good-byes and went to the railway station. When he bought his ticket, the agent refused to check his trunk because regulations stipulated that the claim check had to be attached to a trunk handle, not to a piece of rope. The trunk would have to be sent separately, by express.

The frustrated, frightened black boy, who wanted so badly to go to high school and who did not have enough money to ship his trunk, sat weeping on the steps of the station. Eventually the lad opened his eyes and saw before him a large pair of work shoes. His eyes slowly made the journey from feet to face. The stranger was a black man dressed in overalls. Looking down on the dejected little soul he said, "Boy, what are you crying about?"

Howard Thurman explained his situation.

"If you're trying to get out of this town to get an education, the least I can do is to help you. Come with me." They went to the ticket window, where the humble man paid for shipping the trunk. When the agent handed him the receipt, he gave it to the happy boy and disappeared, never to be seen again.

Little did the anonymous steward know he was contributing to the preparation of a world-renowned philosopher, educator, and preacher!

Bear Fruit

Many years ago Henry Sloan Coffin said, "Every Christian is called by the Master to follow Him, and that following may be in a carpenter's shop as well as in preaching and teaching. All Christians are ordained to bear fruit."

Still Your Missionary

Missionary biographies warm the hearts of Christians the world over. In the late 1800s James Chalmers, missionary to New Guinea, proclaimed with triumph his unalterable choice: "Recall the twenty-one years, give me back all its experiences, give me its shipwrecks, give me its standings in the face of death, give me back my surroundment of savages with spears and clubs, give me back again the spears flying about me with the club knocking me to the ground—give it all back to me, and I will still be Your missionary!"

Cheerful Competitiveness

Aware of the difficulty in doing God's work in the bustling city, a Chicago minister had this sentence on the outside bulletin board of his church: "The competition is terrible, but we are open every Sunday."

Every Minister

The minister must demonstrate in language and life that he is familiar with and faithful to the crucial event of all history— the coming of Christ into the world! Like Horace Bushnell, every minister should be able to say, "I know Jesus Christ better than any man in [town] Hartford."

Everyone Can Minister

"You shall be my witnesses in Jerusalem and in all Judea and Samaria and to the end of the earth" (Acts 1:8).

A witness is one who testifies to an act or an experience or a person. A witness usually determines the outcome of justice in a court of law. This means that a Christian is one who testifies to the presence and power of Christ. It also means one must attempt to share his/her experience with others.

There was a remarkable story in the May 19, 1982, issue of *The Wall Street Journal* concerning Richard Block, cofounder of H.

& R. Block. A few years ago he had lung cancer and struck a bargain with Fate: "Let me live and I will devote my life to fighting cancer." His was a frightening scenario—symptoms, reports from specialists, and ultimately the heavy announcement from one physician, "If I were you, I would get my estate in order."

Today he is well enough to play tennis. More importantly, he has opened a cancer management center in Kansas City. Another aspect of this unique program is a nationwide communication linkup to give rural physicians the latest information on the treatment of cancer. Still another innovative facet of his program is the establishment of a hotline for cancer patients. Each month, newly diagnosed cancer patients are matched with volunteers who have been treated for the same kind of cancer. Block characterizes his mission as: "Help the next person who gets cancer."

Finding Your Place

When in the Belgian Congo (now Zaire), I traveled with a physician from Florida who had left a lucrative practice to work for a few months in the Ecumenical Hospital in Kimpese. We shared the same lonely cabin. After several days, I said, "John (not his real name), tell me, what are you doing over here?"

There was a long silence, much too long. Then, in a well-modulated Southern voice, he said, "That's a good question. I sometimes wonder myself. You see, I have never quite found myself. I left my family to serve in World War II. All the while I was wrestling with the problem of vocation. There were times when I considered being a medical missionary. Consequently, when I read about 'Operation Doctor,' I thought this would afford an opportunity for me to settle once and for all if I should be a missionary. I closed my offices in Florida and here I am."

God Is Working Still

"I'm still convinced," says Mother Teresa, "that it is He and not I. That's why I was not afraid; I knew that if the work was mine it would die with me. But I knew it was His work, that it will live and bring much good. . . . If the work is looked at just by our own eyes and only from our own way, naturally, we ourselves can do nothing. But in Christ we can do all things. That's why this work has become possible, because we are convinced that it is He, He who is working with us and through us in the poor and for the poor."[2]

Great Things for God

While standing in Carey's Chapel in Calcutta, the remarkable life of William Carey was illumined before me. At first blush Carey would seem an unlikely missionary candidate. Born in 1761 in Paulerspury, England, an inland village, he was thus deprived of the spaciousness of mind and spirit that characterizes seaport communities. He nevertheless was an eager student, though he quit school in his early teens. His manners were provincial and crude; he was physically unimpressive. At fourteen he was apprenticed to a cobbler where he learned to make shoes. As a youngster, he was known to be dishonest. At seventeen he was greatly impressed by the writings of Jonathan Edwards. He married when he was twenty and began to preach and teach at twenty-three. At last, in Nottingham, in 1791, Carey preached his now-famous sermon to a Baptist association on the text, "Enlarge the place of your tent" (Isa. 54:2). One sentence from that sermon has lived through the years, challenging and inspiring many: "Expect great things from God; attempt great things for God."

Subsequently, Carey offered himself as a missionary to the London Missionary Society. His first wife, an illiterate, reluctantly agreed to accompany him to India, arriving in Calcutta in 1794. The years that followed were hard and discouraging.

Hardships, together with Mrs. Carey's inability to adjust to a strange new world, drove her insane. William Carey refused to put her in an institution. Instead he looked after her himself, a burden which he carried gracefully for fourteen years.

Yet this slender man with an inquisitive mind and dedicated heart was a tremendous scholar. He taught himself Latin, Greek, Hebrew, Dutch, French, and Italian. Even while tilling the soil, he translated the Scriptures. All the while he was witnessing, working, organizing, and struggling with the problems of slavery and extortion. There were six years before he made his first convert. But Carey lived with the vision of attempting great things for God. He did not blame others for the problems of the world; rather he endeavored to correct them.

Have Come to Help

Some years ago, a New York newspaperman by the name of Jacob Riis wrote a moving and condemning series of articles depicting deplorable conditions in the tenement sections of New York City. Eventually he wrote his famous book, *How the Other Half Lives.* Theodore Roosevelt, among the first to read the new volume, was impressed and went to the office of the author for a conference. Riis was not in, whereupon, Roosevelt left his personal calling card, on which he wrote: "Have read your book and have come to help."

Interruptions

One day a woman intercepted Jesus on His way to visit a family in need. She was desperate, caught between helplessness and hope. The suffering soul was living at the interface, the edge of the old and the beginning of the new. She had been ill for twelve years; doctors were unable to help her. She was diseased and discouraged. Her faith inspired courage, so she barely touched the hem of Jesus' garment as He pressed through the crowd. But something happened in that encounter. The Lord perceived that power had gone from Him, the power of love, the power of compassion, the power of healing.

The church has always been the center of action, whether in a cathedral, storefront, a dusty road in Palestine, a ron-da-vel in Africa, or a hospital room in New York City. Wherever believing persons experience and truly respond to the presence of Christ, miracles continue to happen. (See Luke 8:40-48.)

A Living Sacrifice

Clark Vandersall Poling was a classmate of mine at Yale Divinity School. In due time he became a chaplain in the army. On a dark February night—the third to be exact—1943, the cargo transport *Dorchester*, carrying 904 men, was torpedoed at 1:15 AM and sank in iceberg-infested waters within twenty-five minutes. The ship was within ninety miles of her Greenland destination. Six hundred and seventy-eight men were reported "lost in action." According to the quartermaster Frank A. Benkler's affidavit, there were four chaplains aboard, including Clark—Jewish, Catholic, and Protestant. Without regard for personal safety, each chaplain unfastened his life jacket and gave it away. The courageous men were last seen standing hand in hand, praying for the safety of their men.

"Greater love has no man than this . . ." (John 15:13).

Master of the Sparrows

A Scottish minister of a previous generation recounted a dream to his congregation. He dreamed he had died and came to the Pearly Gates. To his dismay, he was denied entrance until he presented his credentials. Proudly the pastor articulated the number of sermons preached and the prominent pulpits occupied. But Saint Peter said no one had heard them in heaven. The discouraged servant enumerated his community involvements. He was told they were not recorded. Sorrowfully, the pastor turned to leave, when Peter said, "Stay a moment, and tell me, are you the man who fed the sparrows?"

"Yes," the Scotsman replied, "but what does that have to do with it?"

"Come in," said Saint Peter, "the Master of the sparrows wants to thank you."

Here is the pertinent, though often overlooked, point: great and prominent positions indicate skill and capacity, but small services suggest the depth of one's consecration.

Ministry to Street People

"Sell all that you have and distribute to the poor, and you will have treasure in heaven; and come, follow me" (Luke 18:22). This command has troubled struggling Christians for nearly two thousand years. The impact of Jesus' words to the rich ruler have seldom been taken more seriously than by Dorothy Day, Roman Catholic activist, who took the command literally and personally.

Daughter of a nonreligious sportswriter, Dorothy was confirmed in the Episcopal Church, became a Socialist agnostic at the University of Illinois, saying, "For me Christ no longer walked the streets of this world. He was two-thousand-years dead and new prophets had risen up in His place."

Living in New York with an atheist whose "ardent love of creation brought me to the Creator of all things," she converted to Catholicism. She gradually identified with the poor and down-and-out people of the streets. She courageously faced criticism and conflict. Eventually a dozen Houses of Hospitality sprang up across America. She lived for years in "Maryhouse," a residence for the destitute on New York City's Lower East Side, where she occupied a small room. Her witness was contagious; her influence incalculable. She was known as the "Street Saint."

Her funeral from the linoleum-floored Church of the Nativity, where she worshiped daily, drew the greats and near greats. Hordes of anonymous souls made up the congregation of worshipers. Yippie Abbie Hoffman declared: "She is the nearest thing this Jewish boy is ever going to get to a saint." A drifter, known simply as Lazarus, with tears streaking his face, said it all: "That fine lady gave me love."

Miserable Bridge Between

Helmut Thielicke, noted German theologian and preacher, in discussing clergy-laity relationships, said in *The Trouble with the Church,*

> . . . despite all the lay movements, church congresses, and evangelical academies, there are only a few miserable footbridges over the chasm between the clergy and the laity. This is where the most blood flows from that wounded Body.[3]

Primarily Spiritual

One of the remarkable Christians of our time is Harold E. Hughes, from Ida Grove, Iowa. He was reared on a farm, then became a truck driver, an alcoholic, the Governor of Iowa, and finally a United States Senator. He became so interested in human beings that he declined to stand for a second term in the Senate. In response to business and political colleagues, he said:

> I have an intuitive, compelling commitment to launch out in a different kind of effort that will be primarily spiritual rather than political. This new work will cut across political and religious creeds; ethnic, and language barriers; and will, I hope, reach into other countries of the world to further international understanding.[4]

Today he is involved with alcoholics, minority groups, and with human justice and ministry throughout the nation and around the world.

Recognition of People

In his book, *Life at Close Quarters,* Arthur Fay Sueltz shared the story of a Dutch sailor during the Second World War. The lonely man drifted in the South Atlantic in a rubber raft for thirty-eight days. Surviving without food and water for much of the time, sunburned and dehydrated, he feared being consumed by sharks that followed him day after day. At last he was rescued. It is said that his greatest joy was not getting out of the sun or being safely separated from the sharks, but realizing the significance of people. Being too weak to talk, he simply listened and observed at first, as he responded to proper care and nourishment. When able to visit, the grateful man said: "I never before realized that people are so important to us."

Retelling the Stories

A memorable experience from my interim ministry in New York City was attending a Seder. A Jewish congregation was using the facility of Park Avenue Christian Church, 1010 Park Avenue. My wife, Sybil, and I were invited. It was a beautiful and meaningful evening. The meal was served on costly, gold-edged china and crystal. The entire program lasted well onto three hours. It was impressive and moving to see families clustered together about the exquisitely appointed tables. Throughout the celebration, whether in ritual, pantomime, or children's recitations, we were reminded of the Exodus; God's guidance of and love for Israel. (Read Deut. 10:12-22; Josh. 4:6 ff.)

The Christian minister is commissioned to retell the story of Jesus.

A Servant Church

St. Paul's Episcopal Church in Richmond, Virginia, is a place of ministry in Christ's name. In its urban setting, St. Paul's lives to heal the broken, bring hope to the despairing, be a place of warm fellowship and reconcile the difficult issues which are so much a part of city life. The parish understands itself as a servant church, the human face of God. Service to others is strengthened by the Breaking of Bread, the preaching of the Word and the Prayers of the People—all pointing toward Jesus, the Word made flesh, who dwells with his joyous Community until the end of time.[5]

Called to Ministry

The call of the preacher is deprecated by many in the secular world. At the beginning of this century a literary critic in a New York paper, after receiving a book about preachers of the day, including Phillips Brooks, added a derogatory remark that "it was a pity so much ability and labor were spent upon men whose work was entirely aside from the main currents of human interest."

When I gave my life to be a preacher, the remark was made to me, "What a pity to throw your life away!" The judgment of so much of the unbelieving world is that the influence of the pulpit has long since been rejected by thinking people, and that the ministry of the pulpit is irrelevant and insipid.

But in the judgment of God those ascension gifts of Christ are the most valued, the most precious, and (bless His name) the most lasting.[6]

—W. A. Criswell

Miscellaneous

Matthew 6:24; Romans 15:18-21; 2 Corinthians 6:16-18;
Revelation 15:2-4

The biggest task of humanity in the next fifty years will be to prove the experts wrong.

—Norman Cousins

The function of socialism is to raise man from the level of fate to that of tragedy.

—Leon Trotsky

The Anvil of Love

The late Rufus M. Jones told a delightful story of a black-smith in Maine who was exceedingly short in stature. In fact, he was almost a midget. He fell in love with the tallest girl in town. It was a quiet romance; no one knew it—not even the girl! One day she came to the blacksmith shop to get some welding done for her father. She was amazed at the black-smith's skill. He proposed to her on the spot and, much to his amazement, she accepted him. He jumped up on the anvil and kissed her. They went for a walk. He wanted to kiss her again. She said, "Not in public!"

"Then," the little man replied, "if there isn't going to be any more kissing, I am not going to carry this anvil any further."

Are You Unique?

The Associated Press announced, on August 8, 1983, the acceptance of an extraordinary young man by Harvard University. Grant Colfax, Booneville, California, who had skipped school for the past eleven years and had spent his time raising goats and studying at home, was one of 2,200 acceptances out of 12,500 applicants for the freshman class at Harvard.

This unusual boy did not watch television. Why? Because there was no electricity in his home. His admissions test scores were in the top 5 percent. The lad is reported to have said, ". . . they didn't take me because I may or may not be intelligent. They took me because I'm unique."

A Denominational Dog!

A disturbed lady asked her pastor if he thought it would be all right to have a funeral service for her dog. Since the dog was "like a member of the family," the preacher agreed "it would be appropriate." The tearful parishioner continued, "Pastor, who do I get to have the funeral?" Not exactly thrilled at the prospect of rendering such a ministry, the pastor replied, "I have a demanding schedule tomorrow. Why not try Brother Smith down the road?" Rejoining, she said, "Very well, Pastor, but tell me, please, how much I should pay the minister for his services—two-hundred or three-hundred dollars?" The eyes of the pastor matched his face. Putting his arm around the bereaved woman, he said, "My dear, why didn't you tell me your dog belonged to our denomination?"

Choices

The late Joseph Fort Newton declared there were but three avenues open to the individual, and "the joy of life" is dependent upon the choice. They are: rebellion, resignation, and reconciliation.

Complaining

It is reported that Matthew Arnold had a weakness for complaining. When he died a neighbor quipped, "Poor Matthew, he won't like God!"

Dimension of Quality

It is an astonishing fact that Leonardo da Vinci produced so few paintings—about twelve. The scope of his curiosity and knowledge, however, is expressed in architecture, engineering, science, art, magic, and machinery.

Like many great painters, Leonardo was challenged by the human body. His knowledge of anatomy was apparent. Horses also fascinated this remarkable man, and his drawings of them seem all but perfect.

Artificial flight obsessed him for twenty-five years, and his designs were invaluable to aeronautical engineering. As one biographer put it, "Leonardo always seemed to go on to other things before he took the final step of bringing his projects to concrete, functioning reality."

He is believed to have lived with the idea of the *Last Supper* for fifteen years before actually beginning the work in 1495.

He painted the masterpiece on the walls of the refectory in the Dominican monastery of Santa Maria della Grazie in Milan; the prodigious undertaking was achieved in about three years.

The days were long. Leonardo frequently worked from dawn to dark without thinking of food. When one considers that the painter worked with live models and individual likenesses, blending them into realistic, emotional participation, the work is all the more phenomenal. Although damaged and restored many times, the nearly five-hundred-year-old masterpiece still communicates his genius.

Leonardo's self-portrait with furrowed face and beard was done when he was about sixty-two years old. Even though he lived an additional five years, he considered himself an anonymous old man without home or fortune.

Through compassion and respect, Francis I, king of France, gave him a home. He lived out his days doing a series of apocalyptic drawings called *Deluge,* frequently referred to as *Leonardo's Last Judgment,* depicting once again the fascinating and frightening forces of nature.

Among his personal possessions at the time of his death in Cloux were his books and three paintings: the *Mona Lisa, St. Anne,* and that strange work called *St. John,* emphasizing the enigma of creation and life itself.

From Leonardo da Vinci comes an inescapable lesson: It is not how much one leaves at death but what one leaves—not quantity but quality.

From Tradition to Truth

We read that the Crusaders put a pelican on their shields and carved a pelican over the archway leading to a replica of the Upper Room. They believed in the tradition that when there was no food to feed its young, the pelican would tear out its own heart to feed them. Not on the level of tradition, but from the infinite heights of truth, Calvary communicates the ultimate sacrifice of love.

Close to the Orwellian World?

The political novel *1984* by George Orwell, written in the late 1940s, is prophetically disturbing. Eric Blair (Orwell's real name) portrayed a world dominated by three giant powers. In it is pictured the enormous face of a man about forty-five with a moustache, handsome and strong, whose eyes are always following you. Beneath the picture are the words: *Big Brother Is Watching You.*

More than ten million copies of *1984* have been sold in America, thus surpassing the sales records of Hemingway, Fitzgerald, Steinbeck, and Salinger. The book is being studied in classrooms from high school to university. Marvin Rosenblum of Chicago plans to produce a movie version of *1984.*

Instead of powerful persons manipulating events and controlling citizens—and they will—there is the more sophisticated, silent method associated with high-tech and the rise of the "computer trail."

Our "nonperson" society is expanding at a frightening pace. "Big Brother," represented by a growing bureaucracy and the development of the computer, has enormous power to obliterate, alter, and control history. There are from fifteen to twenty files on every citizen in the U. S. There is emerging a new vocabulary designed to distort, if not destroy, truth: such as, Newspeak, Doublethink, Doublespeak. The electronic eye is watching!

Multiple Marriages

United Press International reported on March 28, 1983, that Judge Rufus Coulter of Phoenix, Arizona, sentenced Giovanni Vigliotto to thirty-four years in prison and a fine of $336,000 on convictions of bigamy and fraud. Vigliotto admitted he had married more than one-hundred women.

Politician and Prophet

Professor Roland H. Bainton reminds us that substantial social change is slow. In *Yesterday, Today, and What Next?* (Augsburg, 1978), the eminent historian cited the conflict and companionship that existed between the statesman/politician William Pitt and the prophet/philanthropist/abolitionist William Wilberforce. The issue? The abolition of slave trade and slavery itself in the British Empire. The men were good friends. Both desired the abolition of slavery. Pitt was prime minister, Wilberforce a member of Parliament. Wilberforce resolved to make slavery the consuming cause of his life. Pitt could not, of course, make it a top priority at every session and remain prime minister. Duels between the giants continued. When nearing death in 1833, Wilberforce received word the House voted to abolish slavery. "Thank God," he said, "that I have lived to witness the day in which England is willing to give twenty million sterling for the abolition of slavery."

The ruler and the prophet were frequently at odds over policy, but each worked in his own manner to achieve common objectives. Through the years of confrontation and challenge, their friendship was not ruptured. And fittingly enough, Wilberforce and Pitt lie side by side in Westminster Abbey.

"Behind the Door?"

Years ago a professor was giving a nature talk to children. His subject was plants and flowers. He explained how the seeds became plants, how the plants became leaves and flowers, and how the plants developed seeds all over again. Then he told about how all the different parts of a plant are built up of tiny cells, and how all these cells are filled with the amazing substance called protoplasm, which is contained in all living bodies and which makes them live and grow. Finally he stated that no one knew what gave protoplasm its power of living and growing. "That is a closed door, and behind the door is an unexplainable mystery." Then one of the children asked, "Please, Sir, does God live behind the door?"

—James Hastings

Replenishing the Pantry

When Watson Fowler was forty-one, he retired as a school-teacher. He was fed up and angrily announced: "I am never going to do a useful thing again." We all get tired of duty and responsibility at times, but to enjoy the fruits of the Christian faith, to participate in love, goodwill, forgiveness, charity, to partake of the blessings of the community and friends without a compensating ministry, is to consume the food in the kitchen without replenishing the larder.

Scriptural Serendipities

Scripture is stippled with unexpected assurances and promises. Here are just a few enduring passages:

As far as the east is from the west, so far does he remove our transgressions from us (Ps. 103:12).

We know that in everything God works for good with those who love him (Rom. 8:28).

But God, who is rich in mercy, out of the great love with which he loved us, even when we were dead through our trespasses, made us alive together with Christ (Eph. 2:4-5).

Cast all your anxieties on him, for he cares about you (1 Pet. 5:7).

In my Father's house are many rooms; if it were not so, would I have told you that I go to prepare a place for you? (John 14:2).

Serendipities: in the Daily Round

In 1754 Horace Walpole coined the word *serendipity*. It emerged from his story called *The Three Princes of Serendip*. The dictionary defines the word as "an aptitude for making desirable discoveries by accident." It carries the meaning of happy, unexpected pleasures and compensations. As the late Edgar DeWitt Jones would put it, it is "stumbling into paradise."

Life is cluttered with surprises, and many of them are significant. Remember how penicillin was discovered? While conducting normal lab work in a London hospital, Alexander Fleming observed that a mold had formed on a bacteria culture and was consuming it. He learned further that this powerful mold destroyed masses of germs. Instead of throwing out the untidy mess, he studied it, thus introducing the marvelous era of antibiotics.

Many claim that Christopher Columbus, the navigator who is believed to have discovered America, never realized what he had accomplished and considered himself a failure. If only he had known! Perhaps he does now.

We once lived in Des Moines, Iowa, where a grade school celebrated a "Serendipity Day." A youngster presented the teacher with a cocoon, saying, "This is what I think serendipity means. This caterpillar thinks it is dying, but it is really being born."

Should Animals Have Rights?

The issue of animals' rights poses complicated questions. As to why, in the scheme of things, a lamb, monkey, cat, or dog should be sacrificed for you or for me? Each year we are advised that 60 million animals, including 161,000 dogs, meet death in research of one kind or another.

Although the Bible teaches that "man has dominion" over the creatures of air, sea, and land, sensitive souls nevertheless flinch at the cruelty to and sacrifice of animals. Saint Francis of Assisi and Albert Schweitzer would doubtless welcome the emergence of the Animal Rights Movement.

Struggles of Rembrandt

Rembrandt van Rijn has left an unbelievable autobiography in art. From ninety self-portraits, one may view the spectrum of human existence, life's journey from the exuberance of youth to the pensiveness of old age. These brilliant paintings eloquently project the personal and stylistic development of Rembrandt.

Born of poor, unlettered Dutch peasants in Leiden, July 15, 1606, the eighth of nine children, Rembrandt knew struggle and hardship. Like many dream-driven souls from impoverished backgrounds, he possessed seemingly inexhaustible energy and determination to excel at all costs.

By 1640, Rembrandt was the most successful artist in Amsterdam. However, tragedy ensued. Saskia, his wife, died in 1642, following the birth of their son, Titus.

The next twenty years were streaked with loneliness, sadness, and hardship. His faithful companion, Hendrickje, died in 1661 and Titus in 1668. The loss of loved ones, money, property, and confiscation of his art collection to satisfy creditors, were not sufficient to drive Rembrandt into isolation or alienate him from society. He bore his desolation nobly without a trace of bitterness.

In forty-five years this master of portraiture produced and maintained a high level of excellence in fourteen-hundred drawings, six-hundred paintings, and perhaps eight-hundred religious and biblical etchings.

At the time of his death in 1669, Rembrandt's popularity was so low, friends so few, that burghers observing the lonely funeral cortege exclaimed, "Who was he?" Little did they know that centuries later the New York Metropolitan Museum would pay $2.3 million for his *Aristotle Contemplating the Bust of Homer*.

When Sacrifice Is Necessary

The Wall Street Journal once projected a striking paradox of our time when it reported: "The elms in South Park, Pittsburgh, must come down because they are obstructing the monument to Joyce Kilmer. They have lifted their leafy arms so high that passersby can no longer read the inscription which begins: 'I think that I shall never see/A poem lovely as a tree.' "

In a world where people surrender their rights to preserve themselves, where cities are bombed to protect people, where nations wage war to preserve peace, where spending determines economy, it is tragically appropriate that trees should be sacrificed for a poem about trees.

When Your Cup Runs Over

Alice Freeman Palmer, once president of Wellesley College, had this to say about her marriage: "I don't know what will happen if life goes on growing so much better and brighter each year. How does your cup manage to hold so much? Mine is running over, and I keep getting larger cups."

Why a Home?

In my book, *Parents Deserve to Know,* a contributor provided this descriptive paragraph which has since been quoted in magazines:

A home? Why do I need a home? I was born in a hospital, educated in a college, courted in an automobile, and married in a church. I get my food at the delicatessen and restaurant. I spend my mornings at golf, my afternoons at the club, and my evenings dancing or at the movies. And when I die, I shall be buried from the undertaker's. Why do I need a home? All I need is a garage!"

While this may be a distorted picture of the American home, it is, nevertheless, sufficiently characteristic to give us concern.

Worry Like a Christian

There appeared a remarkable story in *Look* in August 20, 1957, under the attractive caption, "I Fly the President." In this carefully written article, Colonel William Draper declared that worry was his business and President Eisenhower's safety his reward. Many interesting and intimate precautions were taken by Colonel Draper's thirty-three-man team responsible for the *Columbine III* preparatory to, during, and after a flight. Every member of the crew was a specialist and a perfectionist. Aeronautical standards are not sufficiently demanding to satisfy those who fly the President. An oil leak in the *Columbine* would keep the crew up all night. Usually two tests were considered adequate to check such a repair. Draper took ten.

The then-thirty-six-year-old pilot was always available. On a trip, he slept with not one, but two alarm clocks. Aircraft Commander Draper said: "People often ask me what it's like to have the responsibility of the President's life in my hands. I think it demands a special dedication. Everyone in the crew down to the newest mechanic must have it."

Missions

Psalms 107:8-9; Matthew 28:16-20; John 3:16-17; John 10:16; Acts 1:8; Acts 17:5-9

The world mission of the church is not carried on in a vacuum, but in relationship to existing political, social, economic, and religious factors at work in a given area.

—A. Dale Fiers, the first general minister and president of The Christian Church (Disciples of Christ)

God sifted a whole nation that He might send choice grain over into this wilderness.

—William Stoughton, election sermon, Boston, April 29, 1669

Are You in the Picture?

Standing one day in the office of Trans-World Airlines, Paris, I observed an unusual picture map. From Paris, lines ran out to the various cities around the globe served by TWA. At the edge of this gigantic map were photographs of recent travelers. Beneath the display was this arresting question: "Will your picture be here next week?"

The church is the center of celestial travel. Are you in the picture?

Beyond Information—Communication

Fred B. Craddock took as his thesis for the 1978 Lyman Beecher Lectures at Yale University Divinity School this quotation from the nineteenth-century Danish philosopher-theologian, Sören Kirkegaard: "There is no lack of information in a Christian land; something else is lacking, and this is a something which the one man cannot directly communicate to the other."[1]

Born in a Storm

Roger Williams, English-born clergyman, founder of the Rhode Island colony, and a pioneering Baptist, did not discover the lessons of freedom in the quiet of his study. Nor was his message well received in academic circles. In fact, critics churned up a storm. But out of that gathering storm came the clear, compelling voice of Roger Williams—the mouthpiece of God, in a dangerous and frightening world.

Storms of controversy frequently spawn enduring values and beloved institutions.

Christian Compassion

Mother Teresa, founder of the Roman Catholic Missionaries of Charity, working saint of the streets in Calcutta, and the recipient of the Nobel peace prize in 1979, says she finds the same thing missing in the lands of plenty as in the lands of poverty—*compassion.* "Maybe they are starved for bread in Africa. You are starved for love in the United States."

Confidence

When Dr. Wilbur Cosby Bell, grand soul of the Episcopal Church and honored professor at Virginia Theological Seminary, learned that he was to die soon, he said, "Tell the boys that I've grown surer of God every year of my life, and I've never been so sure as I am right now."

The Contagion of Goodness

David Livingstone was buried in Westminster Abbey, April 18, 1874. The body of this noble soul had been brought back from Africa. Zanzibar, servant of the remarkable missionary, asked for the privilege of accompanying his master's body to its resting place. It was an impressive scene. In the chaste atmosphere of the great cathedral stood a humble black man at the head of the casket!

In the matter of talents, the two men were hardly comparable. Livingstone was a five-talented person if ever there was one. He excelled in medical skill, charm, and courage, while the simple servant had but one talent. His mind was thought to be dense, his color thought to be a curse. His only gift was obedience. However unequal in grace, the two men were one in courage and in faithfulness.

Costly Missions

The HH-3F settled on its pad like a mighty bird returning

from an exhausting flight. Though noisy, the landing was beautiful.

The giant helicopter, weighing approximately sixteen thousand pounds, carrying four thousand additional pounds of fuel, had safely borne her crew back from a hazardous, attempted-rescue mission at sea. For three hours, six courageous and highly skilled men had penetrated the fog, searching for a fishing vessel. Its captain had contacted the Coast Guard station at Saint Petersburg, Florida, reporting that a member of his crew had sustained a broken leg and needed medical attention.

Back on the ground, occupants of the aircraft gracefully and carefully disembarked. There were brief comments and admiring gestures between air and ground crews. The last man to leave the craft was the flight surgeon, dressed in fire-resistant gear topped off with an extraordinary white helmet.

At the first opportunity, I asked, "How did it go, Son?"

"Not too well," he replied. "The fog was too dense. . . . They would not allow us to approach, let alone make a rescue."

Memory of this dramatic and daring adventure brings into focus the incalculable, persistent love of God, who sent His Son on the greatest of all search and rescue missions.

From the beginning of recorded history, good people in the context of time and in proportion to their abilities have endeavored to save one another from despair and destruction.

Do All the Good You Can

In 1773, John Wesley sent George Shadford, a man of gracious temperament and remarkable dedication, to America. Here is Wesley's letter of embarkation and farewell:

Dear George,—The time is arrived for you to embark for America. You must go down to Bristol, where you will meet with Thomas Rankin, Captain Webb and his wife.

I let you loose, George, on the great continent of America. Publish
your message in the open face of the sun, and do all the good you can.

I am, dear George,
Yours affectionately,[2]

Gas of Immorality

In a letter to Adlai Stevenson, John Steinbeck wrote: "There
is a creeping, all-pervading gas of immorality, which starts in
the nursery and does not stop until it reaches the highest
offices, both corporate and governmental."[3]

Hearing and Responding

Mary McClellan lived in Mississippi more than one-hundred years ago. In her Methodist church one morning, she
heard a moving sermon on missions. When the special offering
was taken, she put in a five dollar bill—a lot of money in those
days—with a note reading, "I give five dollars and myself,
Mary I. McClellan." Indeed she did! She became a wonderful
Christian. Eventually, she and her minister husband went out
as missionaries. They were among the pioneers for Methodism
in the Orient.

Home Missionary

A marvelous ministry was reported in the *Richmond Times-
Dispatch* (Virginia), July 25, 1983. The admired servant was Mrs.
Nona Tanner of Kenbridge, Virginia, who had been tutoring
students for forty-five years, without pay. She interviewed
students seeking help before deciding on the ten or so she
works with each year. The scope of her assistance ranged from
elementary to college students.

Mrs. Tanner, a graduate of the College of William and Mary
who taught in high school before starting her free tutorial
program, said: "The only thing I want to see is a child do well,
and most of them only need a little motivation."

Little wonder this remarkable educator is a member of the U. S. Congressional Advisory Board!

Worth More than a Navy

Decades ago a British naval officer, Admiral Hunter, was court martialed for allegedly "endangering one of his vessels." At the trial, evidence was presented that the particular ship had been seriously damaged. The admiral's defense was: "Gentlemen, all the evidence you have heard is true, but you have not heard the reason why the vessel was injured. I ordered the vessel to be put about. Why? There was a man overboard, and I had hoped to save him; and, gentlemen, I deem that the life of an individual sailor in Her Majesty's navy is worth all the vessels that float upon the seas."

"It Belongs to Mankind"

Just prior to the turn of the twentieth century, two well-known but unsung scientists in Paris informed the French Academy of their findings, which led them to the belief in the existence of radium. Pierre and Marie Curie continued to perfect the process of isolating radium from pitchblende. At last the world believed and shared their joy.

Soon the Curies faced a difficult decision. If ever a couple had a chance to profit, they did. Being the only people in the world who knew the secret formula, they were in a position to become instantly wealthy. At the time, the commercial value of radium was one-hundred-fifty thousand dollars per gram. Their options? They could go public, make known their research without reservations; or they could copyright their findings, patent the process, and thus control the production of radium throughout the world.

Instantly, Marie maintained that the latter proposal was "contrary to the scientific spirit." After thoughtful consideration, the generous couple came to this magnanimous decision, "It belongs to mankind."

Their duty was clear, their mission complete.

Keeping Alive

Everett Palmer, author-minister in South Dakota, told the story of Brother Oglesby, an undersized giant, quietly demonstrating how to live in the present. At the age of sixty-five, Oglesby retired from the staff of a prominent university in California. Being a specialist in agronomy, he pursued some personal ideas of orcharding and made one-hundred thousand dollars. At age seventy-seven he retired again—this time to Southern California—and offered himself in full-time Christian service to his church. Eventually he was licensed as a local preacher in the Methodist communion. Each year he would go to the superintendent and ask for the hardest job in the district. It was usually a small, struggling church; and he would go from door to door trying to generate interest in the Lord's work. At the end of a year, Brother Oglesby would ask his superintendent for a new assignment, and the process was repeated.

For a period of twelve consecutive years, single-handedly, he started a new Methodist church each year. He was once asked how many calls he made during a year in the interest of his work. From thirty-five hundred to fifty-five hundred was the answer, and with a twinkle in his eye, he said: "It is one way to prove you are alive."

Lamp Lighters

Church historians remind us that only in the last two-hundred years has the world witness of the church approached the missionary spirit that characterized the early church. Among the pioneers and stalwarts were: William Carey, who started his work in India in 1782; Robert Morrison, to China in 1807; Adoniram Judson, who went out to Calcutta in 1812; Robert Moffat, to Africa in 1818; David Livingstone, to Africa in 1841; J. Hudson Taylor, who started the China Inland Mission in

1853; John G. Paton, who went to the New Hebrides in 1859; and Bishop William Taylor, to Africa in 1884.

Among more recent missionary-saints are: E. Stanley Jones, who went to India in 1907; Albert Schweitzer, who sailed for Lambaréné, Africa, on Good Friday, 1913; Mother Teresa, who while teaching in St. Mary's High School in Calcutta, decided on September 10, 1946, to request permission to live outside the cloister and to work in the slums, and Dr. William Wallace, Southern Baptist medical missionary to China, who was martyred in 1950. Permission was approved in Rome, and Missionaries of Charity was organized in 1950. The work of Mother Teresa and her sisters has caught the eye of the world and respect of countless millions of Christians.

This saint of the street is fond of saying, "Welfare is for a purpose—an admirable and a necessary one—whereas Christian love is for a person."

Not Sensing the Mission

Elton Trueblood told of an American community with five churches and fifty-six clubs. Naturally, in such a setting, the church suffers and largely because professing Christians fail to comprehend the nature and the mission of the Church.

One-Man Mission

He was one of the first to welcome us via telephone when we arrived in town. His melodious voice vibrated with good cheer and enthusiasm. Having identified himself as a neighbor, we stopped by at our earliest opportunity. Without explanation or apology, his wife greeted us warmly and escorted us to Mr. Black's bedroom. Later we were to learn his story.

Twenty-five years before our arrival in the community, Black was helping his minister start a stubborn car. At last, he pushed the automobile downhill. Something happened to his back—he never walked again. Yet, he was free of self-pity and cynicism. He carried on a profitable business from his bed, was involved in everything good in the community, had a direct line to the pulpit of his church, and provided funds for a country chapel which bears his name. What an ambassador for Christ! He was the actualization of 2 Corinthians 4:8-10.

Put Yourself in the Plate

Many years ago, during worship in a little church, as the ushers were returning to the front with the offering, a small boy tugged at the sleeve of one of the men, whispering, "Please put the plate down on the floor." Shocked and perplexed, the usher obeyed. And to further complicate matters, the lad stepped into the offering plate. It was his way of saying, "I give my whole life to You, Lord. Not just the coins in my pocket, but my time, strength, and all the days of my life."

That enthusiastic and consecrated boy was none other than Robert Moffat, who became a pioneer missionary to Africa and father-in-law of the saintly missionary, David Livingstone.

Win Some

The temptation is always to be agreeable with people, gentle and general. Daily someone says, "I never discuss politics or religion with anyone." This is not only untrue, but a sad commentary on people with convictions. Every Christian, as Paul said to Timothy, is entrusted with the gospel and is expected to win laborers for His kingdom. (See 1 Tim. 1:8-11.)

With No Apologies

Isaac Owen was an early Methodist missionary to California. When asked for an autobiographical sketch, he wrote:

Isaac Owen was born in Vermont; raised in Coonrange on White River in the wilderness of Indiana; costumed in buckskin; fed on pounded cake; educated in a log schoolhouse—the principal study in the course was Webster's spelling book; converted to God in the woods; licensed to preach on a log; first circuit embraced a part of five counties. Last heard of, a missionary in California, and, on a review of his life, has no apologies to offer for having been born.[4]

Money

Genesis 23:12-16; Matthew 17:24-27; John 2:13-16; 1 Timothy 6:10

The power of that heretic [John Calvin] lay in the fact that he was indifferent to money.

—Pope Pius IV

No man is rich enough to buy back his past.

—Oscar Wilde

Affluent Americans

Despite economic blues, *Wall Street Week* reported there were 25 percent more affluent Americans in 1982 than in 1981.

All You Need

In his penetrating book, *For the Love of Money*, psychiatrist James Knight told of a visit to Bergen, Norway. The guide spoke of a family that lived on the top of a mountain. The altitude and terrain were such that it was very difficult to reach the summit, even with horses. It required two hours to walk to their home. There were no modern conveniences. The family raised or made practically everything they needed. The mother had learned to knit while walking up and down the hill. An American tourist made bold to ask: "Does it pay to live here and put up with all of this?" Without a moment's hesitation, the kind lady replied, "Life itself is pay enough."

American Millionaires

Cleveland Amory, writing in *Parade* magazine for October 17, 1982, said that the U. S. Trust Company estimates there were

520,000 millionaires in America in 1979. *Forbes* published a list of four-hundred centimillionaires—people worth more than $100 million—in the U. S. in 1985.

The Big Kick

William Allen White, the great journalist and philanthropist of Emporia, Kansas, demonstrated Christian insight when he gave Peter Pan Park to the city in memory of his daughter, Mary, who was killed in a horseback riding accident. When he presented the deed of the property to the mayor, he said:

> This is the last kick in a fistful of dollars I am getting rid of today. I have always tried to teach you that there are three kicks in every dollar—one when you make it . . . the second kick is when you have it . . . the third kick comes when you give it away. . . . The big kick is the last one.[1]

Cash: Changing

Our highly complicated, competitive, technological society has revolutionized procedures and expanded definitions. There was a time, for instance, when money could be rather clearly defined. Not so any longer. Louis Rukeyser, in his syndicated column for June 1, 1982, quoted the respected economist of New York's Irving Trust Company, George W. McKinney, Jr., as saying:

> A couple of hundred years ago you talked about money and you talked about coins of some kind or other. Then you start adding in currency; then you add in bank deposits; now there are a lot of things that you never even heard of before. These changes are coming so fast these days that if you talk only in terms of what was money yesterday, the definition's walked out from under you today.

Comments

Any man who knows what he's worth, isn't worth much.
—J. Paul Getty

Money—money, like everything else—is a deception and a disappointment.

—H. G. Wells

Make all you can, save all you can, give all you can.

—John Wesley

Do You Know Its Price?

One of my favorite preachers, the late Leslie Weatherhead of London, told the story of a poor South African woman who was fined for a misdemeanor. The frightened soul paid her fine with a gold coin which she finally produced from beneath a weird layer of skirts. As she turned to leave, the clerk called: "Wait a minute, the price of gold has gone up." The poor woman did not realize that she had paid too much.

Fiscal Responsibility

In his *News Letter to Virginians* for July 1982, Senator Harry F. Byrd, Jr., reported that the national debt as of April 30, 1982, was $1 trillion, 65 billion. It requires $115 billion a year to service the debt. Recently, the debt has reached $2 *trillion!*

How much is a trillion dollars? I don't know. But some genius has said if a person were to count, "One, one, . . ." every second of the day and night for thirty-two years—that would be a trillion!

Has It Made You Happy?

Charles Albertson once interviewed Cecil Rhodes, who built a vast empire in South Africa. In congratulating Rhodes he said: "You ought to be happy."

Rhodes replied:

Happy! No! I spent my life amassing a fortune only to find that I have spent half of it on doctors to keep me out of the grave, and the other half on lawyers to keep me out of jail!

How We Spend Our Money

Two theater-packing movies in 1982—*E. T., The Extraterrestrial,* and the comedy, *Tootsie,* masquerading gender—broke previous box office records. During a time when approximately twelve million Americans were unemployed, *E. T.* brought in $130 million in thirty-eight days, and *Tootsie* grossed $39.8 million in the first seventeen days of its showing.

Longevity Demands It

In the play, *Cat on a Hot Tin Roof,* Tennessee Williams has Margaret say to her husband, Brick, "You can be young without money, but you can't be old without it."

The Mystique

Aristotle saw money-making as an unnatural perversion; for Luther, it was secular, demonic; for Freud, wealth was dammed-up or misappropriated libido; for Norman Brown, the "money complex" is rooted in the psychology of guilt. Adam Smith reminded us in *The Money Game* that many adept players never get around to spending the money they have made.[2]

Nit-picking

In *Parkinson's Law* is a chapter entitled, "High Finance and the Point of Vanishing Interest." The humorous, though provocative, professor illustrated the law of triviality. The finance committee of a corporation assembled. Item nine on the agenda was a report on an automatic reactor priced at $10 million. It was a formal, impressive, perfunctory meeting with data sheets, maps, blueprints, and resource leaders. Not counting time for examining charts and rustling papers, item nine required two-and-one-half minutes to pass. Item ten on the agenda was the consideration of a bicycle shed for use of the clerical staff. An estimate of $2,350 had been received. After forty-five minutes of tedious, petty, dollar-pinching debate, and after shaving off three-hundred dollars, item ten passed.

Pursuit of Money

Economist John Kenneth Galbraith said:

That the love of money is the root of evil can, conceivably, be disputed. . . . What is not in doubt is that the pursuit of money, or any enduring association with it, is capable of inducing not alone bizarre but ripely perverse behavior.[3]

Preferential Treatment

Representative Les Aspin, Democratic Congressman of Wisconsin, shocked many Americans when he revealed to the news media June 7, 1982, that the Pentagon spends about $3.3 million a year to provide low-cost veterinary care for pets owned by members of the armed services. At a time when cutbacks are commonplace, spending has become a way of life. Aspin declared it was "not only ironic but also offensive that subsidized pet care in the military remains a sacrosanct federal program. Medicare gets the ax, but 'Peticare' marches on."

Real Money

What is real money? Gold and silver! Substitutes carry labels, "francs" or "marks" or "dollars." However defined, it is power. It is a divisive commonality, a commodity accepted and exchanged for something else. Money is a measure of value, legal tender with which we barter for the necessities and luxuries of life. It is also the combined product of personal energy, planned initiative, and skill translated into currency.

Responsibility

John D. Rockefeller, Jr., said: "I was always so afraid that money would spoil my children." Consequently, he maintained a highly disciplined family. He saw that each child kept a ledger. At the end of a week, those who had made mistakes in their accounting would be fined five cents, and those who had accurate accounts would be rewarded with a bonus of five cents. Basic business principles were practiced with the children. Later, when the boys desired money for some project, their father would make them a loan at the going rate of interest.[4]

Too Much Too Soon!

Eugene Evans of London earns $52,500 a year designing computer games. Not bad? So, what's the problem? The sixteen-year-old whiz kid is too young by a year to drive, which makes it senseless to buy a car, and two years too young to qualify for credit cards, a mortgage, or the "check card" required for cashing personal checks.

What It Won't Buy

Money can buy a number of things: property, personal pleasure, hardware, software, TV ads, and travel, but it cannot buy public office or love. The 1982 elections dispelled claims that public offices can be bought. Oil tycoon Bill Clements supposedly spent $14 million, losing in his bid for reelection as governor of Texas. Shopping center magnate of Minnesota, Mark Dayton, laid out $7 million, not enough to secure for him a seat in the U. S. Senate. Real estate heir Adam Levin invested $1 million for a New Jersey House seat—it was inadequate. Nor did Lewis Lehrman's drugstore fortune win for him the governorship of New York.

What You Do With It

The late J. Paul Getty, one of the world's richest men, wrote in his memoirs, *As I See It*, that he had tried to live by his father's credo: "It's not how much money a man has, it's what he does with it that counts."[5]

Peace

Leviticus 26:6; Psalm 34:13-14; Isaiah 52:7; Micah 4:3-4; Luke 2:14;
Luke 19:41-44; John 14:27

Thank God for peace! Thank God for peace,
when the great gray ships come in!
—Guy Wetmore Carryl

If there is anything we have learned from history, it's that we learn
nothing from history.
—Benjamin E. Mays

A Boutonniere of Peace

England's William Gladstone is not only recognized as one
of the more perceptive statesmen of all time, but also as a
persistent apostle of peace. One day as the courageous man
stood in Parliament arguing for the freedom of Ireland, a rose
dropped from the lapel of his coat. After Gladstone had left the
chamber, a fellow member of the House retrieved it, saying: "It
keeps me mindful of a great heart pleading for a better world."

A Costly Experiment

According to John Adams, a third of the American colonists
was against the Revolution, another third was indifferent, but
the other third was active in the Revolution; and it is to them
that we are indebted for our way of life. The freedom, the
peace they cherished and purchased, was a costly, daring thing.

Denied

Some of us are old enough to remember the ecstasy following World War I, the hopes and dreams, the prophetic stance
and spirit of Woodrow Wilson and a handful of Americans;
but the time was not ripe and the nation said "no" to proposals

of peace, and America's voice was one of the loudest. Wilson, the dreamer, shriveled away, as did our chances of a more permanent peace.

Identifying Love

The first Palm Sunday was, as the author James Stewart has suggested, "a passion of self-identifying love." Jesus' mission was a dangerous one. Danger always brings out one's best or worst. As the late Dag Hammarskjöld stated, "It is when we all play safe that we create a world of utmost insecurity."

"It Must Never Happen Again"

Standing on a dock in Hoboken, New Jersey, as caskets containing Americans slain in France during World War I were being unloaded, President Warren Gamaliel Harding was heard to say, "It must never happen again."

But it has!

Litany on Peace (from the Scriptures)

Leader: The way of peace they know not/and there is no justice in their paths;/they have made their roads crooked,/no one who goes in them knows peace (Is. 59:8).

Response: Depart from evil, and do good;/seek peace and pursue it (Ps. 34:14).

Leader: Where jealousy and selfish ambition exist, there will be disorder and every vile practice. But the wisdom from above is first pure, then peaceful, gentle, open to reason, full of mercy and good fruits, without uncertainty or insincerity (Jas. 3:16-17).

Response: And the harvest of righteousness is sown in peace by those who make peace (Jas. 3:18).

Leader: Blessed are the peacemakers, for they shall be called children of God. (Matt. 5:9).

Response: Strive for peace with all men, and for the holiness without which no one will see the Lord (Heb. 12:14).

Leader: If you are offering your gift at the altar, and there remember that your brother has something against you (Matt. 5:23).

Response: *Leave your gift there before the altar and go; first be reconciled to your brother, and then come and offer your gift (Matt. 5:24).*

Leader: He is our peace, who has made us both one, and has broken down the dividing wall of hostility (Eph. 2:14).

Response: *And he came and preached peace to you who were far off and peace to those who were near (Eph. 2:17).*

Leader: And the peace of God, which passes all understanding, will keep your hearts and your minds in Christ Jesus (Phil. 4:7).

Response: *The God of peace be with you all. Amen. (Rom. 15:33).*[1]

Look at the Prince of Peace

In commenting on the peace of God, Spurgeon testified: "I looked at Christ, and the dove of peace flew into my heart; I looked at the dove of peace, and it flew away."

Lord, Take My Hand!

Ralph Sockman told the story of a New York lawyer who, when he first came to the city, would take his young son on long walks. In order to keep up, the small fellow would hold his father's little finger. By and by the lad would grow weary, and his steps would lag. At last he looked into the benign face of his father and asked, "You'll have to take hold of my hand now, Daddy, for I can't hold on much longer."

Is not this a picture of ourselves? We have been holding onto the little fingers of security so long that we are losing our grip on things that matter. Now we must ask God to take our hand and lead us. "Thou dost keep him in perfect peace,/whose mind is stayed on thee" (Isa. 26:3).

Perfect Peace

John Henry Newman wrote perceptively: " 'These things write we unto you, that your joy may be full.' What is fulness of joy but *peace?* Joy is tumultuous only when it is not full; but peace is the privilege of those who are 'filled with the knowledge of the glory of the Lord, as the waters cover the sea.'

'Thou wilt keep him in perfect peace, whose mind is stayed on Thee, because he trusteth in Thee.' "

Armageddon at Our Door

At the close of World War II General Douglas MacArthur said: "We have had our last chance. If we do not now devise some greater and more equitable system, Armageddon will be at our door. The problem basically is theological and involves a spiritual recrudescence and improvement of human character. . . . It must be of the spirit if we are to save the flesh."

Peace Without Justice!

Professor Davie Napier, Yale Divinity School, said to the graduating class at Lexington (Ky.) Theological Seminary in June of 1982 that it is not an easy time for ministry. Peace, always tenuous, fragile, at best fleeting, may be lost to perpetual darkness. And it is a rough time for ministry when quite apparently in our own and most countries of the world, peace is wanted and somehow expected without justice.

Persistent Peacemakers

The stimulating and challenging Trappist monk, scholar, and writer, Thomas Merton, once wrote a story which I wish to retell, largely in my own words. Two men, one drunk, the other sober, were going through a forest. They were attacked, beaten, robbed—even stripped of their clothing. When they finally emerged from the woods, they were asked if they encountered any difficulties on their journey.

The drunk replied: "Everything went fine, no trouble at all." The interrogator asked, "Why then are you naked and covered in blood?" No reply.

The sober traveler declared that his companion was drunk and not to believe him. "The trip was a disaster, we were beaten within an inch of our lives. . . . Be aware of what happened to us, and look out for yourselves."

"Will you ever go back into the woods?" the sober man was asked.

"Yes," he replied, "in the morning!"

The dream of peace is elusive and only persistent peacemakers will bring it to pass.

Personal Peace

Peace is far more than protection from annihilation. Peace is more than the cessation of hostilities. Peace is more than a state of mind or the tranquility of a countryside. Peace is commitment to a way of life which precludes war, poverty, slavery, prejudice, and fear. Peace is action. Peace is the fruit of love.

Augustine, saturated with pagan philosophies and motivated by unmanageable lusts, met this Prince of peace in a fourth-century garden and the civil war in his heart ceased. He became a mighty giant of God.

The Power of Fairness

The late E. Stanley Jones declared that trust was Mahatma Gandhi's great strategy and nonviolence was his method. It is said that when he prepared a speech on a crucial subject, Gandhi would write out the address verbatim, send copies to his enemies, and ask them if it was a fair statement. The method was so disarming that controversial statements frequently went unchallenged.

The Price of Peace

In 1965, Thomas Merton saw war, the avoidance of massive violence, as "the number one problem of our time." In *Peace and Protest* he wrote: "The human race today is like an alcoholic who knows that drink will destroy him and yet always has 'good reasons' why he must continue drinking."

We seem to be addicted to war, and thus incapable of seeing and pursuing constructive alternatives.

Profiles of Peace

Josef Goebbels received a Ph.D. from Heidelberg University in 1920. Following graduation he became active in the National Socialist Party. In 1926 Hitler placed him in charge of party organization for Berlin, and three years later he headed the propaganda campaign for the entire party. Goebbels entered the Reichstag in 1930. He rose to the rank of general, being one of Hitler's most trusted colleagues. During those turbulent days, Goebbels wrote in his diary that Mahatma Gandhi was a man of extraordinary abilities; if he would only use his skills to organize a military force, he would succeed.

At last, when Hitler's dreams of world conquest turned into nightmares, and the German machine was devastated, General Goebbels is said to have committed suicide just before the fall of Berlin in May 1945.

Without firing a shot, Mahatma Gandhi, through passive resistance, discipline, and unflinching courage, brought to India what armies had not accomplished—freedom! Goebbels's death went unnoticed. But when Gandhi was assassinated, January 30, 1948, the world wept. The advocate and practitioner of peace had fallen. His influence continues.

Reflections

Anyone who has visited the Palace of Versailles outside Paris, where the peace treaty following World War I was signed, is reminded of that difficult period. Upon visiting this historic place for the first time, the late Halford E. Luccock observed that the trouble with the conference was—it was held in the great Hall of Mirrors, and everyone was watching himself!

Speak Kindly

Jeremy Taylor, seventeenth-century English bishop, used to

counsel aspiring ministers to "speak kindly to everyone you meet for everyone has a problem."

Sworn at the Feet of Christ

The Christ of the Andes is an impressive symbol of peace. Once Chile and Argentina were enemies and fought constantly. At last they decided it was in their mutual interest to live in peace. So, high upon their natural boundaries, the Andes, they erected a marvelous statue of Christ with outstretched arms. The inscription reads: "Sooner shall these mountains crumble into dust than the Argentines and Chileans break the peace sworn at the feet of Christ the Redeemer."

What Do You Want?

When Dante knocked at the door of the Franciscan monastery at Lunigiana he was asked, "What do you want?" He replied, "Peace!"

Perseverance

Proverbs 24:16; Luke 21:19; Ephesians 6:18-19; Revelation 14:12

Step after step the ladder is ascended.
    —George Herbert

Born for Victory

Have we forgotten the series of tragedies that assailed Ralph Waldo Emerson, the American poet and essayist? Emerson's early years were filled with books and a demanding daily routine. Poor health plagued him. After being sanctioned to preach, he was forced to go south because of tuberculosis. In 1829 he became pastor of Old North Church in Boston. The same year he married Ellen Tucker. Two years later she died of tuberculosis. A theological controversy cost him his pulpit in Boston. One biographer wrote, "A doom seemed to hover over his family and his life. But under the surface, dark as it was at the moment, a purpose was taking form in his mind. He knew he was born for victory."

Christian Contagion

William Barclay told of a bright young woman who contracted a crippling disease that left her partially paralyzed. She had been an outdoor person, loving sunshine and sports, but now her world had turned into shadows. One day a friend brought her a book on the theme of Christian joy, written in a vivid, radiant style. As the girl took the book in her gnarled fingers, she spoke quietly, "Certainly, I know this book."

Her friend replied, "Have you read it before?"

"Yes," replied the cripple. "You see, I wrote it."

Despite Declinations

A comic novel, *A Confederacy of Dunces,* written over twenty years ago by John Kennedy Toole, won the 1981 Pulitzer Prize for fiction. The author, age thirty-two, became so discouraged receiving rejections from publishers that he eventually took his own life in 1969. Whereupon his mother, Mrs. Thelma Toole, though in a wheelchair, assumed the challenge of having her son's work published. Going from publisher to publisher, she finally succeeded in inducing the novelist Walker Percy to read it. He liked it and persuaded the Louisiana State University Press to publish it.

From Darkness to Light

Frank Sinatra maintains that Ray Charles is "the only genius in the music business." Blind from an accident at age seven, Charles is not bitter, is productive, and is tremendously beloved. When fourteen, Ray lost his parents in still another accident. He remembers, and is forever challenged, by his mother's early admonition: "You're blind, Son, not stupid. You lost your sight, not your mind!"

Hang in There

Dr. Norman Vincent Peale reported on a visit with a former president of the United States, the late Herbert Hoover. It is said that President Hoover's Christian faith and practice were commendable. During their conversation, the popular preacher asked, "Mr. President, can you state in one sentence the secret of your success in life?" Quickly he answered: "With the help of God, I never gave up."[1]

It's Daily

In his book, *Starting Over*, Charles R. Swindoll wrote about boyhood vacations at his grandfather's cottage near the Gulf in South Texas. Coats, the black cook, was friendly and unique. While barbecuing one day, the loquacious hired man, after sharing some of his ups and downs, knelt down to the lad's height and said: "Little Charles, the hardest thing about life is that it's so daily."

And so it is!

Keep Scratching

The black abolitionist woman, Sojourner Truth, trudged across nineteenth-century America telling the story of slavery —not always a popular cause. At one stopover, an antagonist contemptuously asked, "Old woman, do you think your talk of slavery does any good? . . . I don't care any more for your talk than I do for the bite of a flea."

Calmly, Sojourner Truth replied, "Perhaps not, but, the Lord willing, I'll keep you scratching."

Keep Trying

An Englishwoman, Betty Tudor, found thirteen was a lucky number for her. After nearly thirty years of driving instruction, including help from a police driving expert, Mrs. Tudor's perseverance finally paid off. She obtained her driving license on a Friday on her thirteenth attempt. Mrs. Tudor had been banned from three driving schools as "unteachable."

Learn the Pace

When I was a distance runner in college, our coach did all within his power to impress us with the importance of recognizing one's pace. Sometimes we would run with a stopwatch; sometimes we would be asked to guess the pace of a teammate. After months of training and experience, it is amazing how one learns one's pace. Good runners do not worry about the last lap; they concentrate on the challenge of the moment.

Life is like a footrace. It requires stamina and a sense of timing. The rhythm of joy and sorrow, thrust and retardation, working and waiting, eating and sleeping, must be carefully calibrated or we lose the delicate balance so necessary in developing patience, courage, and strength.

Living with Pain

Trouble and pain are inexorably intertwined. Overcoming, or breaking the pain barrier, is one of the secrets of victorious living. It is estimated that one of every four-hundred thousand babies born will have a rare genetic disease called dysantonomia. Victims are unable to feel pain and usually die early. Persons, athletes in particular, have their careers altered because they take drugs to dull pain rather than discovering and treating the source of the problem. Pain is not God's way of punishing people; but rather His way of warning persons that something is wrong physically, mentally, or spiritually.

Jesus did not shy away from difficulties. "Now is my soul troubled. And what shall I say? Father, save me from this hour? No, for this purpose I have come to this hour" (John 12:27-28).

Loyalty Inspires

In his book, *Vision and Betrayal in America,* former Congressman John B. Anderson of Illinois reminds us of the "black year" of the American Revolution—1777-1778—when there were fewer than five-hundred men in the colonies who were willing to pledge their lives, fortunes, and sacred honor for the cause of the nascent republic. Although small in number, the colonists' commitment inspired others, and the foundations of liberty were successfully laid.

No Retreat

In his memoirs, *A Life in Our Times,* John Kenneth Galbraith referred to an eloquent speech made by a West Virginia supporter of John F. Kennedy. At a time in the presidential campaign when it would have been easy to become disenchanted, if not discouraged, the politician-historian of the Mountain State reminded his audience of Napoleon's battle at Waterloo. Surveying the battlefield, the tough little general said to his drummer, "The English are standing firm. The Old Guard is making no progress. We are defeated; sound the retreat."

Hesitantly, the lad looked at Napoleon and protested, "Master, in all our campaigns in Europe, I have never learned to sound the retreat."

Deeply touched by the comment, Napoleon said, "All right, drummer boy, sound the advance."

The Persisters

The well-known writer Arthur Gordon, when seventy years old, was asked to enumerate life qualities he most admired in people. After quietly rehearsing such characteristics as honesty, courage, and compassion, he mentioned "persistence." He was referring, of course, to positive, constructive persistence.

Without this dogged trait, little of lasting significance is ever accomplished. I am reminded of a comment by Elton Trueblood in a writer's conference. In emphasizing the importance of learning discipline, he challenged: "If you want to write, put glue on the seat of your pants and sit in a chair!" No amount of talent or conducive atmosphere can make up for hard work —stick-to-it-ive-ness!

To understand the will to persist, Gordon reminded us of two stalwarts: Thomas Carlyle and Noah Webster. As Carlyle neared completion of his absorbing masterpiece, *The French Revolution,* an undiscerning, thoughtless maid gathered up the papers and tossed them into the fire. Disappointed, heartsick to be sure, but Carlyle did not pamper himself with self-pity nor did he shoot the maid—he sat down and rewrote it from memory.

Noah Webster thought he could complete his dictionary in "three to five years." It required twenty-one!

What persistence!

Personal Grit

In 1941 the book, *Born that Way,* appeared. One could not read its pages without being profoundly moved, for it concerned a terribly twisted boy with cerebral palsy. He was five years old before he could balance himself to shuffle. However, in the boy's heart lived a giant. He battled handicaps and embarrassment. His struggles at Princeton University and Yale Medical School revealed a drama in determination. Slowly he climbed the staircase of schooling and study. Ultimately, Dr. Earl R. Carlson was considered one of the foremost authorities in the country on cerebral palsy.

Personal Persistence

Christy Brown, a cripple from Dublin, Ireland, was born with inconceivable handicaps. He was unable to walk, dress himself, or feed himself, talked in a guttural sound, never attended school a day in his life, but wrote a literary masterpiece that received world acclaim. In his autobiographical novel, *Down All the Days,* the author told the story of what it was like to be all but helpless; to be one of twenty-two children; and to live in the slums. It required Christy Brown fifteen years to write his book, for he typed it with the little toe of his left foot.

Self-Identification

When Abraham Lincoln was shot, his body was taken by train to Springfield, Illinois, via several large cities, thus affording many citizens opportunity to share the grief of the national tragedy. The pattern was usually a procession from the railroad station to city hall where the body would lie in state. As the hearse was moving through the streets of New York, a large, husky woodsman pressed forward with little regard for those around him. One resentful man yelled out, "Don't walk on my feet!" The big fellow apologized awkwardly and finally said, "Excuse me, Sir, but I must see the coffin." "Why must you?" asked the irritated man. "Two of my brothers died in the same cause he did," replied the lumberjack. "Besides," he proudly added, "he was one of my craft, and I could never go back to the woods without seeing and blessing his coffin."

Stick-to-it-ive-ness

Louis Spencer, son of a former president of Franklin College, as a youngster lost an arm and a leg when the bicycle he was riding slipped and threw him under a switch engine. It was a painful and horrible experience for all involved. After the misery of operations, and when it was evident the lad would live, Louis looked up at his father and said, "Dad, you can do a lot in this world with one arm and one leg!" With an artificial limb, Louis won the Ping-Pong championship of Indiana. Later, he went to college and to graduate school at Northwestern, where he earned a Ph.D. in physics.

Triumph of Justice

The legendary Indian athlete, Jim Thorpe, won two gold medals for the pentathlon and decathlon events in the 1912 Olympics. An unprecedented accomplishment! Subsequently, it was discovered that the young man had played semipro baseball in 1910 for two dollars a game; and he was consequently stripped of his medals. The marvelous Olympian lived with this injustice and hurt until his death in 1953 at age sixty-four.

Sports-loving fans, friends, and family, however, took up the fight to clear the record and to have Thorpe's medals returned. After seventy years of struggle, at a special ceremony in Los Angeles, January 18, 1983, surrounded by six of the seven Thorpe children, Juan Antonio Samaranch, president of the International Olympic Committee, officially returned replicas of the original medals. (The original ones were given to second-place finishers.)

Triumph of Truth

The late Martin Niemöller was one of Hitler's prized prisoners. The famous German minister vigorously resisted tyranny. He was imprisoned for seven-and-a-half years at a camp where 238,756 persons were put to death. Yet he carried on a daring ministry at Dachau.

Pastor Niemöller was more than a former prisoner of war. He was a living testimony to truth. To talk with Niemöller was to visit a man who looked death in the face day after day and knew the power of the resurrected Christ. His remarkable life reassures us of the triumph of truth.

A Winner at Last!

As a young man, Abraham Lincoln went to the Black Hawk War a captain and, through no fault of his own, returned home a private. His military career was over. Subsequently, he went into business, which did not endure. As a lawyer in Springfield, Illinois, he was considered too impractical, too temperamental to be a success. Turning to politics, Lincoln was defeated in his first campaign for the state legislature. He was defeated in his desire to be commissioner of the General Land Office. He was defeated for the United States Senate in 1854; defeated for the vice-presidency of the United States in 1856. He was again defeated in his effort to become senator from Illinois in 1858. Yet, in 1860, Abraham Lincoln was elected president of the United States.

Power

Exodus 9:13-16; Deuteronomy 8:18-19; Luke 4:14-15; John 1:12;
1 Corinthians 1:22-25

I teach them POWER to will and do,
But only now to learn anew
My own great weakness through and through.
                    —Leslie Pinckney Hill

Power admits no equal, and dismisses friendship for flattery.
                    —Edward Moore

Advance on Your Knees

Dr. Joseph R. Sizoo, great preacher of Saint Nicholas Collegiate Church (Reformed), New York, told of visiting an army training camp during World War II. It was early morning, the grass heavy with dew. Even so, they sat in heavy weeds, listening to the officer lecture the men on how to take a given military objective. To demonstrate correct procedure, a group of seasoned soldiers on their hands and knees, hugging the wet ground, could hardly be seen in the dawn's early light. The officer called out, somewhat casually, "If you advance on your knees, you are always safe."

Any Word from the Lord?

King Zedekiah lived about twenty-six-hundred years ago. He came to the throne at the tender age of twenty-one. Judah's days were numbered. The young king climbed the ramparts of beseiged Jerusalem. After surveying the panorama of imminent doom, he ordered Jeremiah, the prophet whom he had imprisoned, brought forth. Wistfully the king asked, "Is there any word from the Lord?"

This probing query opens the door of our imaginations. The secret meeting between the king and the prophet was, in itself, a moving drama. Zedekiah was apprehensive. His advisors had persuaded him to follow the fortunes of war, yet in his heart the king wanted to heed the counsel of Jeremiah. Picture the prophet in this momentous juncture: gaunt, marked by maltreatment, humble, yet courageous, without malice or arrogance, or fear of personal harm, facing the king who asked, "Is there any word from the Lord?"

Jeremiah answered, "There is." Then he said, "You shall be delivered into the hand of the King of Babylon" (Jer. 37:17).

Like Zedekiah, amid confusion and uncertainty, we too scan the horizon for hope. We turn not to a single prophet, but to the church, and ask, "Is there any word from the Lord?"

Are You Happy with Yourself?

We are told that Frederick the Great, honored soldier, craved praise as a man of letters. Napoleon wanted to be a musician. Whistler, the painter, wanted to be a soldier. When Whistler failed at West Point, he followed engineering, but he found himself in art. Ty Cobb, the remarkable baseball player known as the "Georgia Peach," wanted to be a physician. A generation ago the world was plunged into war by a former house painter who wanted to be a military genius and dictator!

The Assessment Continues

The Archbishop of Canterbury, Geoffrey Francis Fisher, addressing the second assembly of the World Council of Churches at Evanston, Illinois, left this perception: "There are only two groups of people in the modern world who know what they are after. One, quite frankly, is the Communist and the other, equally frankly, is the convinced Christian. The rest of the world are amiable nonentities."

Breaking the Patterns

Do you remember Dostoevsky's differentiation between people and ants? The Russian novelist opined that it lies in the human capacity to break old patterns. This is the change Jesus makes in life. He provides the power to forget, but also the will to remember that He is with us and that to bless.

It is the Spirit himself bearing witness with our spirit that we are children of God, and if children, then heirs, heirs of God and fellow heirs with Christ, provided we suffer with him in order that we may also be glorified with him (Rom. 8:16-17).

Constructive Anger

The remarkable chairman of the Chrysler Corporation, Lee Iacocca, when addressing the graduating class at the University of Michigan, as reported in *Time,* June 20, 1983, said, among other things:

I want you to get mad about the current state of affairs. I want you to get so mad that you kick your elders in their figurative posteriors and move America off dead center. Our nation was born when 56 patriots got mad enough to sign the Declaration of Independence. We put a man on the moon because Sputnik made us mad at being No. 2 in space. Getting mad in a constructive way is good for the soul—and the country.

Financial Power

The latest financial facts indicate that women control at least 75 percent of all investments in the United States. This speaks volumes concerning the influence and expertise of women in a free society. At the same time, however, at least 50 percent of women in the lower echelons of the work force do not receive the same pay for the same work as men.

A Gift from God

City Temple, London, was bombed not once, but twice, in 1941. The twenty-two-hundred-member congregation, who for the most part lived vast distances from the church, had no place to worship save a small hall. For his first sermon in this interim situation, the pastor, Leslie Weatherhead, chose as his subject, "The Power of God." He said, "We felt gloriously close to the church of the first century as we prayed and sang, with London burning all around us."

Nuclear Giants and Ethical Infants

The late Joseph R. Sizoo spoke perceptively when he wrote in *Still We Can Hope:*

> We have grasped the mystery of the atom but we have rejected the Sermon on the Mount. We have achieved brilliance without wisdom and power without conscience. Ours is a world of nuclear giants and ethical infants.

Obedience Generates Power

Luke shared the experience of fishermen who toiled all night without reward. Their failure was perfectly honorable. They were not embarrassed, simply weary. In fact, they had left their boats by the edge of Lake Gennesaret and were washing their nets when Jesus appeared. He sat in one of the boats and taught those who gathered. Afterward He said to Simon, in whose boat He was sitting, "Put out into the deep and let down your nets for a catch." Simon said: "Master, we toiled all night and took nothing!" (Luke 5:4-5).

Peter was not ashamed. It was not his fault they had failed. He was not an amateur fisherman demonstrating new gear. Peter and his companions were professionals; fishing was their business. Knowing they had failed, Jesus did not criticize but encouraged them to try again, in deeper water. The catch was phenomenal, and Peter exclaimed: "Depart from me, for I am a sinful man" (Luke 5:8).

The Paradox of Power

During my ministry in Saint Louis, a devastating storm struck the southwest side of the city. Listening to the radio, a very polite, calm announcer suggested that prayer might be a good indulgence. Later, when the threat of a tornado had passed, from the same station came a solicitous beer commercial.

This is the paradox of peace and power. When surrounded by danger, we conform. When the danger passes, we revert to normalcy (Read John 14:27).

Pentagon and Pentecost

The Pentagon, standing in Arlington, Virginia, on the fringe of our nation's capital, is one of the largest and most famous buildings in the world. Lieutenant General Brehan Sommerville pushed through the initial construction of this amazing five-faced, five-story building in sixteen months. Many caustic and humorous remarks surround what has been called "Sommerville's folly." Among the humorous stories is that of a Western Union messenger boy who went in the Pentagon to deliver a message, got lost, and finally emerged a colonel!

This "city in itself" covers about forty-two acres of ground, with 120 acres of lawn to cut. The building originally represented an expenditure of approximately $100 million. The inconceivable dimensions of the huge building are even more impressive when one is reminded that the *Queen Mary*, Empire State Building, and the Washington Monument could all be housed within its walls. The Pentagon contains thirty-four acres of floor space and seventeen-and-one-half miles of corridors. Despite its enormous size, the Pentagon is said to be exceedingly well-managed. Its two-hundred telephone operators handle more than three-hundred-fifty thousand calls a day. From ten to twelve tons of wastepaper is salvaged every twenty-four hours.

Defense of the Western world is planned and patrolled from the Pentagon. It is an intricate and guarded communications center. Thus the Pentagon is far more than an incomprehensible building housing an amazing assortment of personnel; it is a symbol of power. There are those who fear lest it should become America's "golden calf"—the object of supreme loyalty and the altar of total sacrifice.

There is an enormous contrast between the pretentiousness of the Pentagon and that anonymous place in Jerusalem where early believers received the Holy Spirit! The Pentagon speaks of preparedness and physical power. Pentecost speaks of personal faith and spiritual power. The Pentagon is primarily identified with the strength and well-being of America. Pentecost speaks of the transforming and saving power of the Person of Galilee who came that the world might have life, peace, and hope.

The Pentagon represents defense; Pentecost, ultimate destiny. One majors in protection, while the other majors in the propagation of the gospel of Jesus Christ.[1]

Personal Power

I received a wonderful letter from the president of a large shoe company. In the course of the communication, he referred to the importance of discovering power for one's life, that which drives one on and on. He made it quite clear that the power referred to was not that commonly called "engineered" or "measured" power. Then he related a conference which he had with his son, who said to him upon graduation from college, "Dad, I don't want to go into business. I want to be a minister." He is preparing for a totally different vocation from the one of which his family had dreamed.

The Power of Belief

In London during World War II, a placard, hung over broadcasting booths, read, "Is what you are saying worth a man's risking his life to hear?" Jesus not only risked His life, indeed, He gave it for the privilege of saying, "I am the resurrection and the life; he who believes in me, though he die, yet shall he live, and whoever lives and believes in me shall never die" (John 11:25-26).

Do you believe this?

Power of the Past

Elizabeth Fry lives in every conscientious effort to improve prison conditions. The Wright brothers live in every plane that pierces the blue. James Watt lives in every steam plant. Thomas Jefferson comes to life in every brilliantly drawn judicial document. Abraham Lincoln is compassionately alive in every constructive effort to liberate the oppressed. Gutenberg lives in every best-seller. Homer speaks in every polished poem, and David sings in every great hymn. Louis Pasteur is praised in every glass of milk. Guglielmo Marconi is heard in every broadcast. The spirit of William Carey lives in every missionary. The anonymous Samaritan of the Scriptures is revealed in ministries of mercy. Mary, the mother of Jesus, lives in dedicated mothers, and trustful Joseph is remembered in good fathers. Jesus lives wherever there is faith to believe He is alive.

Royal Clothes

There is a remarkable reference to Emperor Hirohito of Japan in John Gunther's *Procession*. In referring to the Emperor's spartan ways, demanding schedule, abstinence from drinking and smoking, Gunther wrote, "One curious item is that he is said never to wear any clothes twice, not even underwear." His used clothing was given to minor officials and considered a precious gift.

Too Many Napoleons

George Bernard Shaw was once asked in what generation he would have preferred to live. The witty Irishman replied: "The age of Napoleon, because then there was only one man who thought he was Napoleon."

What Is Left?

In the fifth century when Rome was destroyed, messengers hurried to tell Augustine, then bishop of Hippo, North Africa. To them everything seemed lost. "What is left?" they cried.

Augustine replied, "What is left? The city of God!"

Without Fences

Don Sanford, White Cloud, Michigan, related the story of three American prisoners who escaped from a German camp during World War II. Because one man was wounded, it was necessary to conceal him by day and carry him by night. At last the escapees made their way to a French village, where an old priest gave them shelter. Even so, the wounded soldier grew weaker, and died during the night.

Desiring their friend to have the best burial possible, the Americans asked if there was any available space in the church cemetery for their comrade. Knowing that the dead lad was a Protestant, the priest shook his head and said, "Only Catholics can be laid to rest in that cemetery, but we can bury him in the lot just outside the fence."

It was agreed, and the service was held. However, the soldiers noticed that the aged priest seemed troubled. The following night, a strange thing happened. The priest assembled several of his parishioners. Together they took down the fence and moved it over to include the grave of the soldier. When the Americans inquired about the compassionate act, the old priest replied, "A Protestant may not be buried in the cemetery, but there is no rule which says we cannot move the fence to include a Protestant."

Women Power

There are, we are told, 6.5 million more women in America than there are men. Although women hold a voting edge in national elections, only twenty-four ladies were members of the ninety-eighth Congress of the United States, which numbers 535 persons. Despite this disparity, women are gaining ground and leadership in the political arena, even as they are in other sectors of society. In 1971, for instance, there were only seven women mayors in America of cities of 30,000 plus. Today there are seventy-six. Since 1971, U. S. women have greatly increased their strength in statehouses across the country. Then there were 362; today there are 994.

Prayer

1 Samuel 7:5; 2 Chronicles 7:1-3; Luke 11:1-4; Luke 22:39-46;
John 17:15

Pray and stay are two blessed monosyllables.
—John Donne

Prayer is exhaling the spirit of man and inhaling the Spirit of God.
—Edwin Keith

Able to Discern

Reinhold Niebuhr's discerning prayer has been quoted frequently:

O God, give us
Serenity to accept what cannot be changed,
Courage to change what should be changed, and
Wisdom to distinguish the one from the other.

Are You Tired of Praying?

A cartoon pictured a little boy kneeling in prayer. Obviously disgruntled with God, he was saying, "Aunt Harriet hasn't gotten married, Uncle Hubert hasn't any work, and Daddy's hair is still falling out. . . . I'm getting tired of praying for this family without getting any results."

Ask and It Will Be Given

The eminent scientist and enviable Christian, Dr. George Washington Carver, holding a peanut in his hand, asked, "Mr. Creator, what's in that peanut?" The Creator replied, "You've got brains, You go and find out." Carver found the answers, and he used them to benefit humankind. And so can we, when our quiet times with God lead to creativity and deeper commitment. (See Matt. 21:22.)

Comments

Prayer is the little implement
Through which men reach
Where presence is denied them.

—Emily Dickinson

Prayer is combat with God. It is struggle. It is not limited to the pious; it is articulating need, recognizing God's ultimate power and authority.

—Jacques Ellul

Pray in the darkness, if there be no light.
—Hartley Coleridge

Certain thoughts are prayers. There are moments when, whatever be the attitude of the body, the soul is on its knees.
—Victor Hugo

Continue the Conversation

Although the discipline of prayer—the pathway to God—may not bring the coveted miracle, the Christian is challenged to continue conversations with God. Not that the Father needs to be reminded of human problems so much as mankind needs to be reminded of God's presence and power.

Jesus referred to the Temple of worship as the house of prayer: where believing souls could confess their inadequacies, quietly or audibly articulate need, and courageously recommit themselves to higher purposes.

Controversial Prayer

The dubious affinity between sports and religion ran into a whirlwind on Monday night, December 2, 1974, when the Miami Dolphins played hosts to the Cincinnati Bengals. As usual, just prior to the game, an invocation was offered. The Reverend Richard J. Bailar of the United Church of Christ asked the Lord's blessings on the night's game. It was a shocker:

Creator God: Father and Mother of us all: We give You thanks for the joy and excitement occasioned by this game. We pray for the physical well-being of all the gladiators who run the gamut of gridiron battle tonight . . . but, knowing that the tigers are voracious beasts of prey, we ask You to be especially watchful over our gentle dolphins. Limit, if You will, the obfuscations of Cosell's acidulous tongue, so that he may describe this night truly and grammatically as it is. . . . A great game, in a great city, played before Your grateful children, on whom we ask peace and shalom. Amen.[1]

Given the Right Words

In his book, *Self-Esteem, the New Reformation,* (Word, 1982), Dr. Robert H. Schuller shared thoughts on a hospital call he made on John Wayne. The veteran film star was facing surgery the following morning. As he traveled to the hospital, Schuller prayed for divine guidance. Should he be direct about Wayne's relationship to Christ, was Wayne prepared to meet God? The "still, small voice" counseled him not to be direct, but to simply "bring Jesus Christ into the mind of John Wayne. He will accept or reject Christ. That is what it's all about."

Dr. Schuller found the old giant lying on the bed. They talked. Then the famous pastor asked, "Duke, may I pray for you?"

"You bet, Bob, I need all the help I can get." The actor closed his eyes; his face was taut with tension.

"Lord, John Wayne knows about You. He has heard about You all his life. He admires You. He respects You. And deep down he knows that You can and want to forgive him of all of his sins. Deep down in his mind he accepts You and believes in You and loves You, now."

Opening his eyes, Pastor Schuller said John Wayne's face was no longer taut, but as peaceful as an Easter sunrise. The preacher had been given the right words and they had been sincerely accepted.[2]

How Long Do You Pray?

A never-to-be-forgotten experience occurred during a conference with a pulpit search committee. Following queries pertaining to theological positions, administrative skills, and family, a saintly lady asked, "Doctor, how long do you pray?" There was an awkward silence. Before I could respond, a member of the "scouting committee" volunteered, "When we heard him in his pulpit, he prayed about four minutes." "That is not what I mean," the gentle soul replied. "How long do you pray for the church, your people, and yourself in private devotions?"

Is It Cheating to Write Out Your Prayers?

After worship one Sunday, someone visited the pulpit and wrote across the typescript of the morning prayer, "Don't cheat, Pastor." It stung me. It still does. But I am thankful, for it has caused me to reevaluate my ministry many times, especially the conduct of public worship. Is it cheating to read the morning prayer?

Jesus, I'm Here!

George McLeod, leader of the Iona community, Scotland, told of a young man observed entering and leaving a Catholic church each day at noon. On one occasion, a priest queried the visitor, who revealed that his lunch hour was the only time he could pray. The observer asked, "What do you say in your prayers?"

"I say, 'Jesus, it's Jimmy!' "

The priest was deeply moved by the man's prayer habits. Months later, when he stood in the humble bedroom of a very ill young man, he sensed a Presence. The priest was certain that as he stood there he heard a voice say, "Jimmy, it's Jesus!"

Leave Your Prayer List

The sexton of a metropolitan church noticed scraps of paper in a certain pew in the sanctuary after each Sunday service. One day he made bold to examine the crumpled pieces of paper. He found such notes as: "Mary—ill; Bob, needs job; her rent due; my needs . . ." After a few weeks of this, the faithful custodian shared the mystery with the pastor, who alerted several members who sat in the area where messages were found to please identify, if possible, the person who was leaving tidbits of information each Sunday. The quiet plan succeeded. In due time, the minister adroitly engaged the lady in conversation in his study about the intriguing practice of leaving notes addressed to various people in her pew.

Smiling, the gentle lady declared that the bits of paper had deep meaning for her. "You will think it silly, but sometime ago I read, 'Take your troubles to church with you.' So I write down my concerns, burdens, and needs on little pieces of paper, take them to church, pray about them, and leave them there. I feel God is taking care of them!"

"My People Aren't Used to It!"

I supplied for a seminary friend one summer while he was on vacation. Reaching the pulpit that first Sunday, I found this note addressed to me on the large, open Bible: "Don't pray over two minutes. My people aren't used to it!"

The Old Hallstand

My parents were ardent practitioners of prayer. As a child, I was greatly impressed by their daily devotions. Eventually I was such a convert that I thought anything that went wrong could be readily remedied, or anything that I desired could be obtained, if Mother prayed about it.

As I grew older, the nature of my problems and concerns changed and, whenever I voiced doubt or fear, Mother would say, "We had better pray about this." Our secret place was an old hallstand near the front door of our country home. This antique, straight and tall, faced with glass, with clusters of hooks on each side for coats, and a receptacle near the right-hand side for umbrellas, also had a chest across the bottom which made it convenient and comfortable to rest the elbows while kneeling. This was our favorite altar. To me, it was a place of miracles.

Praying for Your Pastor

It is said that the backbone of Charles Spurgeon's magnificent ministry was the concern of an invalid in his church who made it her business to solicit prayers for her pastor and church.

Praying on the Porch

A few years ago, I visited the physician of my childhood, whom I had not seen since I was twelve years old. This tall, handsome gentleman, crowned with culture, wearing the uniform of his country, made a lasting impression on me as a boy. He had come to practice medicine in our little community following World War I. There was something different about him and his wife. I loved them. It was a sad day when the brilliant young doctor left to practice surgery in New York City. Following retirement, he resumed practice in Virginia.

Driving through the community where he and his brother operated a small hospital, I telephoned him. When I told him who I was, he immediately invited me over. As I approached his lovely home, there he stood on the porch in his shirtsleeves, charming as ever. He wept as I approached, and he hugged me fondly. We reminisced. He told me of his wife's death and said: "Curtis, I am so lonely. I have been so busy through the years that I never realized the deeper needs of people 'til now." As naturally and confidently as asking a nurse for a surgical instrument, he said, "Please pray for me."

We bowed and prayed together.

A Soldier's Prayer

I asked God for strength, that I might achieve,
I was made weak, that I might learn humbly to obey.
I asked for health, that I might do great things,
I was given infirmity, that I might do better things.
I asked for riches, that I might be happy,
I was given poverty, that I might be wise.
I asked for power, that I might have the praise of men,
I was given weakness, that I might feel the need of God.
I asked for all things, that I might enjoy life,

I was given life, that I might enjoy all things.
I got nothing that I asked for, but everything I had hoped for.
Almost despite myself, my unspoken prayers were answered.
I am among all men, most richly blessed.[3]

So Much to Do

Scholars remind us, "Luther was above all else a man of prayer." Martin Luther was an insatiable worker. He drove himself mercilessly. Up at daybreak, he put in long hours studying, translating, and writing. Think of his massive commentaries. Think of translating the entire New Testament from Erasmus's Greek into a common language in eleven short weeks! Yet Luther took time to pray an hour or two each day. He said he prayed a lot because he had so much to do.

"Thanks for the Task"

I shall long remember standing with the Reverend N. M. Townsend of the Kingsgate Christian Church in Kingston, Jamaica. Before entering the sanctuary, and surrounded by a number of his leaders, the pastor turned to one of his men and said, "Will you please lead us in prayer?" He replied, "Thanks for the task."

Typical Table Prayers

Bless us, O Lord, and these Thy gifts, which we are about to receive from Thy bounty. Through Christ our Lord. Amen.—Catholic

O Christ our God, bless the food and drink of Thy Servants, For Thou art Holy always, now and ever and unto ages of ages. Amen.—Orthodox

Lift up your hands toward the sanctuary and bless the Lord. Blessed art Thou, O Lord our God, King of the universe, who bringest forth bread from the earth. Amen.—Hebrew

Bless, O Lord, this food to our use, and us to Thy service, and make us ever mindful of the needs of others, in Jesus' name. Amen.—Protestant

When It's Hard to Pray

A distraught mother with a small child answered the door. I identified myself. Asking me in, she commented, "The Lord must have sent you." Weeping, she disclosed a terrible thing that had happened in her family that day. It was necessary to take legal action. She asked me to pray. Have you ever tried to pray in such a situation, with a television going and a youngster playing? In a sense, I was trapped, I was cornered. Or was it the way God intended it to be?

Preaching

Matthew 3:1-3; Mark 1:14-15; Luke 20:1-8; Acts 8:4; Romans 10:17; 1 Corinthians 1:21

The ministry of print can reach where the ministry of the voice can never penetrate.

—William Barclay

I preached as never sure to preach again, and as a dying man to dying men.

—Richard Baxter

What many ministers seem to lack is a sense of occasion.

—William F. Dunkle, Jr.

All the Grammar

A listener to Dwight L. Moody was most critical of his grammar and reprimanded him for it. "My dear fellow," replied Moody, "I wish my grammar were better. I wish I had a better education, but I am using all the grammar I have for the glory of God. Are you doing as much with yours?"

An Art and a Labor

Edgar Dewitt Jones, a prince among preachers, told this story on himself. As a young pastor in Kentucky, and while visiting with one of his elders, he commented, "I expect to be a good preacher by the time I am fifty years old." The elder, blunt but true as steel, grunted, "I certainly hope so."

A Chinese Coolie

Dr. Baker James Cauthen, Baptist foreign mission executive, once wrote: "I see myself as a Chinese coolie carrying a heavy load on a pole. If I put office work on one end and preaching on the other, they can balance each other."

Communicating the Gospel

There is a dramatic story concerning the life and influence of King George V. In the latter years of his reign, it was his custom to broadcast a Christmas message to the empire. During one of these broadcasts, when the ears of the world were waiting to hear the voice of the king, an engineer observed that an important wire had snapped. America was cut off! Time was of the essence. Suddenly, as though nudged by an angel, a mechanic seized the broken wires. Holding one in each hand, he was thus able to complete the circuit which permitted the royal message to be transmitted to the United States. The voice of the king passed through the body of the engineer.

In the broken connections of our world, how can the Word of the Lord be heard unless it passes through the preacher?

Giving Something of Self

John Claypool titled his Lyman Beecher Lectures, given at Yale University and published in 1980, *The Preaching Event.* John says, "I go into the pulpit to give something of myself, not to get something for myself."

God Tapped Him

Peter Marshall was a powerful preacher of the previous generation. Born in Scotland, a few miles from Glasgow, he was four years old when his father died. In due time his mother remarried. The lad did not like his domineering, alcoholic stepfather. Peter Marshall's home life was miserable.

In those days a young man could join the Royal Navy at age fifteen years, nine months. Though underage, Peter quit school and ran away to join the Navy. Within a few days his true age was discovered; the young man was in a dilemma. Not having the courage to face the homefolk under the circumstances, Peter found a job and attended night school.

Meanwhile, Peter Marshall heard a missionary from China speak in his church. He was deeply moved by what he heard and offered himself as a missionary candidate to the London Missionary Society. At the time, neither the Society nor the Marshall family were able to finance Peter's schooling. Consequently, he compromised on the preaching ministry.

At long last, while out walking one Sunday afternoon in Scotland, three weeks after he had prayed fervently for vocational guidance, in his own dramatic phrase, "God tapped me on the shoulder."

An opportunity opened for him to come to America. He had three manual jobs in New Jersey within a span of five months. Eventually he made his way to Birmingham, Alabama, where interested persons assisted in his education. At age thirty-five, Peter Marshall became pastor of the First Presbyterian Church in the nation's capital (see Matt. 13:44-45).

Good News

Bishop William Taylor of the Methodist Church was a heroic Christian who went to California in the gold rush of 1849 and settled in San Francisco. He discovered there was no church for him to preach in, and not many people wanted to hear him. So, on Sunday morning, he would roll a wooden barrel down to a street corner, climb up on it, and shout, "What's the news?" Then, as nomads and natives gathered around, the preacher would announce, "Thank God, my brethren, I have good news for you this morning!" And he would proceed to preach.

The Image of the Preacher

Henri Nouwen's volume, *The Wounded Healer*, communicates the necessity of identifying with need; as preachers, we are and must minister as "wounded healers."

In General

In general, a community is no better than its churches. In general, a church is no better than its minister. In general, a minister is no better than his preparation.

Jesus Is Passing By!

A stranger visiting a Methodist community in Britain asked an old Cornishman to explain the obvious morality and spirit of the villagers. He replied, "A man named Wesley passed this way." And so must the church of Jesus Christ constantly remind the observing world that Jesus of Nazareth is passing by. There is an irresistible contagion about the Christian. Above all others, the preacher—by word and ministry—must preach: Jesus is here! (See Luke 18:37*ff.*)

Key to Preaching

Roland Bainton, among the world's foremost authorities on Martin Luther, was quoted in the December 15, 1982, issue of *The New York Times* as saying: "The key to Luther's preaching was his imagination." He "loved to think how he would have felt if he had been there—Mary, Joseph, the Shepherds and the wise men."

The Ministry of Listening

The late Carlyle Marney used to say if preachers would listen to their people twenty hours a week, then they would have a right to speak to them for twenty minutes on Sunday morning.

The Vigor of Truth

J. H. Jowett described Henry Drummond's speaking to orphans and runaway children in Edinburgh, Scotland. "He spoke to them with a simplicity and finished refinement which added the spell of beauty to the vigor of truth."

Personal Credentials

When Billy Graham was planning for his mission in India, he wrote the eminent Christian from Ceylon, D. T. Niles, for counsel. The scholarly churchman replied: "Yes, there is one thing which you must be aware of. When you are in India, people will expect to see some sign of austerity in your way of life as part of your credentials in claiming to be a man of God."

Person to Person

In *Reconstruction of the Church on What Pattern?* E. Stanley Jones referred to a conversation he had with a multimillionaire secularist who said: "If Brother Stanley can't convert me, I will sue him."

Trumpets in the Morning

Harper Shannon entitled his book on the pastoral calling *Trumpets in the Morning.* How descriptive of the divine discipline within the life of the God-called preacher! Preachers who have left the pastoral ministry for one reason or another, but still realize God has indeed called them, hear the sound of "trumpets in the morning." A truly called servant of God can never escape the clarion call, regardless of circumstances.

Prophet, Pastor, Preacher

A prophet excites people, but he is seldom promoted by the bureaucracy of the church. The teacher is tolerated and usually appreciated in retrospect. The pastor is beloved; the preacher admired. Yet in a sense the ordained leader is all four.

Role Playing

Kierkegaard told the story of a small circus that traveled from one little town to another in Denmark. Advanced promotion usually consisted of handing out information pieces, detailing performances, to citizens of the community where the circus would show that evening, while the crew put up a tent on the edge of the village.

On one occasion the circus tent caught fire an hour or so before show time. It so happened that the clown was the only one sufficiently dressed to seek help. The clown hurried into the village, begging people to fetch their water pails and help quell the fire. The villagers interpreted the clown's appearance as part of his act.

As Kierkegaard put it, "they heard the clown with their eyes." And not until they observed the red glow of the sky did they shift their minds from entertainment to crisis. At last the people of the Danish village saw more than a clown—they saw a human being earnestly seeking help.

Ministers must be aware of being stereotyped, such role players that their influence is narrowed and interaction with persons held suspect.

Weigh Your Words

Calvin Coolidge wisely expressed it: "One of the first lessons a president has to learn is that every word he says weighs a ton."

And so do those of the preacher!

Words and Deeds

Saint Augustine's counsel regarding the duty of the clergy is equally binding on all Christians: "to teach what is right and to refute what is wrong, and in the performance of this task to conciliate the hostile [and] to rouse the careless."

Revival

Matthew 4:18-19; Matthew 19:23-30; John 1:41; Acts 4:12; 2 Timothy 4:5

Religion can exist in our lives either as a dull habit or as an acute fever.

—William James

We die daily. Happy are those who daily come to life as well.

—George McDonald

Booth Saw King Jesus

And when Booth halted by the curb for prayer
He saw his Master thro' the flag-filled air.
Christ came gently with a robe and crown
For Booth the soldier, while the throng knelt down.
He saw King Jesus. They were face to face,
And he knelt a-weeping in that holy place.
Are you washed in the blood of the Lamb?[1]

Captured by Photographs of a Man

While leafing through a copy of *Life* magazine in 1947, William Mellon, age thirty-seven, of the famous Pittsburg family, who was living in the lap of luxury, was fascinated by a picture of Albert Schweitzer with an antelope. Mellon said he thought of Schweitzer as an organist. The perceptive man began to study the phenomenal European. He was so impacted by Schweitzer's work that he went to Africa to visit the multitalented missionary. Returning home, he enrolled in medical school, was baptized in the Park Avenue Christian Church, New York City, and eventually went to Haiti and built a hospital, largely at his own expense, and named it "Schweitzer."

Learning of the project, among other things, Schweitzer wrote Mellon: "I am truly moved, more than I can tell you at this expression of understanding."

Christ Changes Life-styles

Mrs. Colleen Evans, wife of the pastor of National Presbyterian Church, Washington, D. C., has a book called *Give Us This Day Our Daily Bread.* In it she shares the story of a friend in California called Bill, who was rather late affiliating with the church. He had been an alcoholic.

After identifying with Christ, he began studying the Bible in earnest. He recognized the tithe as a basic right of the Lord. Gradually he began to adjust his life-style, and eventually altered the accepted biblical standard of tithing, the giving of a tenth to God and operating on the 90 percent left, into operating on 10 percent and giving away 90 percent! Not everyone could do this, of course, but what a marvelous answer to Malachi's query, "Will a man rob God?" (3:8); and to Paul's declaration—"Thanks be to God for his inexpressible gift!" (2 Cor. 9:15).

Don't Miss Anyone!

John Killinger shared the story of a parishioner whose son was taken to summer camp. The little chap was not at all sure he would like the experience of being away from home for a week, but friends and parents assured him it was a good place and he would enjoy it. He went.

When the parents returned, much to their surprise they found their son standing where they had left him, wearing the same clothes. The punctilious mother asked, "Son, there were plenty of other clothes in your bag. Why didn't you change?"

"I wanted to be sure," the little fellow said, "that you didn't miss me."

Glory to God

Billy Graham told the story of Billy Bray, a saintly minister of another generation, who sat by the bedside of a dying friend who had been timid and reluctant to witness for Christ. The dying man said, "If I had the power I'd shout glory to God." Whereupon Pastor Bray replied: "It's a pity you didn't shout glory when you had the power."

"Night comes, when no one can work" (John 9:4).

Growing in Grace

How well I remember a board meeting in a metropolitan parish. Concern was voiced that we were not reaching a sufficient number of persons for Christ. We were in general agreement as to what should be done, but no one was willing to commit himself to the task. There were searching moments of silence. Then, quite unexpectedly, a prominent physician stood and said, "I don't know much about evangelism, but I love Christ and His church. Pastor, if you will teach me how to become an evangelist and if you, the members of this board, will cooperate, I will head up our evangelism program for next year."

It was an exciting statement! Like a blood transfusion, he injected new life and enthusiasm into the group. We experienced a great ingathering of souls that year. Moreover, the physician grew in Christian grace and loyalty, as did the congregation.

If Not, Why Not?

Many years ago, physicians throughout the world celebrated the anniversary of the death of Thomas Linacre, founder and first president of the Royal College of Physicians. When sixty years of age, the good doctor decided to become a clergyman.

He applied himself to New Testament studies. Once, after reading the Sermon on the Mount, he exclaimed: "Either this is not the gospel or we are not Christian."

"Just As I Am"

During a revival at a rural church, while examining the prospect list with some of the members, the name of a well-to-do farmer kept surfacing. He was reported as being a good man who attended church regularly and supported it generously. I was impressed by the sincerity of the man.

One night during a thunderstorm the lights went out in the church. There were "ohs" and "ahs" from the congregation. I assured the brethren that since I preach without notes, the darkness posed no handicap. After a few moments of confusion, the service proceeded. A candle was lighted so the pianist could see how to play. While the invitation hymn, "Just As I Am," was being sung, one person responded. You guessed it—the well-to-do farmer!

Looking Down the Gun Barrel

Halford E. Luccock reminded us of the report by Clifford Dowdey in his book, *Experiment in Rebellion.* The shocking incident occurred during the War Between the States. When the Union army, under the command of General McClellan, was marching on Richmond, and it appeared that the capital of the Confederacy would be captured, Jefferson Davis, president of the Confederate States, was baptized in his home by the rector of a neighboring church. With threatening danger only twenty miles away, Davis decided to become a Christian.

Personal Glory

Archibald Rutledge, the poet laureate of South Carolina, in *My Colonel and His Lady,* told the story of a black ferryboat captain, who took passengers across the Santee River. The ferry was usually dirty. But on this day, Rutledge found it completely transformed. It was clean from stem to stern. The boat fairly glistened in the sunlight. No less miraculous was the transformation of the captain himself. He was neat, clean, and quiet. When asked the meaning of the sudden change, the humble man replied, "Well, you see, Sir, I have a glory."

Quit It!

Sam Jones was a popular evangelist in the South years ago. During the course of a revival meeting, he would designate a "Quitter's Night." Persons were asked to bring symbols, or pictures, of their sins: cards, dice, whiskey bottles, pictures of other men's wives, and so forth. As the fiery evangelist exhorted the brethren to come forward and leave evidence of their sins, one of the saints of the church responded. The preacher was surprised and asked, "Aunt Sarah, what are you repenting of?" She replied, "I ain't done nothing, and I'm gonna quit it!"

Reducing the Population of Hell

Born in East Northfield, Massachusetts, February 5, 1837, Dwight Lyman Moody lost his father in 1841. As a boy, young Moody was independent and mischievous. His schooling was very limited, but his energy was boundless. At age seventeen, he became a shoe salesman in Boston. After his conversion in 1855, he moved to Chicago where he entered business and started a Sunday School which grew into a church. A man who earnestly believed the Lord would provide, in 1860 he gave up business and devoted himself to missionary work in Chicago and, subsequently, assisted soldiers during the Civil War.

Ira David Sankey, a musician, joined Moody in 1870, and together they produced a book of *Gospel Hymns*. These stalwart Christians conducted a series of huge revival meetings, which, according to friends of Moody, "reduced the population of hell by a million souls."

Dwight L. Moody also founded the Northfield Seminary for Girls in 1879, and two years later started a similar, practical,

Bible-centered school for boys known as Mount Hermon. This visionary, hardworking servant of the Lord opened the Chicago Bible Institute as well as a conference center for Christian workers in Northfield. His practical skills, common touch, organizational abilities, perception of individual need, gentleness, earnest preaching of the gospel, and the winning of souls marked him great, despite his scholastic deficiencies.

Reenlistment

Captain John Callender of the Massachusetts Militia was guilty of cowardice at the Battle of Bunker Hill. One of General Washington's first duties as he assumed command of the American forces at Cambridge was to order the court-martial of Captain Callender. This is an infamous crime to a soldier, the most humiliating of all, so the captain was stripped of his commission and expelled in disgrace. However, there was another side to this man. In the meanwhile, something happened. He observed Washington, and later Callender reenlisted in the army as a private. During the Battle of Long Island, Callender demonstrated such conspicuous courage that Washington publicly revoked the sentence and restored him as an officer in his army.

The Sawdust Trail

William Ashley (Billy) Sunday was born in Ames, Iowa, November 19, 1862, and died in Chicago, November 6, 1935. His father, a brickmason, was killed while fighting in the Union Army in 1862. Young Billy spent four years in an orphan's home, grew up on a farm, completed high school, and worked in a funeral home before becoming a professional baseball player.

In 1896 Billy Sunday began conducting revival meetings in cities across America. Joined by the songleader, Homer A. Rodeheaver, and other specialists over the years, following the example of Moody, Sunday held three-hundred revivals, totaling an estimated attendance of one-hundred million. Faithful to the Fundamentalist wing of evangelical Christianity, Sunday claimed that "One-million souls hit the sawdust trail" to profess their faith in Jesus Christ as a result of his preaching.

A Sense of Grace

John R. Claypool has related the story of his friend, Sam Keen. Like many, Keen felt that if he could obtain a doctorate from an Ivy League school and join a respected college faculty, he would be happy, would lose that sense of "nobodiness." He achieved these objectives, but he remained unhappy, unsatisfied. Then one night, alone in a hotel room, like another bright man of yesteryear, he found himself asking, "What must I do to be saved?" The answer came abundantly clear. "Nothing, nothing at all. It comes with the territory or it does not come at all." Subsequently, he said "he had been like a man riding on an ox, looking for an ox."

Slaves and Beggars

Simone Weil has noted that Christianity is a religion for slaves. "We have to make ourselves slaves and beggars to follow Christ."

Think Hard

Walter Winchell once quipped, "If you have a son in Korea, write to him; if you have one at Camp Breckinridge, pray for him." Remembering this, my days were not without refreshing humor at Breckinridge. During a Tri-Faith Mission, wherein I was the Protestant representative, a company commander lined up his men and barked, "All right, you guys, you have three days to decide whether you are Catholic, Jewish, or Protestant! And you atheists better think hard!"

The Transforming Power

Beneath the Marquand Chapel at Yale Divinity School is an undecorated prayer chamber. Some refer to it as the catacombs. The octagonal room rises to an immense height. Its unadorned walls are broken only by small openings for light. As we approach the entrance, we are conscious of the fact that our shadow is diminishing in size until by the time we reach the altar, it is actually much less than normal. This phenomenon is accomplished through unique lighting at the end of the corridor.

Is not this a parable of the transformation that occurs within when Christ becomes the center of our living? We decrease while Christ increases!

Yes, We Do

You may remember that in *The Robe,* Lloyd C. Douglas had Marcellus accepting the invitation of Christ to be a disciple. The strong man wrote to Diana, his lover in Rome, of his conversion. With penetrating pertinence she replied: "What I feared was that it might somehow affect your life—and mine, too. It is a beautiful story, Marcellus, a beautiful mystery. Let it remain so. We don't have to understand it. And we don't have to do anything about it; do we?"[2]

You Need Three

It has been said that every professing Christian needs three conversions: (1) Be converted to Jesus Christ. (2) Be converted to the church, and through baptism be thus identified with the community of faith. (3) Be converted to the world, that is, return to the world as a caring Christian.

Sin

1 Samuel 15:25; Jeremiah 31:29-31; Matthew 12:31; John 1:29;
John 8:7; Galatians 2:17-21

The entire story of Sodom and Gomorrah is the story of perversion.
—Bill R. Austin

The proper process of unsinning sin is to begin well doing.
—Robert Browning

I never feel virtuous unless I have a sense of guilt.
—John Steinbeck

Asking for Money, a Sin?

Some years ago I went with our son, David, to see *The Adventures of a Young Man,* which was showing in a theater in Saint Louis, Missouri. It depicted the life of Ernest Hemingway. At an unexpected place in the show, the lights went on, and a picture of James Stewart was flashed on the screen. Whereupon the popular actor made an appeal for a hospital for theatrical people, their relatives and friends. We overheard someone back of us blurt out: "The theaters are getting worse than the churches. They are always asking for money."

Comments

No matter how many new translations of the Bible come out, the people still sin the same way.

—Anonymous

He that sins is human; he that grieves over sin is a saint; he that boasts of sin is of the devil; He that forgives sin is God.

The heart and the eye are the agents of sin.

—old proverbs

The worst sin toward our fellow creatures is not to hate them, but to be indifferent to them.

—George Bernard Shaw

Cursing Silently

Writing about Queen Elizabeth's bedroom intruder in July of 1982, Bob Green, syndicated columnist, commented,

The lesson is . . . that nothing works for anybody. . . . The world has fallen into such disrepair and slovenliness that the Queen herself is right down there with the rest of us, gritting her teeth and cursing silently at what life has come to.[1]

Does It Make You Nervous?

A faithful parishioner surprised his pastor by asking: "Doesn't it make you nervous preaching on sin with all those experts sitting out there in the congregation?"

Duplicity

When I think of faithfulness, I am reminded of Napoleon's classical description of one of France's great statesmen. He said: "Talleyrand is a silk stocking full of mud."

Gaining Strength

Saint Francis of Assisi suggested that we should go outside to weep over our faults in order to be ready to meet with joy those who come to draw strength from us.

The Harder They Fall

Our college football coach, and many others, used to say: "The bigger they are, the harder they fall!" This applies with equal relevance to the business and professional arenas. If you question the claim, ask flamboyant automobile entrepreneur John DeLorean, who left the corporate nest at General Motors to start his own automobile manufacturing company in Northern Ireland. The dream burned out, while debts flared. His company went into receivership. DeLorean was also indicted on alleged drug trafficking but was acquitted.

Ask Jake Butcher, another bright entrepreneur, a banker who enjoyed living in the fast lane. Butcher worked for years to bring the World's Fair to Knoxville, Tennessee. He stood by President Reagan as he formally opened the Fair in 1982. Subsequently, Butcher flew to Louisville in his private jet to attend the Kentucky Derby with his friend, Governor John Y. Brown. On February 14, 1983, much to the amazement of the people of Knoxville and the nation, Butcher's United American Bank was declared insolvent by the State Banking Commissioner and closed. The Federal Deposit Insurance Corporation sold it to a Memphis holding company, First Tennessee National Corporation, which opened it the following day. Butcher has since been sentenced to a federal prison term for bank fraud.

These dramatic reversals emphasize the truth of Solomon's warning: "Pride goes before destruction, and a haughty spirit before a fall" (Prov. 16:18).

Success is a moving target!

Love Crucified

E. Stanley Jones shared the story of a government employee in India whose work involved much travel. He became unfaithful to his wife. Being a sensitive man, he could not live with himself and decided to tell his wife. With agonizing awkwardness the man divulged the whole story. When his words began to penetrate, the wife turned pale, shook with grief, and collapsed. "In that moment," confessed the offender, "I saw the meaning of the cross. I saw love crucified by sin."

Loyalty to Self

In *Shantung Compound,* Langdon Gilkey defined sin as devotion to a finite interest; it is an overriding loyalty or concern for the self, its existence and its prestige.[2]

Manifested as Pride

Pride, usually considered a virtue, is, under some circumstances, a basic form of sin. Dr. Karl Menninger, in *Whatever Became of Sin?*, reminded us that vanity, egocentricity, arrogance, self-adoration, selfishness, and self-love are really synonyms for pride. Theologically, pride asserts itself into pride of power, knowledge, and virtue.

Writing in *Power, A New Social Analysis,* Bertrand Russell noted, "Every man would like to be God if it were possible; some few find it difficult to admit the impossibility."

No Forwarding Address

The popular television program, "Real People," showed a package that had been sent to a person in prison. The package was "returned to sender" with this dramatic message stamped on it: "Escaped; Left No Forwarding Address." When we escape from the imprisonment sin creates, we must leave no forwarding address. Paul stated it succinctly: "Make no provision for the flesh, to gratify its desires" (Rom. 13:14).

On Being Fed Up

Ralph Barton was a popular cartoonist for *The New Yorker.* He is reported to have committed suicide, leaving behind his well-known and publicized confession:

> I have had few real difficulties. I have had, on the contrary, an exceptionally glamorous life, as life goes, and I have had more than my share of affection and appreciation. The most charming, intelligent, and important people that I have known have liked me. . . . I have run from wife to wife, from house to house, and from country to country in a ridiculous effort to escape myself. . . . No one thing is responsible for this suicide and no person except myself. . . . I did it because I am fed

up with inventing devices for getting through twenty-four hours a day.

On Being Too Critical

Thomas Carlyle, nineteenth-century Scottish essayist and historian, and his wife Jane Welsh, once entertained a prominent guest whom Carlyle wanted to impress. During a pause in table conversation, Carlyle heard his wife breathing heavily. Whereupon he chided, "Jane, I wish you would not breathe so noisily."

Years later, when Jane ceased breathing altogether, Carlyle read in her diary how much his statement about her breathing had hurt. He wept for another chance, but it was too late! Reflecting on their years together, he realized his had been a long marriage of criticism.

A Quiet Death

In examining the subtle and not too subtle examples of sin, the famed psychiatrist Karl Menninger declared: "To injure someone's self-respect, his pride, his status among friends and equals may be to quietly kill him. No crime. But sin, I say."

Refusal to Love

Sin has a willful, defiant, or disloyal quality; someone is defied, offended, or hurt. The willful disregard or sacrifice of the welfare of others for the welfare or satisfaction of the self is an essential quality of the concept sin. . . . And sin is thus, at heart, a refusal of the love of others.[3]

Shining Red Shoes

One of Hans Christian Andersen's famous fairy tales is *The Red Shoes*. In the story, Karen, a lovely, poor girl, dreamed of having a pair of red shoes. After her mother's death, she went to live with a wealthy woman. Her guardian nurtured her in the atmosphere of the church. When Karen was ready to be confirmed, her foster mother purchased suitable clothes for the occasion, including the orphan's murmured wish for red shoes.

The shoes attracted considerable attention. Karen wore them to church. She thought they were silhouetted in the chalice from which she sipped communion for the first time. Out on the street Karen began to dance. Try as she might, she could not stop. Her foster mother managed to take the red shoes off and hide them.

After her guardian's death, Karen found the coveted shoes and began to dance again. She danced through the streets, out of town, and finally into the woods. Karen became frightened. At last she encountered an angel who said, "Dance in your red shoes, dance on, until you are pale and cold and your flesh shrivels." The possessed girl begged for help. Exhausted, she asked the village executioner to cut off her feet. He obliged. But even so, Karen's dancing feet went off into the night. The girl was compelled to use crutches the rest of her life, but she was happy to be free of her obsession.

Andersen has given us a continuing sermon in the fantasy of *The Red Shoes*. Every person, regardless of age or ambition, station or schooling, owns at least one pair of red shoes. Any absorbing idea, anything which shackles an individual, monopolizes his/her time, warps the mind and shrivels the soul—is an obsession. Good or bad, obsessions are shining red shoes—sins!

The Trick About Sin

In *A Month of Sundays*, John Updike said to Mooney, "Deceit has done you in. That's the trick about sin, it does in the doer."

Unkissed Imagination

John Ciardi, the poet, said an ulcer is "an unkissed imagination" which is taking revenge for having been jilted! It could be an unwritten letter, an unuttered prayer, the denial of reality, an unfinished task, or a hounding promise. Whatever, life cannot go on forever without beauty and reality.

Wickedness Going Faster

The distinguished journalist, James Reston, having found few answers to the world's pain and problems, interviewed his mother in California when she was ninety-four. Among other trenchant comments, she said: "All this 'progress' is merely a wickedness going faster."

A Wrong Is a Wrong!

My seminary classmate, the late Arthur W. Mielkie, told of a visit to America by the Reverend Kyoshi Tanimoto, a Methodist minister who had miraculously survived the Hiroshima conflagration. The pastor asked to meet Albert Einstein, the man whose knowledge had much to do with the construction of the first atom bomb. Einstein was pleased to welcome the minister from Japan. Imagine the high drama and excitement as the two men met in the professor's home at Princeton, New Jersey! It was reported that Einstein suggested the bomb should never have been dropped on a city. Graciously Tanimoto countered, the Japanese would have dropped it on America if they had possessed the bomb.

With firmness and moral conviction, Einstein answered, "Even if you might have done it to us, this would still have been no excuse for us to drop the bomb."

Sports

Judges 15:12-17; 1 Corinthians 3:16-17; 2 Timothy 4:6-8; Hebrews 12:1-2

When the One Great Scorer comes to write against your name—
He marks—not that you won or lost—but how you played the game.
—Grantland Rice

Accepting Defeat

Jack Dempsey, "The Manassa Mauler," who ruled boxing's heavyweight division from 1919 to 1926, died Tuesday, May 31, 1983, at age eighty-seven. This gentle man out of the ring amassed a career total of sixty victories in eighty-one fights, forty-nine by knockouts. He also boxed hundreds of exhibitions, sometimes accommodating as many as a half-dozen hungry aspirants on a single night. Yet, Dempsey enjoyed more admiration and popularity after his defeat by the former Marine and student of Shakespeare, Gene Tunney, than while he was champion. Having been punched almost blind by the "Fighting Marine," Dempsey told his trainer, "Lead me out there, I want to shake his hand."

Baseball

Forty-three-year-old Gaylord Perry notched his three-hundredth career pitching victory against the New York Yankees, Thursday night, May 6, 1982. Consequently, the cagey hurler for the Seattle Mariners joined the elite group of major league 300-game winners.

Basketball

Richard "Digger" Phelps (his father is a mortician, hence the nickname), colorful basketball coach at Notre Dame, declares he lived a narrow life for years, living "basketball 365 days a year." After traveling in Europe, seeing historic places and paintings of the masters, his world began to expand. He still loves basketball and wants to win. But there are other equally important things in life. The press quoted him as saying: "Give me a choice now between winning the NCAA Championship —and getting a Van Gogh for my wall, and I'm going to have to do some heavy thinking."

Boxing's Champion

The late Joe Louis (Barrow) was heavyweight boxing champion for twelve years. He defended his title twenty-five times and retired undefeated as a champion. While in conversation with Joe, Red Smith commented that he (Louis) was fifteen years before his time in the marketing of fights; he missed the multimillion-dollar, closed-circuit television shows.

"No," commented Louis, "when I was boxing I made five million dollars and wound up broke, owing the Government a million. If I was boxing today I'd make ten million and wind up broke, owing the Government two million."[1]

Challenging Limitations

Dack Axselle of Ashland, Virginia, was one of hundreds who participated in the Richmond Newspapers' Marathon, October 1982. As an eight-year-old, his distance was five miles. Unlike his competitors, Dack was a winner before he started! Born with spina bifida, a congenital birth defect that damages the nervous system, Dack has never been able to walk without leg braces and crutches. Even though he has no feeling in his legs from the knees down, he is forever challenging his limitations. With the extraordinary support of his family, he trained hard for the marathon, and finished the grueling five miles amid generous applause.

Update: Dack Axselle completed 13.1 miles in the 1983 Marathon. The screws in his braces had to be replaced!

Dedication

Now and again, baseball broadcasters will mention the fabulous career of Christy Mathewson, the amazing pitcher for the New York Giants at the turn of the century. He won thirty-seven games in 1908. This remarkable man was admired on and off the field. Of all the stories attributed to Mathewson, the one I appreciate most concerns a highly contested game when

Christy was a runner on third base. The manager called for a squeeze play. Mathewson implemented the sign to the best of his ability.

Dust enveloped home plate. The umpire could not be certain what happened. We are told that an unprecedented conference was held between umpires. It was agreed that Christy should make the decision. The fierce competitor walked around home plate adjusting his trousers, dusting off his uniform; finally, removing his cap, he announced: "He got me." Later, in the dressing room, his teammates asked him why he divulged the secret; whereupon the great athlete, with considerable pride, said: "I am an elder in the Presbyterian Church."

Football Computer

Roger Shank, age thirty-seven, is chairman of Yale's Computer Science Department and father of the football computer. The project is an effort to reconstruct the memory of a football coach, reminding him of plays that worked and why, as well as visualizing possible options. At a deeper level, the professor is endeavoring "to create a computer model of the human understanding of process." Shank says that, in a sense, "artificial intelligence" is a field of vanishing horizons.

The professor's capacity for mathematics surfaced early. His mother recalls a visit to their dentist when Roger was four years old. Preparing to leave, they were reminded to return "two weeks from Wednesday." Immediately, the boy said: "You mean the twenty-eighth." It seems he had been studying the calendar, memorizing the dates of each day of the month.[2]

Get Back in the Game!

In the annual Rose Bowl classic of 1929, a most unusual play occurred. In the second quarter of that closely contested game between California and Georgia Tech, a California back recovered a fumble. Shocked by the impact of scrimmage, he brought the crowd to its feet by running in the wrong direction. What's more, he ran brilliantly! At last he was tackled by his own teammates.

At halftime the respective teams filed into their locker rooms. Roy Riegels, who made the "boo-boo," sat by himself, waiting for the coach's blast. When the California team left for the field, Clarence Price, the head coach, went over to the dejected player and, placing his arm around his shoulders, said: "Remember, old man, the game's only half over. Get back in the game!"

With such understanding and encouragement, needless to note, Riegels played perhaps the best half of his career, even though Tech won 8-7.

Humility

"Grantland Rice was the greatest man I have known, the greatest talent, the greatest gentleman." This is the appraisal of the late Red Smith. Many felt the only thing greater than his talent was his generous heart. Rice was the epitome of courtesy.

The story goes that the noted journalist's working pass ticket for the Army-Notre Dame football game went astray. This man, who virtually created that classic game, did not complain. Instead he went down Broadway, bought a ticket from a scalper, and watched the game from the stands with his typewriter on his knee. Afterwards, he went to the press box to complete his story. Hearing of the experience, a friend asked, "Why didn't you throw some weight around?"

"Tell you the truth," Granny came back, "I don't weigh much."[3]

Integrity

Once in a football game between the University of Chicago, where the legendary Amos Alonzo Stagg was head coach, and the University of Illinois, an official sustained an injury. Coach Stagg was asked to step in and referee his own game—a crowning act of confidence! It would be like asking an attorney to judge a case in which he was involved, or a farmer to determine the price support for his crops and those of his neighbors, or asking a parent to evaluate his child's conduct. Alonzo Stagg had so identified himself with integrity that a rival coach could trust him to place the demands of fair play above victory and self-interest.

A Legend Bows Out

As previously announced, following Alabama's 21-15 triumph over Illinois in the Liberty Bowl, December 29, 1982, Paul William "Bear" Bryant bowed out of college coaching after a fabulous thirty-eight year career. The unexcelled, majestic line in the record book reads: 323 victories, eighty-five defeats, and seventeen ties. Add to these graphics twenty-seven bowls, twelve Southeastern Conference championships, and six national titles. When asked how he would like to be remembered, he drawled, "That I helped more people than I hurt."

"My Own Referee"

Billy Conn, an excellent former heavyweight boxer, who in seventy-four fights was knocked out only twice, both times by Joe Louis, wrote of the "quiet humor, dignity and honor" of the "Brown Bomber" in the July, 1983, issue of the *Reader's Digest*. Joe was a remarkable person.

Louis defended his title a month following Pearl Harbor. He devoted his purse to the Navy Relief Fund. About two months later he fought again, and this time donated his purse to the Army Relief Society.

According to Conn, fighters worry about who will referee and judge their performances. Holding up his fists, Joe would exclaim, "I bring my own referee."

Apology

Jake Powell, who used to play outfield for the Yankees and the Washington Senators, frequently acted on impulse. Eventually he killed himself. But there is a story worth remembering about this controversial athlete.

In Comiskey Park, Chicago, one day right before a game, a radio broadcaster grabbed him for an unrehearsed interview in which Powell made a thoughtless, slurring comment that alienated the black community. Emotions ran high. Threats of boycotts were voiced wherever Powell played. When next in New York, Jake, unannounced and unescorted, worked Harlem from north to south. Stopping here and there, he would identify himself, apologize for a foolish mistake, and say he was sorry.[4]

Prayer Huddles

My telephone rang. It was the sports editor for the *National Observer* calling to ascertain my reaction to the Redskins' prayer huddle following their victory over the Dallas Cowboys, Sunday, December 31, 1972.

Reflecting on his query, for I was not expecting the call, I attempted to convey some of the more obvious psychological aspects involved; how some individuals, particularly coaches, are prone to exploit any mystique imaginable to "psyche" up their players.

Reborn

In the rash of mail and communications following Vince Lombardi's acceptance of the coaching position in Washington, D. C., one fan took it upon himself to point out all the reasons why he could not succeed: the reputation of the team, the park, but most of all, the players, whom he said did not need to be "remade" but "reborn."

The Right Thing at the Right Time

In his book, *Putting Faith to Work,* Robert McCracken shared a story concerning Leo Durocher. Everyone who follows baseball knows Durocher, how once he was brash, arrogant, loud, impetuous, impatient, and a merciless slave driver. His philosophy was wrapped up in his description of Mel Ott: "Nice guys finish last."

He never dreamed that one day he would be a "nice guy" and finish first, and when that day arrived he had matured enough to give the team credit. He explained that all he did was to wave them home from third base.

But the crux of the story concerned the fabulous center fielder, Willie Mays, of the Giants. After joining the club, there was a period when he made only one hit in twenty-six times at bat. The old Durocher would have banished him, benched him, or sent him back to the minors, but he did none of these. One day, the twenty-year-old player came to his manager, weeping, and begged to be benched. The new Durocher draped a fatherly arm about the strong young man's shoulders: "Don't worry, Son, you are my center fielder, even if you don't get another hit all season."

Willie strode from Leo's office with buoyant step and promptly began hitting the ball. He became one of baseball's immortals, because at a strategic moment in Willie's life, Durocher was keen enough and understanding enough to do the right thing at the right time.

A Senior Swimmer

At age 94 Jamison Handy, believed to be the oldest living Olympian, still plunges into the water for a half-mile swim each day. He said, "Swimming, the water, is the most wonderful thing in my life. It's hard to communicate how I feel about it."

Handy has the unique distinction of winning two Olympic

medals twenty years apart: his first, a bronze for swimming; a second medal as a member of the U. S. polo team in 1924. A teammate was Johnny Weissmuller of Hollywood fame. Handy "is credited with developing the modern freestyle breathing technique, the legless crawl for distance swimmers and the idea of painting pool bottoms with the lines that sprinters use as guides."[5]

Track

He was an excellent student, one of the finest athletes I ever coached. In his junior year in preparatory school, he qualified to participate in the All-New England Track Meet. He lost his favorite race—the 440—by half a chest. It was a record race, magnificent to watch. I was sick not only because we lost, but also because of the disappointment suffered by this splendid young man. We reviewed the race and concluded that perhaps we made a tactical error. The year passed.

Soon it was track season again and, as expected, our captain qualified once more for the all-important meet. My star, now a senior, about 6'-3", 200 pounds, was the epitome of strength and grace. As the big event drew near, we made careful preparations. At last the gun sounded, and the same two boys who battled the previous year were again running stride-for-stride. Result? My lad lost!

As we walked off the race, this young man said something I shall never forget: "Coach, he is half-a-chest better."

What Nationality Is Your God?

Lee Trevino won the 1972 British Open Golf Tournament. This exciting player exhibited phenomenal skill in overtaking and closing the door on Jack Nicklaus.

Colorful Trevino, whose austere upbringing adds competitiveness, steel, and spirit to the game, also brings rich deposits of compassion, generosity, and cheer wherever he plays.

In an interview following his fantastic victory at Muirfield,

Scotland, a smiling Lee quipped, "God must be Mexican." He was referring to his incredible chip shot on the seventeenth hole when Jack Nicklaus and Tony Jacklin seemed to have disposed of the former champion.

Observing this confident man and reflecting on his remark— "God must be Mexican!"—the thought came to me: *Is not this the heart of the human situation? Whether in jest or seriousness, in sport or religion, we are all conditioned to think in terms of nationality, race, religion, and politics.*

You Pitch Thursday

Carl and Will, good friends, lived in the same retirement complex. Having played baseball in their youth, both naturally enjoyed following the game. They attended all local games from Little League play to college contests. One day Will inquired, "Carl, do you think they'll play baseball in heaven?"

"I certainly hope so," replied Carl.

Shortly thereafter, Carl died. One night Will was awakened by a familiar voice, that of Carl. Following a general conversation, Will asked, "Carl, what's the good word from up there?"

"I have good news and bad news, Will. The good news is we play baseball every day! The bad news is you are scheduled to pitch next Thursday."

Stewardship

Malachi 3:7-10; Luke 16:2; John 3:16; 2 Corinthians 9:6

It is in giving that we receive. . . . It is in dying that we are born to eternal life.

—Francis of Assisi

All that I Have . . .

The late D. T. Niles reminds us of the heartbroken father, Mathew Sands, praying on his knees. In his hands he held a telegram which read: "Your son David reported missing, believed dead." Mathew Sands was inarticulate as he quietly recalled the life of his son, a pilot in the Air Force. At last he turned the telegram over and wrote on the back of it, "All that I have and all that I am, I give to God and for His service."

These words of recommitment brought comfort to his harrowed heart. Presently the telephone rang. It conveyed the interest of a neighboring university in Mathew Sands, a retired pastor. En route to the university for an interview, he came upon an abandoned church. Beside it a sign read: "For sale by auction." He entered the church to pray and while there decided to buy it and restore it to its holy mission.

Later, another man entered, Andrew Jelks. He had come to appraise the property. If acquired, Jelks planned to turn the building into "Andy's Amusement Arcade." Sands determined to write the trustees and make them an offer.

When the day of the sale arrived, a curious group of people gathered about the church. Mathew Sands, standing among them, put his hand into his pocket only to find the letter addressed to the trustees. In his confused state of mind, he had inadvertently enclosed the wire from the War Office instead of his offer. He was disappointed and disgusted with himself, but it was too late. Anyway, he decided to stay for the auction.

The man in charge of the sale finally announced that the church had been sold to Mathew Sands, declaring that his was the highest offer. He then read aloud the bid: "All that I have and all that I am, I give to God for his service."

The Best I Have

Some of us remember the bitter conflict between Russia and Finland in 1939. At last, Finnish officials ordered evacuation of their beloved homeland, including that of an old lady living alone. She had only a few hours to gather together her belongings. She was also told that to prevent the house from falling into Russian hands, it would be burned when she left. When the soldiers returned to pick up the dear soul, she was on her knees scrubbing the floor. Being astonished, they asked: "Mother, did you not understand we must burn your home?"

"Yes," she said, "but if I must give it to my country, I want it to be the best I have to give."

A Bigger Shovel

A wealthy elder in a church we once served used to quote the phrase, "You can't outgive God." His remark is reminiscent of another generous steward who, when asked if he was not in danger of "beggaring" himself through multiple gifts, replied, "Not at all. I shovel out and God shovels in, and He uses a bigger shovel than I do. And God started the shoveling first."

Checkbooks Speak

Philip Guedalla, an eminent biographer, declared that the hardest problem the biographer faces is that of discovering the real person about whom he is to write. It is fairly easy, he said, to find out what the subject did, where the subject went, and what the subject said; but what kind of person lives inside is a different matter. Guedalla illustrated his point by citing his biography of the Duke of Wellington. He came across unimpeachable evidence when he discovered Wellington's old checkbooks.

A Christian Makes a Will

The average person is allergic to the idea of a will. To him or her it is surrounded with mysticism. Some feel that the drawing of a will is so personal that no one should talk to them about it. Others feel that writing a will is so simple they need no assistance. Still others feel that a will is for the well-to-do.

While a will is a legal instrument, and the most important one an individual can draft or cause to be written, it is more of a record of faith than a declaration of fortune. It is the individual's assurance of extending his or her influence into the future after death. It is, therefore, one's legal and spiritual resurrection.

Enjoy Your Philanthropy

Arnaud Marts published a provocative book entitled *The Generosity of Americans* (Prentice Hall, 1966), in which he reminded us that Americans give away more than $11 billion a year for the public good. With considerable beauty and detail, he shared an experience with the late H. W. Hoover, president of the Hoover Suction Sweeping Company of North Canton, Ohio. Hoover desired to discuss several matters with Marts. The industrialist went on to say he was born just a mile east of his factory and that life had been good to him. He wanted to register appreciation in his will and wondered if giving a hospital would be appropriate. Marts agreed to explore the idea. During the second conversation, the financial consultant pointed out that North Canton and Canton were only a few miles apart, that they had two fine hospitals, and that he might want to consider giving a YMCA to the community. He accepted the challenge and gave it while he was still alive.

To express its gratitude, the community published one copy of a *We Thank You* book. On its pages were the signatures of every person in the community—all two-thousand of them—except four who refused to sign. When this was presented to Mr. Hoover, he was too overcome to articulate his feelings. As the old man grew older and had more free time on his hands, he would go over to the lobby of the YMCA and watch men and boys come and go.

Development of the Tithe

First, ancient folk were admonished to bring the first fruits of their fields and flocks to worship. "The first of the first fruits of your ground you shall bring into the house of the Lord, your God" (Ex. 23:19). Scholars believe that the reference to the house of the Lord meant local shrines that were scattered throughout the country.

The second stage in the development of the tithe is seen in the directive to bring offerings to the Temple in Jerusalem. This was at least seven centuries before Christ. It also included a tithe, a tenth of all their possessions. Moreover, every third year a special tithe was taken for relief of the Levites, strangers, orphans, and widows.

The third stage in the development of the tithe is revealed in the acknowledgment of the Temple as the center of religion for Israel. "So shall you also present an offering to the Lord from all your tithes, which you receive from the people of Israel; and from it you shall give the Lord's offering to Aaron the priest" (Num. 18:28).

Feeding the Poor

During the 1971 World Synod of Bishops, England's Cardinal John Heenan shocked his fellow prelates by proposing that the Roman Catholic Church sell its valuable art treasures to feed the poor.

Giving Money

Christian giving is always a response. The motivation for our giving is that we have received. This doesn't mean we try to pay God back, for that is an impossibility. It does mean that our giving begins in gratitude.[1]

A Jar of Peaches

My first job out of seminary was to recruit students and raise money for Lynchburg College. It was a discouraging task in the 1930s. I shall never forget an elderly lady on whom I called for a special gift to the college. After listening to my presentation, the beautiful, dear soul explained: "Young man, I believe in what you are doing. I would like to help but I have lost everything." Then she excused herself from the room and presently returned, holding in her hands a jar of pickled peaches. "Would you accept this as a reminder of one who loves the church and the college but is unable to give at this time?"

Miracles Continue

Every denomination can boast of exceptionally committed stewards. Some are persons of average means who, according to the standards of the world, give beyond their means; and others, immensely wealthy, demonstrate astonishing generosity. Among many consistent stewards and philanthropists, the Christian Church (Disciples of Christ) points with pride and thanksgiving to Theodore Prentis Beasley, founder of The Republic National Life Insurance Company, Dallas, Texas, who, after fifty years of leadership, continued as board chairman emeritus, and who has given millions to church-related causes and institutions of the Christian Church. In fact, more than any other person.

A humble but confident man, Beasley testifies, "I have never had a bad day in the life insurance business. Of course, there have been trying days, but never bad days." Accompanying this attitude has been a prodding faith. "Miracles happen to those who believe in them."

My Largest Honorarium

When preaching in Latumbe, Africa, I was alerted by my host, John Ross, to the possibility of a visit from members of the church. Sure enough, about mid morning the following day, a delegation of some twenty members of the congregation came to the Ross home. They sang a hymn, thanked God for my visit, and prayed for my safe return. The spokesman of the group presented me with thirty francs—about sixty cents. I was inarticulate. Later I was told that it took these dear people about half a day to raise thirty francs; in fact, they had begun the previous afternoon. I was humbled and overcome as I realized there are people in the world who are that poor—yet that dedicated.

I shall never spend those thirty francs. I shall keep the gift to remind me of a people who sacrificed to lavish love on a stranger. This gift is recorded in my heart as the largest and most appreciated honorarium ever received.

Pledge Sunday

During a Sunday morning worship service in our sanctuary, a child wrote some notes. Among them was a brief message to God. The card was placed in an offering envelope which eventually reached me. It read, "Dear God, I love You. Do You love me? Answer yes."

When you are asked to write God a message on a pledge card, write it in such a way that He will know how much you love Him.

The Precious Moment

Charles Mercer said his father used to be a collector of sundial inscriptions, and for many years my favorite was: "It is later than you think." But more recently I've changed my mind. Today I prefer one that goes: "It's a long time till sundown."

Share Your Gratitude!

Canterbury Cathedral is a beautiful and historic place. Portions of this imposing structure date back to the twelfth century. Saint Thomas á Becket, Archbishop of Canterbury, was murdered in this cathedral four days after Christmas in 1170.

When Thomas was a baby, his mother would weigh him in a basket on his birthdays, then fill the basket with coins, food, and clothing to the identical weight of the child. Then she would go and share her good fortune and joy with the poor.

The Signature of Faith

In one large, prestigious church during our ministry the pastors buried 135 people, some of them extremely wealthy. Yet, to my knowledge, only fourteen left that church any of their worldly possessions. No one is ready to die until he or she has made a Christian will. Of course, it does not insure eternal life, but it does register faith in the future.

Step Out with God

Marcus Bach, longtime professor at the University of Iowa, shared this story. One budget Sunday, a man sat in his usual pew, thinking: *In what way is my life different from that of men who never go to church? What have I ever done that is unusual or startlingly religious?* He couldn't think of a single, solitary instance in which he felt he had distinguished himself as a Christian. He had attended church hundreds of times, but the services had never really taken hold of him. He recalled struggles, sacrifices, gambles in business, but he could not recall a single gamble for God! While in this mood, he noticed a blank pledge card in the pew rack before him. He picked it up, fingered it, then wrote five thousand dollars and dropped it in the offering plate.

That afternoon there was a knock at the layman's door. Pledge card in hand, there stood the minister, who had been told to clarify the pledge. He asked, hesitatingly, "Tell me, what's the meaning of this? Did you mean fifty dollars, or maybe five hundred? It says five *thousand* dollars!" "The amount is correct," replied the resentful layman, who allowed that he had been challenged many times "to step out with God," and "now that I have, you and the boys at church want to know if the amount of my pledge is correct."

Time: Not for Sale

The phenomenal philanthropist, Andrew Carnegie, desperately wanted more life. He felt he could make a lasting contribution to society if he had ten more years. He offered $200 million for another decade! That was $54,794 a day, thirty-eight dollars a minute. But no one could accommodate him.

Unredeemed Treasures

Some years ago, a ninety-four-year-old widow died in her home in Chicago. She was known as a collector of antiques. The administrator of her estate found an astonishing collection to things. There was a fifty-year-old collection of chinaware, paintings, and unopened trunks. It was reported that altogether there were twenty rooms packed with rare and expensive furnishings. A fortune in diamonds was found in the false bottom of an old trunk. A desk revealed five thousand dollars in cash, as well as many uncashed checks and money orders. Some of the checks were so old they were worthless, and many of the money orders were sent to Washington for redemption. What would you have done with such a vast fortune? Do you think the poor, rich woman knew what life was all about?

Like the eccentric lady in Chicago, we, too, are connoisseurs of what we term valuables, yet fail to use them properly, leaving the gifts and promises of God unclaimed.

Watch Out for the Status Quo

Once I stood in Carey's Chapel, Calcutta, listening to the pastor retell the courageous life of that noble pioneer. As never before, his life took on new light for me. But have Christians forgotten that in 1789, when William Carey announced he was going as a missionary to India, the East India Company vigorously protested? It was considered imprudent. An idealistic

missionary might jeopardize the high profits of their investments. Every generation has its Sadducees, guardians of the
status quo, coiners of the Temple tax, who persist in protecting
their vested interests.

Success

Genesis 2:1-3; Joshua 1:8; John 5:17; John 9:4

The door into life generally opens behind us . . . The sole wisdom
for [one] haunted with . . . the scent of unseen roses, is work.
—George MacDonald

I would rather fail in a cause that will ultimately succeed than to
succeed in a cause that will ultimately fail.
—Woodrow Wilson

Any Regrets?

The late Edgar Dewitt Jones, with whom I was associated in
Detroit, used to tell of his visit with the famous baseball player, Tyrus Raymond Cobb, better known as "Ty." They talked
baseball, of course, while other guests were arriving. Jones
congratulated him on his playing abilities. The soft-spoken
Georgian was in a pensive mood: "I have had a good time, and
I have been well paid, but I wish I had been a doctor and had
won distinction in that field. Then I could look back on years
that had been spent in helping people, setting broken bones,
and healing their hurts."

Are We Self-Destructing?

On a bitterly cold January day in Milwaukee, Wisconsin,
1983, twenty thousand persons waited in line to apply for
two-hundred jobs. Unemployment is a frightening Franken-
stein! Approximately twelve million persons were out of work

at the beginning of 1983. Unfortunately, and because of the changing industrial and social patterns, some of the old jobs will never return. Unemployment is not only the result of world recession, but also a creature of demography, changing life-styles, and automation.

While unemployment is at an all-time high, so is employment. More and more people are entering the marketplace. Approximately half of the 84 million women in America have entered the work force. Again, America is rapidly becoming a country that is service oriented rather than production oriented. This phenomenal transformation is taking its toll.

Have we inadvertently invited self-destruction? Have the prophets of industry lost their vision and verve? Has management become too rich and corpulent? Has labor's insistence on higher and higher wages priced their products beyond the reach of the populace? Are too many women placing their careers before their children? In one way or another, by philosophy or participation, we all have contributed to the plight of those who stand in unemployment lines.

Comments

It is work which gives flavor to life.
—Henri Amiel

I never did anything worth doing by accident nor did any of my inventions come by accident.
—Thomas A. Edison

Here on earth God's work must be truly our own.
—John F. Kennedy

No man is born into the world whose work is not born with him; there is always work, and tools to work . . . for those who will.
—James Russell Lowell

Do Something!

In *Poor Richard's Almanac,* Benjamin Franklin said,

If you would not be forgotten,
As soon as you are dead and rotten,
Either write things worth reading,
Or do things worth the writing.

Forced Labor

The New York Times News Service reported in November of 1982 that the CIA estimated that four million Soviet citizens were being compelled to perform some kind of forced labor.

It's Inside

Mike Douglas said in *When the Going Gets Tough* (Word, 1982) that the big houses and millions of dollars he has made don't mean success to him. "Success is something inside you. Success is the good things that people do for other people."

Knowing Where to Tap

A certain town in New England experienced a prolonged electrical failure. The best engineers at the power plant were unable to restore the power, whereupon one citizen recalled that a former engineer, now in retirement but living only a few miles away, might be consulted. He was brought in. He inspected the plant, the generators; then he took a wooden mallet and tapped in several places. Instantly the lights came on, whereupon he submitted this itemized bill to the town fathers: "2¢ for tapping; $1,000 for knowing where to tap."

Learning from Failure

"Whatever success I've attained," avowed George Hamid, "I owe to my failures. A hungry showman learns more from one resounding failure than he does from two successes!"

Looking for a Harbor

Arthur Miller's *Death of a Salesman* tells the pathetic story of the deterioration of a man obsessed with success—Willy Loman. He eventually loses his job. Desiring to be supportive, a son takes Willy out for an evening. As they prepare to leave, Willy's wife requests, "Be kind to your father, Son; he is only a little boat looking for a harbor."

One's Second Choice

Sir Walter Scott is remembered as a highly productive novelist. I shall never forget the feeling that captured me when I visited his beautiful home and magnificent library at Abbotsford, Scotland. This relatively frail man, who wrote over one-hundred books, wanted to be a poet. But it was his misfortune —or was it his good fortune?—that Byron was a better poet. So Scott took his second choice, storytelling, and mastered it.

On the Road Befriending Humankind

Paul Swanson, age seventy-nine, is a legend in North Carolina, known as the "rolling barrister." Since 1971, he has been practicing law on the road from his office in a battered 1969 Volkswagen bus which is equipped with an old typewriter, a sleeping bag, a kerosene heater, and law books. He is generally known and beloved. John Brubaker of Statesville, North Carolina, said: "Paul Swanson is a legend. That's what he is. There's no one like him."[1]

Order Out of Chaos

Harry Reasoner concluded his book, *Before the Colors Fade* (Alfred A. Knopf, 1981), with a Catholic theologian's definition of work: "Work is the effort of men and women to bring order out of the chaos left by original sin." You do not have to agree with this declaration to be challenged by it.

Phenomenal Production

Frequently referred to as the Michelangelo of the twentieth century, Pablo Picasso drove himself mercilessly toward perfection. Beyond personal assessment and criticism, Picasso's professional accomplishments are inconceivable. Think of a man producing two-hundred-thousand pieces of art in seventy-five years!

Pride in Your Work?

The preliminary results of a recent Gallup poll indicate that 84 percent of Americans—that's about five out of six—feel a great pride in their work. The author of *Why I'd Rather Work*, Henry Lee, wrote: "So I went back to work. The aches and pains gradually disappeared, the dreams sweetened." At seventy-one he felt a sense of purpose and pride in his life that only work gives.

Sex Discrimination

We are constantly reminded of sex discrimination, especially in corporate America. Ask Mary Cunningham, former Bendix executive. Obvious and subtle barriers to advancement are common. A financial manager of an industrial plant in Pittsburg said she worked for an executive who warned her, "Don't ever make any decisions without coming to Daddy."

Successful Failure!

Media reported in June of 1983 the bizarre story of Mortimer J. Adler, who completed the four-year curriculum at Columbia University in three years and was invited to join Phi Beta Kappa, but did not graduate with the class of 1923. The reason? He flunked the swimming test! He went on, however, to receive his Ph.D. at Columbia in 1928. Subsequently he wrote such scholarly works as: *Six Great Ideas* and *Aristotle for Everybody*. At the time of this writing he was chairman of the board of editors of *Encyclopedia Britannica* and director of the Institute for Philosophical Research in Chicago.

Incidently, after much delay and discussion, Columbia awarded the youthful scholar, Mortimer J. Adler, a bachelor's degree with the class of 1983.

Dr. Adler has also learned to swim!

The Supreme Worker

Jesus declared, "My Father is working still, and I am working" (John 5:17). Professing Christians must be workers not only for their own dignity and support but also because of the example of Jesus.

Taking a Chance

Remember the Great Depression? I do. My father, not a wealthy man but a well-to-do farmer, who also operated a fertilizer business, like so many lost everything except his good name and real estate. The economic crash came when I was a sophomore in college. In a tender, but realistic, mood, Father allowed: "Son, we have always wanted you to have the best of everything, but we have suffered heavy losses. I still have credit, and I can borrow whatever you need to finish school; or perhaps you would like to assume the responsibility yourself." I chose the latter course. Through academic, athletic, and ministerial scholarships, I saw myself through the rest of college and seminary.

How well I remember that frightening day in 1933 when I arrived in New Haven, Connecticut, via bus from Virginia. I had plenty of time to review my situation as I carried two heavy bags from the downtown common up Prospect Street to Yale University Divinity School. Was I presumptuous to be enrolling in one of the country's most prestigious and expensive schools when I had but five dollars in my pocket? What if I did not make it? These were low hurdles compared to my commitment and goal.

Watch Your Step

Actress Bette Davis quipped: "When you get to the top of the ladder, you will wish you had the things you dropped on the way up."

Content

I was too ambitious in my deed,
And thought to distance all men in success,
Till God came on me, marked the place, and said,
"Ill-doer, henceforth keep within this line,
Attempting less than others"—and I stand
And work among Christ's little ones, content.

—Elizabeth Barrett Browning

Time

*Numbers 7:10-12; Psalm 90:4; Ecclesiastes 3:1-8; John 11:9-10;
1 Corinthians 7:29-31*

A life of ease is not for any man, nor for any God.

—Thomas Carlyle

Time alone is irreplaceable.

—Douglas Southall Freeman

If all the year were playing holidays,/To sport would be as tedious as to work.

—William Shakespeare

Above Time

Writing in *The Eternal Now,* Paul Tillich declared: "There is no time after time, but there is eternity above time."

Are You Double-Parked?

Perhaps you saw the cartoon in *The New Yorker* depicting an

American couple dashing up the steps of the Louvre in Paris shouting, "Where's the *Mona Lisa?* We're double-parked!"

Physically, mentally, and emotionally we are all double-parked. We are in a hurry! Schedule is our master, the clock our altar. If we miss the signal light, we are uptight. We do not have time for conversation, for people, for family, or for the church.

Comments

Comedy writer Goodman Ace came up with a wonderful idea. He suggested that we have a thirteenth month, inserted between December and January. "It would be a month of quiet reflection," he proposed, "to remember things you've forgotten that would tidy up your life."

Benjamin Franklin referred to time as money.

Carl Sandburg compared time to a sandpile we run our fingers through, and it's gone.

> We have so little time and so much left to do.
> > —Henry Spencer Moore, British
> > octogenarian sculptor

> If nobody asks me about it, I know. If I want to explain it to somebody who asks me about it, I don't know.
> > —Augustine

> An hour can destroy them.
> > —Seneca

Day After Day

"We must work the works of him who sent me, while it is day; night comes, when no one can work" (see John 9:1-12). This tremendous passage inspired Elton Trueblood to entitle his autobiography *While It Is Day.* This eighth-generation Quaker, distinguished author, pastor, and professor took seriously John's admonition. To read the life of Trueblood is to become better acquainted with one who values time and the relevance of the gospel. He is a confirmed believer in discovering one's prime time and using it for first-class work.

Enough Time to . . .

In her syndicated column for November 11, 1971, Erma Bombeck reminded us that time hangs heavy over the heads of bored people, eludes the busy, flies by for the young, and runs out for the old. Perhaps we should view it, she counseled, through a child's eyes.

"When I was young, Daddy was going to throw me in the air and catch me and I would giggle until I couldn't giggle anymore; but he had to change the furnace filter, and there wasn't time."

There is always something else to do!

Miraculous Time

Matthew Arnold referred to time as "a daily miracle." Benjamin Franklin, in *Poor Richard's Almanac,* mused, "Don't squander time, for that's the stuff life's made of." Various proverbs and maxims have spoken of time as impossible to recall, to retrieve. The Christian should treasure every second of time, savoring the moments for the glory of his Lord. These "few precious days," to quote a phrase from a song, are but a prelude to eternity.

How Do You Measure It?

The astronomer measures time by light-years, the geologist by vast cycles, the historian by epics and centuries, the industrialist by the fiscal year, the salaried person by the month, the laborer by the weekly paycheck, the child by the birthday party. But for most of us the common measure of time begins with the awkward motions of rising in the morning and the weary movements at night. In this dimension we determine our day. While the vast majority of the hours are predetermined, planned for us, we nevertheless have precious tidbits of time which we are free to use and which ultimately determine the quality of our character and the degree of our commitment. The Lord measures time in terms of responsible living.

It Takes Time

The acorn becomes a giant oak tree; a seed of wheat germinates and with a colony of grains is worth the going price of a bushel. What a remarkable miracle occurs between the conception of a child and his growth to be a two-hundred-twenty-five-pound fullback!

Keeping the System Going

H. G. Wells predicted in his *The Time Machine* two species: the bright, joyous, delicate "eloi," living above ground in leisure and luxury; and the pale "morlocks," living below in dark caves, bending over machines that keep the system going.

Are we approaching this stratification in society? Are we losing identity, if not purpose, because we must keep the system going? Does it have to be this way?

Living with Two Questions

President James A. Garfield claimed that the whole history of humanity could be described as a struggle to answer two questions: (1) How can we gain a little leisure from our toil?, and (2) What do we do with leisure once we get it?

Love, Live, and Toil

The late Will Rogers had these lines engraved on a huge watch which he presented to David Rubinoff, the consummate violinist:

The Clock of Life is wound but once,
And no man has the power

To tell just when the hands will stop,
At late or early hour.

Now is the only time we own;
Love, life, toil with a will;
Do not wait until tomorrow,
For the Clock may then be still.

Make the Most of It

There is a remarkable headstone in the cemetery of Christ Church, Frederica, Georgia. A marble ball depicting the globe stands about four feet high. Written in circular fashion near the top of the sphere are these words: "Lois Mary McClain, born 11 May, 1930, married 29 December, 1956, died 25 July, 1960. The greatest maxim I can give is make the most of the hours you live."

Make Up Your Mind

You may recall that Alice in Wonderland said to the Cheshire Cat, "Would you tell me, please, which way I should go from here?"

"That depends a good deal on where you want to get to," said the cat.

"I don't much care where," said Alice.

"Then, it doesn't matter which way you go," the cat replied.

We don't live in a wonderland. We live in a hostile world with stern limitations. We cannot go just anywhere we want to go. The past is a closed door, and the future depends on what we do today and what it does to us. Time marches on!

Present Hour

The eminent American psychologist-philosopher William James once said: "The present hour is the decisive hour, and every day is doomsday."

Time and Eternity!

On one occasion a person who visited the Court of Sessions in England, returned late in the afternoon and found the same case still on and the same lawyer talking. He remarked to the eminent Lord Cockburn, "Surely he is wasting a great deal of time." "Time," the jurist replied. "Long ago has he exhausted time. Now he is encroaching upon eternity."

Statistics Speak

According to government statistics, the average American male works in a career for a period of thirty-eight years, while a female career worker averages twenty-eight years.

Take Your Time!

A cub reporter sat nervously at his desk. He had just returned from viewing a horrible accident. It was his big chance to make the front page of the newspaper. Noticing the false starts on the typewriter and anxiety etched in the lad's face, a seasoned reporter went over to the young man, and placed a hand on his shoulder, saying, "Take your time, Son. You have exactly five minutes."

The Time Is Now!

It is reported that every 8.6 seconds someone dies from starvation. Every minute, seven people die in the underdeveloped countries of the world as a result of illness related to malnutrition. That represents 417 deaths every hour.

> Come, O blessed of my Father, inherit the kingdom prepared for you from the foundation of the world; for I was hungry and you gave me food, I was thirsty and you gave me drink, I was a stranger and you welcomed me, I was naked and you clothed me, I was sick and you visited me, I was in prison and you came to me (Matt. 25:34-36).

Wasted by Time

Herman Wouk, in *The Caine Mutiny*, told about Willie Keigh, who was aboard a minesweeper when he received word from his doctor-father that he had an incurable disease that would soon claim his life. In this letter the father offered his son three bits of advice:

> There is nothing, nothing more precious than time.... Wasted hours destroy your life just as surely at the beginning as at the end.
> . . .
> Religion. I am afraid we haven't given you much, not having had much ourselves. But I think, after all, I will mail you a Bible before I go into the hospital.... get familiar with the words. You'll never regret it. I came to the Bible as I did to everything in life, too late. . . .
> Think of me and of what I might have been. . . . For my sake, for the sake of the father who took the wrong turns, take the right ones. . . . Good-bye, my son. Be a man.
>
> Dad.[1]

"What Time Is It?"

After delivering an energetic address, a popular speaker, turning to the audience, asked smilingly, "Are there any questions? Anyone have a question?" The silence was embarrassing. Finally a man toward the back of the room stood and stated, "I have a question." "Fine," retorted the encouraged guest. "And what is your question?"

"What time is it?"

The man's query was wiser than he knew. He was concerned about conditions in a yawning world, not the clock that sleepy people faced. Pressed by myriad appeals, bewildered by the proliferation of inventions and weaponry, disgusted by the pettifogging of politicians, this embattled American was asking: "In view of conflicting ideologies and national problems, what are our chances for a decent existence and survival?"

Vocation

Genesis 2:1-3; Genesis 3:19; John 5:17; John 9:4; 1 Corinthians 3:13; 2 Timothy 2:15

A career is usually considered the continuum along which an individual lives out his or her occupational choice.

—G. Curtis Jones

Thank God for work!

—Abbie Farwell Brown

Are You Haunted?

Most of us would fit into Charles Dickens's description of the *Haunted Man.* In this story, the skillful, provocative writer told of a chemistry professor by the name of Redlaw, who was widely known for his brilliance and leadership. Students flocked to his classes. Deep within, however, Professor Redlaw was haunted. He was tortured by memories. Outwardly he was a howling success; inwardly he was a flop, and he knew it!

Behind the Blue Jeans

"Blue jeans" were created by two impoverished men, one a tailor, the other a peddler. Levi Strauss, a Bavarian Jew, emigrated to the U. S. in 1848. He eked out a poor living selling "dry goods" from door to door. Later, in San Francisco, "he stitched a pair of heavy canvas and created the first pair of Levi pants." In 1872, a tailor by the name of Jacob W. Davis, who, after much hardship, had become successful with his own brand of three-dollar denims, wrote Strauss: "The Secratt of them pents is the Rivits that I put in those pockets." The two men became partners and there have been few design changes since 1873. Incidently, in the 1880s Levis sold for $13.50 a dozen![1]

Courage to Change Careers

The Englishman John Keats, born to the operator of a livery stable in 1795, through toil and discipline studied to be a surgeon. Meanwhile he met the literary giant, Leigh Hunt. Keats began to move in literary circles. In 1816 he gave up medicine and turned to poetry. He died at age twenty-six, but his poems will live forever.

Did She Answer Your Question?

Sally K. Ride, a thirty-one-year-old astrophysicist, has earned her right to be America's first woman in space, if not in the world. It is true that twenty years ago the Soviets launched Valentina Tereshkova into the "blue yonder," but her credentials were so weak—a millworker who jumped out of airplanes as a hobby—that no one outside of Russia took her accomplishment seriously. Not so with Sally Ride.

To begin with, she is brilliant, having excelled in such tough subjects as X-ray astronomy and free-electron lasers at Stanford University, from which she holds graduate degrees, including a Ph.D. Out of eight thousand applicants, she was chosen as one of thirty-five in the 1978 class of astronauts. NASA officials gave her high marks, indeed, saying she had "the right stuff."

Sally K. Ride's experiments in space not only raised high the banner of women's expertise but also signaled a perceptible change in America's social attitudes. Are brains, skill, courage, and stamina matters of gender?

Don't Cheat Yourself

A wealthy man commissioned a contractor to build the finest house he could imagine, whereupon the rich man went away for an extended period of time. When he returned from his world tour, the house was completed. With considerable pride, the builder showed the owner through it. Following inspection, the owner gave the builder back the keys saying, "The house is yours, but you must live in it." Then the botches stared at the builder. He remembered where he had cheated in the use of materials and workmanship.

Life has an uncanny way of forcing us to live in what we build.

Don't Let Down

Professor Cyrus Daniel, Nashville, Tennessee, is a marvelous musician. He was head of the music department at Vanderbilt University for twenty-five years. I had not seen him for a long, long time. As always, I asked him to play for me; and, at age eighty-three, he played a number of pieces on the grand piano, ranging from Bach to Yale's "Boola, Boola," from memory. His graceful fingers seemed as strong and supple as ever. Then he went to his study to play the organ. My first request was "Amazing Grace." Again, he played flawlessly. What's the secret? Music is his life; he still practices every day.

Do Someone a Favor

It was eleven o'clock Saturday night. Having covered more than six-hundred miles that day, we were road-weary and looked for a place to sleep. In the quiet city that claims to have more churches than gasoline stations—Memphis, Tennessee— we inquired about accommodations at an attractive motor court. Though the hour was late, the manager-owner was in and courteously informed us, "We are filled up and have been since six-thirty." Instead of being curt and disagreeable, the friendly man had his secretary telephone several places in an effort to place us for the night. The sixth call was successful.

I was greatly impressed by the general demeanor of the stranger and engaged him in conversation. Among other things, he said, "I came up the hard way. I have been here twenty-two years. We are now filled practically every night. I could have gone home at six o'clock, but I stayed and have assisted thirty people in finding lodging. . . . Whenever I feel my prosperity and good fortune, I think back on the hard days of this business and I stay around to do someone a favor."

Each Must Contribute

Pierre Teilhard de Chardin said in *The Future of Man:*

> If each of us can believe that he is working so that the Universe may be raised, in and through him, to a higher level—then a new spring of energy will well forth in the heart of Earth's workers.

Enjoy Your Work

The space shuttle *Challenger,* not being able to land in Florida, concluded its 2.5 million-mile trip at Edwards Air Force Base, California, Friday, June 24, 1983, after accomplishing fifty-six of its fifty-eight objectives. The five-member crew was professional, and happy, as they were interviewed. Sally Ride, America's first woman in space, summarized her reactions succinctly: "It was fun and I'm sure it will be the most fun I'll ever have in my life."

Entrepreneurs: The Survivors

There seems to be a never-ending list of entrepreneurs—those who make it big. Many who experience phenomenal success are beneficiaries of legacies, stumbled into paradise, learned from the mistakes of others, or were willing to take greater risks than some. And of course they all had a willingness to work harder. It is also frequently a matter of timing.

William C. Durant, founder of General Motors Corporation in 1916, was initially a manufacturer of wheelbarrows.

Bread and pastry products that bear the label Pepperidge Farm were not started by Mr. or Mrs. Pepperidge, but by Margaret Rudin, a Connecticut housewife who started baking whole wheat bread for her family. Requests for her bread increased over the years.

For every acclaimed entrepreneur, many more aspirants have failed. Durant was one of six-hundred Americans who entered the automobile manufacturing industry at the turn of the century. Henry Ford's success would not have been so spectacular without hundreds of failures before him.

Form of a Servant

The genetics of history continue to play a remarkable role in human groupings and responses. Primitive people found it necessary to band together for survival, and so do certain interest groups today. Ours is a self-serving society. We send our youth, if possible, to prestigious schools with the hope such an identity will automatically send them to the head of the class in the real world. We specialize in management training, not in servanthood.

In such a highly calibrated, competitive society, how are we to articulate, let alone emulate, the freedom, faith, and courage of Jesus? How are we to penetrate the tribal customs of the modern world with the gospel?

Knowing the difficulties involved in living not only in the secular world, but also in the community of faith, Paul rose to great literary and spiritual heights in writing to the prosperous Philippians. Aware of their sin and personal problems, the noble Christian articulated a gentle rebuff by recapitulating the nature and mission of Christ:

> Have this mind among yourselves, which is yours in Christ Jesus, who, though he was in the form of God, did not count equality with God a thing to be grasped, but emptied himself, taking the form of a servant (Phil. 2:5-7).

From Drudge to Genius

It was once my privilege to hear the great Ignace Jan Paderewski play the piano. This Polish artist and perfectionist practiced relentlessly. After he played for the Queen of England, she gushed, "Mr. Paderewski, you're a genius."

"That may be," he politely replied, "but before I was a genius I was a drudge."

Imagine That!

Elton Trueblood declared in *The New Man for Our Time* (Harper & Row, 1970) that the vocation of the Christian is threefold: "He is called to pray, to serve, and to think, and he is called to do all three together." Therefore, regardless of one's profession, calling, or means of livelihood, the central vocation of every Christian must be to witness to the glory and presence of Christ.

Long before I was senior pastor of University Christian Church (now First Christian), Des Moines, Iowa, I had heard of the work of Roy Huntoon, Sr. An active member of a Bible class, as well as the entire program of that large congregation, he eventually became concerned for the unchurched, volunteering his services, and preparing himself as a personal evangelist. Through the cooperation and support of his Sunday School class and the church staff, this man, a butcher by trade, organized his work and eventually devoted from two to four hours every working day to evangelism. Think of a man bringing in six-hundred additions to his church over a period of three years! While Roy was calling on prospects every afternoon, there were support teams at work screening prospects, organizing itineraries, and, above all, praying for his effectiveness. Imagine a layperson making evangelism his avocation!

Professional Togetherness

Within thirty minutes after President Reagan was shot March 30, 1981, he was in the operating room at George Washington University Hospital. The speed and efficiency of the rescue mission was phenomenal. However, that which impressed me was the teamwork of five physicians. George

Morales, fifty-four, an anesthesiologist formerly of Mexico, kept the President alive while Joseph Giordano, thirty-nine, a vascular surgeon from Union City, New Jersey, explored the abdomen for bleeding. Benjamin Aaron, from Kansas City, Missouri, and Kathleen Cheyney, thirty-two, from Washington, New Jersey, both thoracic surgeons, probed for the flattened twenty-two-caliber bullet in the President's lung. Sol Edelstein, thirty-four, from Detroit, chief of the emergency room, made sure all went smoothly. Five persons, highly skilled and committed to saving life, disregarding individual differences, functioned as a well-calibrated unit.[2]

Tuit

A contagious Christian handed me a lovely piece of white wood about the size of a half dollar which he frequently gives to confused individuals. On the front is printed in red letters TUIT. On the back is this statement: "I will put God first in my life when I get a round tuit."

Volunteers

In his book, *Point of the Lance,* Sargent Shriver said the secret and strength of the Peace Corps lies in the concept and contagion of volunteers. There is something chivalrous about answering the call to serve.

What Do You Think About?

Ralph Waldo Emerson was correct in asserting, "Man is what he thinks about all day long." That which he or she feeds on, the context of his/her experience, the playbacks from previous contacts, all have frightening and sometimes wonderful means of shaping and strengthening life.

Why?

In his autobiography, *As I See It,* J. Paul Getty referred to his five marriages and five divorces: "In short, five failures." Then one of the world's wealthiest persons asked this probing question: "How and why is it that I have been able to build my own automobile, drill oil wells, run an aircraft plant, build and head a business empire—yet remain unable to maintain even one satisfactory marital relationship?"[3]

Wise Builders

The Centennial of the Brooklyn Bridge was celebrated in May 1983. This amazing structure, measuring 5,989 feet long, has 14,361 miles of wire running through its cables, has an anchor plate that weighs twenty-three tons. It required fourteen years to build and cost $15 million. It was also expensive in human life—claiming some twenty persons over the span of its construction, including that of its architect, a German immigrant, John Roebling, who died before work began. The project also broke the health of his son, Colonel William A. Roebling, who assumed the project following his father's death. Colonel Roebling's wife, Emily, became the daily liaison between her husband and the on-job engineers.

I like this observation as reported in *Newsweek,* May 30, 1983: "Whoever has walked the bridge at sunset and seen Manhattan catch fire through this intricate set of abstract lines knows that Roebling had created a work of art."

There she stands, as majestic and strong as ever, documenting the admonition to build wisely. It is frequently referred to as the "Eighth Wonder of the World" (Read Matt. 7:21-29).

Would You Rather Be Somebody Else?

Living at a time when the general atmosphere and circumstances stimulate the antiself, some people regret they did not pursue a different career. The Danish philosopher of the nineteenth century, Sören Kierkegaard, declared he would have been happier if he had been a police spy. Richard Nixon always wanted to be a sportswriter. Norman Vincent Peale anticipated being a salesman, and Lena Horne a schoolteacher. Opera sing-er, Grace Bumbry, cherishes the thought of being a race-car driver. Bill Veeck of the baseball world dreamed of being a newspaperman.

Would you rather be somebody or something else?[4]

War

Exodus 32:15-18; Isaiah 41:12; Matthew 26:51-52; 2 Corinthians 10:3-6; Ephesians 6:10-20; James 4:1-4

We tend to become what we oppose.
                                        —French proverb

I am not a hawk or a dove. I just don't want my country to be a pigeon.
                                        —Senator Henry M. Jackson

It is not an army that we must train for war; it is a nation.
                                        —Woodrow Wilson

All but 168 Years

The late honored historians, Will and Ariel Durant, declared that of man's reported thirty-four hundred years-plus of written history, he has been at war all but 168 years.

Beyond Numbers

However spacious and democratic our philosophy of peace, compassionate our people, the truth is we were born in war and have continued in conflict. From the Revolutionary War of 1775, War of 1812, Mexican War of 1846, American Civil War of 1861, Spanish-American War of 1898, World Wars I and II, the Korean "Police Action," and the Vietnam conflict, some 37,355,049 men and women have been involved. We have suffered approximately 2,375,546 casualties. We lost 57,939 persons in Vietnam. What else did we lose?

War's Commands

How many mothers in how many lands
Have bowed with Mary in her agony,
In silence borne the wrath of war's commands,
When every hill is made a Calvary.

—Clyde McGee

Conscientious Objector Wins Medal

Private First Class Desmond T. Doss refused to fight for religious reasons in World War II. Joining the Medical Corps, he requested front-line duty, and distinguished himself as among the bravest of the brave. On Okinawa he lowered seventy-five wounded men from their besieged positions, one by one, to safety. Again he dodged grenades to rescue four fallen soldiers. When struck in the legs by grenade fragments, he waited five hours for assistance, only to give his stretcher to another wounded comrade. On another occasion, Doss was hit in the arm. Fashioning a splint for himself, he then crawled three-hundred yards to an aid station.

On October 12, 1945, President Harry Truman presented to Private Doss the nation's highest wartime decoration—the Medal of Honor. He was the first conscientious objector to be so recognized.

Disturbing Dictators

America was born in conflict. We have cherished and maintained the concept of revolution. If he were a dictator, Quentin Reynolds once indicated, the first book he would burn would be the Bible. "I would burn it because I would realize that the whole concept of democracy came out of that Book. The Greeks gave us the name for it, but the Bible gave us the philosophy."

From Finite to Infinite

There was a time when war was man's finite means of obtaining objectives. But with the advent of the atom and subsequent weaponry, modern war is now an infinite end in itself, as well as the end of everything as we know it. This is the gruesome prospect that awaits us.

Humiliating Memories

Horrors and deaths reported in the American Civil War continue to stagger the mind and condemn the conscience. It portrays inhumanity in its cruelest form. "God-fearing people" demanded that their enemies be made to suffer. Suffer they did. Not only in hand-to-hand fighting on battlefields, but also in stinky prison camps. One of the more infamous was at Andersonville, Georgia. Captured Union soldiers were herded together in open pens, exposed to the elements, half-naked, and half-starved. Disease and death were rampant. A Confederate surgeon reported to his superiors that he found thirty-thousand men jammed together on twenty-seven acres of land "with little or no attention to hygiene." Some ten thousand died in seven months; five thousand were found seriously ill with diarrhea. There were from ninety to 130 deaths at Andersonville every day.

Chicago civilians urged the Federal government to subject Confederate captives to similar treatment. Although not as large, the Southern prison camp at Elmira, New York, was equally as brutal and sickening. An Army surgeon inspected the camp of 8,344 men and found two thousand cases of scurvy. He asserted that at the current death rate the entire command would be committed to the hospital within the year and 36 percent would die. The camp surgeon had made frequent complaints to those in authority, "and his requisitions for medicines had been entirely ignored."[1]

Inequities of War

There are approximately 4.7 million people in El Salvador. The per capita income is supposedly about $655 per year. The State Department estimates there are five-thousand rebels and thirteen thousand government troops in the beleagured land. Media reports that we are putting $225 million a year into the Duarte government—this translates into about $50 per person, $17,300 per government soldier or $45,000 per rebel.[2]

Insensitivity

The year was 1941. The place: the Polish village of Minsk. Adolf Eichmann, Hitler's aide on Jewish affairs for the Third Reich, had been sent to witness the execution of five-thousand Jews. Although it was a cold morning, the condemned men, women, and children were ordered to dress down to their underwear. The hapless people walked the last hundred yards of the death march, then jumped into a pit that had been prepared. Observer Eichmann was impressed by the obedience and orderliness of the victims, who apparently had made their peace with death. Then came a barrage of gunfire. Children screamed. Eichmann saw one woman hold her baby high, pleading, "Shoot me, but please let my baby live. Take my baby. Please take my baby."

Eichmann had children of his own, and for a moment he seemed to have felt a twinge of compassion. But before he could voice an order, the baby was hit. "I scarcely spoke a word to the chauffeur on the trip back," he later reported. "I was thinking. I was reflecting about the meaning of life in general."

Merchants of Death

The United Business Service of Boston reports that the No. 1 growth industry in America is defense. Defense expenditures increased 51.8 percent in dollars between fiscal years 1978 and

1981. Another jump of 38.4 percent is anticipated from 1983 to 1985.

Monetary Costs

Some ingenious statistician has estimated that in Julius Caesar's day it cost seventy-five cents to kill a man in battle; in Napoleon's, three-thousand dollars; the Civil War, five-thousand dollars; World War I, twenty-one-thousand dollars; World War II, fifty-thousand dollars; and considerably more in the Korean and Vietnam Wars. Who would dare estimate the cost of World War III?

My Brother

A British soldier who had gone through the terrible ordeal of Dunkirk during World War II, when safely back in England, was asked, "What did it feel like out there on the beach with the sea in front of you, the German army in back of you, and bombs overhead?" He answered, "It was a strange feeling. I felt that every man on the beach was my brother."

No Cheering Dreams

Following Neville Chamberlain's resignation, Sir Winston Spencer Churchill became prime minister of Great Britain, May 10, 1940. In rhetoric that rings with poetry, Churchill described his feelings as he left "the political wilderness" to assume the awesome leadership of his country. "I felt as if I were walking with destiny, and that all my past life had been a preparation for this hour and for this trial. . . . Therefore, although impatient for the morning I slept soundly and had no need for cheering dreams. Facts are better than dreams."[3]

Punishment Continues

Dr. Roland H. Bainton reminded us that the early church was the first peace society. The New Testament is a book without a battle. History indicates that until AD 175 the church was completely pacifistic. Until that date, no Christian could become a soldier after baptism. Another distinguished church historian, Kenneth Scott Latourette, told of a young Christian who was killed in AD 295 because he refused to enroll as a soldier.

There has been little change in civic attitudes: pacifists are imprisoned or otherwise punished for their refusal to register or to fight.

"Rules of War"

Gideon Hausner's *Justice in Jerusalem* (Harper & Row, 1966) is a dramatic and brilliant recounting of events preceding and during the trial of Adolf Eichmann for his role in the massacre of millions of Jews. As chief prosecutor in the case, Hausner detailed the trial as well as the demeanor of Eichmann, who was told on May 31, 1962, that his petition had been refused and that his execution would take place about midnight.

Having declined religious counsel, he asked that fetters be loosened from his ankles so he could stand straight. He refused the customary black hood; sent greetings to his family, and to Germany, Austria, and Argentina, countries that had befriended him. Moments before the execution he said: "I had to obey the rules of war and my flag."

Survival not Enough

In his book, *The Price of Peace,* Ambassador James Wadsworth said it is our responsibility to "take the lead in organizing the world's instinct for survival."

A Theft from Humankind

Dwight D. Eisenhower said during his presidency that every gun that is made, every warship launched, every rocket fired, signifies in the final sense, a theft from those who hunger and are not fed, those who are cold and are not clothed.

Three Positions

Roland H. Bainton, who still wrote, lectured, and traveled in his eighties, said there are three common positions on war and peace.

The first is represented by *Crusaders*. A Crusader is absolutely certain that his/her position is the correct one, and therefore does not hesitate to impose it on others. Since they are confident of their interpretation of justice, they believe it is also God's. Wars fought in this spirit have been and continue to be merciless.

A second position is at the opposite end of the spectrum, *Pacifism*. The heart of this belief is that any form of violence, especially organized violence, such as war, is unchristian. Not all pacifists oppose all forms of force, only force that involves violence and death.

In between these extremes is the position represented by the attitude of a *Just War*. This, too, is tricky, because every war, I suppose, in the eyes of some, was or is justified. The quintessence of this posture is that when all else fails, war may be necessary.

Without Guns

Reports indicate that the civilian toll from the Lebanese massacre of 1982 left these grim graphics: the dead, ten thousand; the wounded, seventeen thousand; the homeless, six-hundred thousand.

What Good Does It Do?

In *The Joyful Christian*, C. S. Lewis, speaking from the viewpoint of one of Satan's demons, said: "War is entertaining. . . . But what permanent good does it do us unless we make use of it for bringing souls to Our Father Below?"

World

2 Samuel 22:16-19; Psalm 9:7-8; Psalm 24:1-2; 2 Corinthians 5:19-21;
1 John 2:15-17

The created world is but a small parenthesis in eternity.
—Sir Thomas Browne

The world is too much with us; late and soon, Getting and spending,
we lay waste our powers.
—William Wordsworth

Are You in This World?

With an unprecedented number of Americans out of work,
a reporter visited the famous Ocean Reef Club, Key Largo,
Florida. This exclusive club has a membership of about thirty-
five hundred, most of whom are millionaires or approaching it.
On this day, the men had just returned from their yachts,
tennis courts, and the links, and were ecstatic over the exotic
buffet of expensive and colorful foods. When asked, "Is there
a recession here?" a member replied, "I don't know of anyone
who has been laid off or anyone who is hungry. That isn't part
of our world."[1]

Bacteria-Filled

Dr. Philip Blaiberg, dentist, Cape Town, South Africa, was
the second man to successfully receive a heart from another
person; and he told his story in the fascinating book, *Looking at
My Heart.*

At last a heart was donated to the dying patient by the wife
of a black man who had sustained a brain injury while playing
on the beach. The long, tedious operation, performed by a team
of fifty-one men and women on January 2, 1968, was successful. That which followed was also remarkable.

After living for weeks in a sterile room where every conceivable precaution was followed to safeguard the patient's health, at the time of his discharge March 16, 1968, doctors and nurses discarded their gowns and masks as Dr. Christiaan Barnard said: "Dr. Blaiberg is passing into a bacteria-filled world."

What an accurate description of our day. However serene, sterile, isolated, protected, we are living in a bacteria-filled world where physical and emotional survival is a challenge and no one can guarantee it.

Brotherhood

There was found among the papers and writings of the late F. Scott Fitzgerald the plot for an unwritten play. It centered about five widely separated members of a family who would inherit a stately house if they agreed to live in it together. This, of course, is more than a figment of Fitzgerald's imagination. It is indeed the perilous plot and plight of the race. Either we must learn the lessons of brotherhood or we shall soon hear the commital service for the neighborhood.

The Challenger and the Carriage

Ironically, during the 1983 textbook-perfect flight of America's space shuttle, *Challenger,* with five persons aboard, traveling at about seventeen-thousand miles an hour, in search of new frontiers for humankind, television pictured Queen Elizabeth en route to Parliament in an ornate horse-drawn carriage. The space explorers were betting their lives on scientific data, experience of others, and their own abilities to survive; the Queen, enveloped in luxury and security, bumped along to the rhythm of horses' hooves.

The contrasting worlds projected brought to mind the comment attributed to Canon Alexander of Saint Paul's Cathedral, London, who estimated, by what standards I do not know, that the historic Cathedral was moving down Fleet Street at the rate of one inch every hundred years!

A Community Perspective

An ingenious soul has endeavored to reduce the world's population into a community of one-hundred people. If this were possible, the community would look something like this:

Six persons would be from the United States; ninety-four from elsewhere.

These six would own half of the money in the world; ninety-four would share the rest.

Six would have fifteen times more material possessions than the other ninety-four put together.

These six would have 72 percent more of the food than required; two-thirds of the ninety-four would live below food standards and several would be starving.

The life span of these six Americans would be seventy years; the life span of the rest would be thirty-nine years.

Of the ninety-four, thirty-three of these people would be from countries where Christian faith is taught. Of the thirty-three, twenty-four would be Catholic, nine would be Protestant.

Less than one half of the ninety-four would have heard of the name Jesus, but the majority of them would know of Lenin.

In the community library there would be at least three Communist documents which would outsell the Bible.

And the perceptive mathematician concluded by conjecturing that by the year 2000, fifty of the one-hundred persons will be Asian.

The Controlling Center

"What has Athens to do with Jerusalem?" This query voiced by Tertullian continues. While Athens may not have much to do with Jerusalem, Jerusalem's cross has everything to do with the destiny of Athens, Washington, Moscow—and the rest of the world.

God's Fathomless World

The *Pioneer 10* spacecraft was launched in 1972 with a five-year mission to visit Jupiter and Saturn. Scientists expected it to stop transmitting years ago. Not so; it continues! In June 1983, *Pioneer 10* became the first man-made object to leave the solar system, passing beyond the 2.8 billion-mile orbit of Neptune. Predictions of the behavior of the small craft are now as mysterious as the deep space it penetrates.

Astrophysicists are hoping that *Pioneer 10* will discover the boundary of "the heliosphere and to find evidence of the suspected tenth planet." Upon leaving the solar system, *Pioneer* will, it is believed, wander through the Milky Way forever, encountering, perhaps, another star system once every million years. Think of it!

How large is your world?

Hardware Overhead

According to *The Sarasota Herald-Tribune* for January 8, 1983, the number of satellites in space is frightening and growing: The United States has 2,652; USSR, 1,967; Japan, forty-eight; International Telephone Space Organization, twenty-eight; France, twenty-five; European Space Association, thirteen; Canada, eleven; United Kingdom, ten; NATO, five; India, five; West Germany, four; China, four; Indonesia, two; France and Germany, two; Italy, one; Australia, one; and Spain, one. This totals 4,779. This is a lot of hardware floating over our heads. Is this the beginning of "star wars"?

Human Population

Demographers maintain that if the present birth rate continues, in nine-hundred years there will be 60 million billion people in the world. This is one-hundred persons for each square yard of the earth's surface. Conjure, if you can, the inconceivable problems of housing, feeding, educating, and teaching this mass of humanity.

What unpredictable forces—disease, famine, genocide, war, pestilence—will prevent this demographic projection?

It Could Be Beautiful!

One of the illustrious prisoners of World War II was Viktor Frankl. He put down in his classic book, *Man's Search for Meaning,* some of his experiences in a Nazi prison camp. He said deprivation made the eye more observant, the ear more attentive. While in a Bavarian camp, a prisoner came running into the building from the compound one evening as they were eating their customary soup and cried for them to rush out in the small yard to see the beauty of the sunset.

Tired as they were, they went out and stood in hushed silence watching the brilliant hues of the evening sky running the spectrum from red to steel blue. In fact, the rays of the sun on the muddy water standing in puddles on the ground looked beautiful. After several undisturbed minutes a prisoner said, "How beautiful the world could be."

Perception

What Benjamin Disraeli once said about Europe over a century ago could apply with equal relevancy to America: "The European talks of progress because by the aid of a few scientific discoveries he has established a society which has mistaken comfort for civilization."

Persons: Greater Than the Universe

Blaise Pascal, seventeenth-century French philosopher and mathematician, was one of the fathers of modern science. He confessed that when he viewed the universe he was terrified and wondered if he were a straw or an atom. But in his finer moments he knew he was greater than the universe because he could think about the universe; the universe did not think about him.

Repay with Kindness

Wherever it is found, the church offers fellowship, creates an atmosphere in which worship is possible and love is communicated. A never-to-be-forgotten experience of a few years ago was to worship in the Central Methodist Church in a city in Ghana, West Africa. It was a large congregation with perhaps a thousand souls in attendance. Insofar as I could tell, I was the only white person present. It was a long service. The last twenty minutes were in English, and I have always felt that portion was for my benefit.

Following worship, many members greeted me, and one invited me to his home for tea. Subsequently my new friend came to the hotel for three straight mornings to inquire of my welfare and to show me around the city. One day I made bold to ask, "You have been so kind to me. Why?"

Whereupon he said, "First of all I am a Christian, and in the next place we have a son studying medicine in London. He would not be there were it not for the support and encouragement of my white friends. The only possible way I can repay them is to be kind to someone else."

Spiritual Convergence

In *The World Challenge,* Jean-Jacques Servan-Schreiber referred to our age as the "age of convergence: the coming together of ancient intuitions and new discoveries in the realms of mathematics, logic and physics." Then he talked about "calculation" being the starting point as well as the end.

What if representatives of the religious traditions and denominations in America, indeed, the world, were to see the increasing necessity to implement the great priestly prayer of our Lord: "Holy Father, keep them in thy name which thou hast given me, that they may be one, even as we are one" (John

17:11*b*). What an invitation to participate in spiritual convergence!

Stored Food and Wasting People

An editorial in *The Wall Street Journal,* March 22, 1983, titled "Dairy Dementia," caught my eye. The author was discussing the subsidization of dairy farmers. The government will soon charge them fifty cents for each hundred pounds of milk they sell. "The levy is supposed to provide a two-for-one reward." The price support has been sufficiently encouraging for farmers to produce more milk than needed. The extra food is stored by the government at enormous costs—$2 billion in price supports in 1982. It is reported that the government has in storage: 415 million pounds of butter; 725 million pounds of cheese; and 1.2 billion pounds of dry milk.

How can one justify such surpluses and expenditures in a hungry world that may have 20 million refugees?

Trading Places

Albert Rosen is a Jew who for several years has worked for a Christian on Christmas Eve. He has traded places with a telephone operator, a guard, a police radio dispatcher, a disc jockey, mail handler, and others.

In 1982 Rosen spent Christmas Eve filling in as a television news reporter. Then sixty-five years old, the housewares salesman said he does the job without pay "in the spirit of brotherhood for my fellowman."[2]

"I'm Sane! I'm Sane!"

In his critically acclaimed 1980 film *The Big One,* director Samuel Fuller used a realistic World War II scenario to demonstrate the absurdity of war. Perhaps the most telling image came from a Belgian insane asylum temporarily being shared by Nazi regulars.

It is mealtime, and the patients routinely shovel down their food, totally oblivious to the German troops sharing the dining hall. When a lady in red enters and begins to dance atop the tables the Germans watch leeringly, but the patients are unmoved. Then in a hail of gunfire a squad of American soldiers storms the dining hall, bodies flying left and right. In the midst of the deadly chaos, the patients continue to eat calmly. Finally, one of their number responds. Lifting a fallen machine gun, he leaps to his feet and begins to fire wildly, shouting all the time, "I'm like you! I'm sane! I'm sane!"[3]

Who Runs the World?

Who runs the world? God used to run it, but now many say, "He is dead." So, who runs it?

Some claim the Communists are running the world. They seem to have a timetable and they appear to be on schedule. Apprehensive souls remind us of their cunningness and cruelty in Afghanistan, Europe, the Middle East, South America, Central America, the United States, and Vietnam.

Some whites are sure the blacks are calling the domestic shots, are telling "Whitey" what he must do in government, housing, and employment.

Still others accuse the Jews of tilting the foreign policy of the United States, especially where Israel is concerned.

Who runs the world? Politicians? Blacks? Labor unions? Students? Environmentalists? The Pentagon? Who runs the world? Be not deceived—God is in control!

Listen to His redeeming Son: "In the world you have tribulation; but be of good cheer, I have overcome the world" (John 16:33*b*).

World Without Frontiers

Space explorations have revealed fascinating facts about the physical world and its inhabitants.

I heard a space scientist say that traveling and living in space is not too far away. The Soviets are flying regular missions to space stations. We are accelerating schedules and experiments. Industry is exploring the manufacturing possibilities of certain products, especially in the area of pharmaceuticals, because of the advantages of the purity of zero gravity.

This same scientist also believes that among the first category of individuals to be recruited for space travel will be those in the fields of communication, those able to record and transmit information to their earth-locked citizens.

Interestingly enough, the elderly, those capable of taking the optioned celestial voyage, would add appreciably to their years, for living in zero gravity is less strenuous. Ultimately it is the weight of gravity that kills us, pulls down the face, shoulders, and heart. For quite a different reason, youth would be eager for the adventure, particularly those wishing to be taller. Living in space for a few months, since it would untangle and straighten the backbone, would add an inch or two to one's height. These and other phenomenal possibilities await the courageous.

A world without frontiers is emerging!

Wouldn't It Be Wonderful?

There is a remarkable scene in Laura Z. Hobson's *Gentlemen's Agreement*. The proud mother reads her son's brilliant manuscript wherein he pleads for tolerance and cooperation among the peoples of the earth. With considerable perception she says: "Wouldn't it be wonderful if this could be everybody's century—not the white man's century or the atomic century, but everybody's century?"

Worship

2 Kings 17:36; Psalm 95:6-7; Isaiah 27:13; Luke 4:8; Acts 17:23; Philippians 3:3

Worship is transcendent wonder.
—Thomas Carlyle

O weary hearts! O slumbering eyes!
O drooping souls whose destinies
Are fraught with fear and pain
Ye shall be loved again!
—Henry Wadsworth Longfellow

Worship is just a dignified, polite but very personal way of getting in touch with God.
—Norman Richardson

Being Aware of God

While visiting an Indian surgeon friend named Dayal Sukhnandan, in Mungeli, I was impressed with this inscription prominently placed on the wall in the stark operating room: "Thou, God, Seest Me."

Have an altar where you work!

Boundless Love

The American Church in Paris is a beautiful edifice. The service is dignified and challenging. It is always a cosmopolitan congregation, with persons from many countries present. In groups of twenty to fifty we walked down the aisle and knelt at the rail by or between strangers to receive the common meal of the church, Communion. No one felt embarrassed and no one felt out of place, for indeed we were at the Lord's table. Afterwards I said to the pastor, "This is the church! It knows no bounds save that of self. It is worship without frontiers."

Centering Moments

Deceitful old Jacob encountered a Presence that would not go away one night as he slept fitfully beneath the clockwork of the stars (Gen. 32).

Young Samuel, aide to old Eli in the Temple, heard a disturbing Voice. He thought it was the priest and ran to Eli's cot. But it was not. After the third call, Eli counseled Samuel to say, "Speak, Lord, for thy servant hears" (see 1 Sam. 3:1-21).

Saul found the Lord—or rather he was overtaken by Him—on the road to Damascus. Saul was suddenly enveloped in light. He heard a voice, "Saul, Saul, why do you persecute Me?" Saul's name was changed to Paul. He became the most powerful Christian of all time, save Christ Himself (see Acts 9:1-22).

A centering moment came to Martin Luther on a sultry day in July of 1505. While walking a dusty road, a thunderstorm developed and a bolt of lightning felled him. Confused and in pain, he cried, "St. Anne, help me! I will become a monk." Luther kept his word, but at last this spacious spirit sought greater freedom than the Roman Church offered.

Choose Your God

Joshua, who had been chosen to succeed Moses and who, unlike his predecessor, had been privileged to enter the Promised Land, assembled his people to remind them of the mighty acts of God. He assured them that Yahweh would continue to bless them if they were faithful.

The Israelites, like all people, were confronted by alternatives. Some were interested in materialistic gods. Joshua knew this and challenged them to choose their god. He did not want them to live by half choices, convenient choices, or popular ones. The climax to his valedictory was "Choose this day whom you will serve, whether the gods your fathers served in the region beyond the River, or the gods of the Amorites

. . . but as for me and my house, we will serve the Lord" (Josh. 24:15).

Encounter Brings Strength and Joy

When we yield ourselves completely to God's guidance, then He creates periods of tranquility. The sabbath and the sabbatical year are examples of the oldest division of time. God enables us to sleep better, to be more alert when awake; He bestows on us an unusual capacity for work, and on the other hand, time for "blissful idleness"; He challenges us to the last extremity, and provides the deepest joy of the moment.

Growing Together

While a student at Yale, I would worship frequently in famed Batell Chapel, to whose pulpit came some of the greatest preachers in the world. A never-to-be-forgotten experience from worshiping there was to see Mrs. J. R. Angel, wife of the president, and their brood, a little staircase of heads, file into their pew. You may say, "But they were unusual children!" Perhaps, but they were children. They wiggled, they whispered, they yawned! They did not, I am sure, know everything that was going on. Neither did I! But something was going on in their little minds and hearts. They were being exposed to an atmosphere, a trust that is all-essential in building family and spiritual togetherness.

Lifting Power

The Panama Canal is a fascinating engineering feat that stands the test of modern engineering. A series of locks lifts a vessel from sea level over the continental divide. It requires seven hours for a ship to go through the locks—a distance of some fifty miles—and once committed, there is no turning back. It cannot go under its own power; it must be guided. Thus the terrain is made even by pushing up water through a series of chambers, connecting in a marvelous way the Pacific and Atlantic oceans.

Likewise, the committed person has been lifted by the grace of God to a new level of life.

Listen to God

We believe so many things absolutely have to be done, and, in addition, we do so many things because they are prompted by our secret motives, that our days and lives are too short. It does not follow that one first should fulfill his duty, then satisfy his own desires, and finally the time that remains listen to God. Generally not much time is left. It should be the other way around: First listen to God and place in His hands our entire lives. Only then will we be able to correctly apportion our time.

With God, the person always comes first and, after that, things. Everything, even the sabbath, exists for the sake of humankind.

Music Makers

When recording artist Pat Boone was two-and-a-half million dollars in debt, this verse was among those that initiated change in his life:

O sing to the Lord a new song;
sing to the Lord, all the earth!
Sing to the Lord, bless his name;
tell of his salvation from day to day (Ps. 96:1-2).

Subsequently, he wrote his book, *A New Song*. There is a sense in which the Bible is a music library; it is filled with poetry, songs of praise, and promise. Aristotle maintained that music was the most moral of all the arts.

Practicing the Presence

John Marshall was not only a distinguished jurist but a splendid churchman. After his wife's death, we are told, he would go to her room every Sunday afternoon and read aloud the Collect and the Gospel for that day as if she were by his side. It may sound sentimental, but can you imagine a Chief Justice being sentimental?

Reflective Moments

Corporate worship is essential to Christian nurture and growth. Important as is church attendance, reflective, private moments of meditation also nourish the spirit.

During our ministry in Richmond, Virginia, the downtown church building was sold to a business firm and the congregation relocated in the west end of the city. The old, Gothic, stone structure was razed and in due time a restaurant stood at the corner of Seventh and Grace Streets. One day a waitress noticed an elderly man sitting at a table with bowed head. After observing him for a few minutes, she reported the unusual posture of the person to the manager. Adroitly, the man in charge asked if he were well and if he could bring him something.

Raising his head, my friend, introducing himself, said: "I am quite all right, thank you. I was an elder in old Seventh Street Christian Church, and this spot is about where the Communion table was, and I am just saying my prayers."

The astonished manager replied: "Friend, you are welcome here at any time, and remember when you come to say your prayers, you are our table guest."

What a unique upper room!

Send Me!

It was the year that King Uzziah died! (Isa. 6:1*ff.*) Uzziah was a great king, the only one Isaiah really knew. It was the end of an epoch. The brilliant past was fading.

On that historic and haunting day, Isaiah saw the Lord. Perhaps the crowds had left the Temple and he was left alone. As he meditated, the walls seemed to fall away and everything assumed giant proportions. Watching the ancient ceremony so rich in color, symbolism, and music, suddenly it all came alive. He was in the presence of God! In those moments of high ecstasy Isaiah felt his unworthiness, confessed his sin, and was immediately cleansed. During the profound and personal dialogue that followed, Isaiah heard a voice asking, "Whom shall I send, and who will go for us?" With deep meaning and commitment, the prophet answered, "Here am I! Send me" (Isa. 6:8).

Sensing His Presence

The word *presence* is variously used today. We refer to a political or a military presence in strategic places of the world. We say she or he has an impressive presence. And then, there is an awareness, an invisible presence without the physical image. T. S. Eliot once commented that we frequently discover and walk with companions not of our own generation.

We know this to be true. Lincoln is as alive to many today as when he walked the streets of Springfield, Illinois. No one can visit those areas in Africa so familiar to Livingstone without visualizing his work and sensing his presence, or Monticello without being impacted by the mighty accomplishments of Jefferson.

Worship is sensing and responding to the presence of God.

Spiritual Nourishment

William Temple once said:

Worship is the nourishment of the mind upon God's truth. Worship is the quickening of the conscience by God's holiness. Worship is the

cleansing of the imagination by God's beauty. Worship is the response
of my life to God's plan for my life.[1]

Stay in Tune

Ted Malone, whose radio show came on early in the morning, told of the Idaho shepherd who wrote: "Will you, on your
broadcast, strike the note 'A'? I'm a sheepherder way out here
on a ranch, far away from a piano. The only comfort I have is
my old violin. It's all out of tune. Would you strike 'A' so that
I might get in tune?"

Malone honored the request. Later he received a "thank-
you" note from the distant shepherd saying, "Now I'm in
tune."

One of the purposes and responsibilities of personal and
public worship is to enable the aspirant to keep tuned to the
Great Shepherd. One of the joys of the Christian life is to help
others recapture the missing note!

A Universal Language

In 1957 the play *The Music Man,* appeared. Written by Mere-
dith Willson, it focused on middle America in the year about
1912. Harold Hill, a salesman, toured the country selling musical instruments and teaching children how to play. The miracle, of course, was that everyone discovered they had some
musical talent. There is something marvelous and bonding
about music, which is a universal language.

Uncoerced

For a number of months I tried to be of comfort to a neighbor
dying with cancer. His costly illness had stretched over ten
years. Although our religious persuasions differed, we were
close friends; and I endeavored to minister to him without
usurping the prerogatives of his pastor. One day, as I stood to
leave, I quoted the twenty-third Psalm. To my amazement, he
followed along with me. On another occasion, at his invitation,

I offered a prayer. When I concluded, he prayed for me. What a touching experience.

Deep, meaningful spiritual encounters frequently occur in unsuspected places and in uncoerced ways.

What Is God's Will?

In the *Sound of Music,* at the close of a frustrating day, the Reverend Mother asks Maria why she has come to the convent. Hesitating, the distraught girl replies, "To discover and do the will of God."

Worship Reminders

Thou shalt not come to service late,
    nor for the amen refuse to wait.
When speaks the organ's sweet refrain,
    the noisy tongue thou shalt refrain.
But when the hymns are sounded out,
    thou shalt lift thy voice and shout
And when the anthem thou shalt hear,
    thy sticky voice thou shalt not clear.
The endmost seat thou shalt leave free,
    for more must share the pew with thee.
The offering plate thou shalt not fear,
    but give thine uttermost with cheer.
Thou shalt the minister give heed,
    nor blame him when thou art disagreed.
Unto thy neighbor thou shalt bend,
    and, if a stranger, make a friend.
Thou shalt in every way be compassionate, kind,
    considerate, and of tender mind.
And so, by all thy spirit's grace,
    thou shalt show God within this place.[2]

You Served Me in Jerusalem

Traveling with a predominantly church group in the Middle and Far East, we found ourselves in Jerusalem one Saturday.

Some felt it would be appropriate to have a worship service near some historic place. The site selected was that of Gordon's Calvary near the Damascus Gate. Preparations were made for worship, including the Lord's Supper. That afternoon I received word that I had been selected as preacher. As much as I appreciated the invitation, without more lead time, my library, and preaching notes, I felt doubly inadequate. But what a place to preach!

Saturday evening was spent contemplating Sunday's message. I finally selected for my theme: "Remember Jesus Christ." The subject, of course, was lifted from Paul's Letter to Timothy:

> Remember Jesus Christ, risen from the dead, descended from David, as preached in my gospel, the gospel for which I am suffering and wearing fetters like a criminal. But the word of God is not fettered (2 Tim. 2:8-9).

The little company of friends, travelers, and a few strangers met at the appointed hour. Following the meditation, as agreed, Communion was served individually. With simple words of invitation, each person came forward, knelt on a rock, and received the loaf and cup. It was a moving experience.

Years later, when we lived in Saint Louis, during the fellowship period following morning worship, a stranger approached, introduced himself, and said: "You served me Communion in Jerusalem." In a far more significant context, we were all served Communion in Jerusalem.

Youth

Genesis 8:20-21; Psalm 25:7; Ecclesiastes 12:1-8; Luke 18:21; 1 Timothy 4:12

Young people need to fall in love with their futures.
—George Burns

Almost everything that is great has been done by youth.
—Benjamin Disraeli

It is better to be a young June-bug than an old bird of paradise.
—Mark Twain

Alone with God

Rufus Jones was one of the most remarkable men of our generation. This brilliant Quaker was a man of unbelievable capacities, endurance, and faith. Imagine a busy man publishing fifty books and six-hundred articles! However, the friendly Quaker did not suddenly appear as God's "Superman." There was a wonderful family behind him.

The story goes that one day Rufus was given the responsibility of weeding the turnip patch. He had scarcely begun his work when a friend came along and persuaded him to go fishing, promising to help him with the weeding later. No fisherman pays much attention to time, and when young Rufus returned home, it was dark. His mother was waiting for him. Silently she led him to his room. He expected the worst, but received the best. His mother put him in a chair, knelt down, put her hands on him, and prayed, "O God, take this boy of mine and make him the boy and man he is divinely designed to be." Then she kissed him and left him alone with God.

Be Good Doctors

Our story comes from the Baylor University School of Medicine. Rick Fox, a superior student and athlete from Colorado, enrolled in the Baylor Medical School, and at the end of his first year he was "top man" in his class. He had always wanted to be a doctor. During his second year, Rick complained of stomach pains, which were eventually diagnosed as terminal cancer.

Upon hearing the news, Rick said to the doctor, "Let me have thirty minutes alone with God." At the end of the period, he called back the doctor and nurses and told them he wanted to offer himself "as a laboratory specimen," declaring he would keep notes of changes and reactions to treatments with the hope it might assist in learning more about the disease. Characteristically, he was always thinking of others.

When, finally, Rick was told he had but a few days to live, he said he wanted to go home to see his family and the mountains. On the day of his departure, an ambulance took him to the airport where sixty students from the medical school lined up to say good-bye. From his wheelchair, he shook hands with each person, calling him by name. As he was taken up into the plane, he turned and said, "Remember, be good doctors."

Beyond Temptation: Responsibility!

Several celebrities, including U. N. Ambassador Jeane Kirkpatrick, were shouted down on a number of college campuses in 1982-83. Therefore, it was all the more refreshing to read of the commendable conduct of ten students from Virginia Polytechnic Institute, who, while returning from vacation in Bimini Island on a chartered sailboat, spotted a two-hundred-pound bale of marijuana floating in the water near Fort Lauderdale. It was said to have a street value of thirty thousand dollars. The honorable students turned it over to Coast Guard officials.

Subsequently this paragraph appeared in Virginia Tech's *Collegiate Times* editorial:

> Many students will call, and are calling, these students fools, idiots, and asses for shunning a quick-money opportunity. In such a materialistic society, such opportunity rarely is turned away, even if it is illegal. . . . It is nice to know some people are responsible.[1]

Shocking Trends

Americans were shocked to read in September, 1983, of a prostitution ring in Brattleboro, Vermont. The operators were ten boys and girls ages eight through thirteen. Sex was also being sold to adults. Within a few days after this shocking report, word came from the Saint Petersburg, Florida, area of a couple of youngsters who had sexually assaulted an eight-month-old girl.

Coping with Stress

Sir William Osler, twentieth-century Canadian physician, was also an effective writer and lecturer. A medical student, and former parishioner, attracted to Dr. Osler's writings, sent me a copy of his essay, "A Way of Life." The noted physician compared life to a rolling ship at sea and urged his readers so to manage the machinery "as to live in day-tight compartments." He continued, "The load of tomorrow, added to that of yesterday, carried today, makes the strongest falter. Shut off the future as tightly as the past."

Although my young friend was a graduate of a prestigious university, a Phi Beta Kappa, and was number one in his class at an equally famous medical school, he took his life sixty days before graduation. Apparently he was unable to take Osler's prescription for living in day-tight compartments. (see Matt. 6:25-31.)

Don't Expect Too Much

Minority persons have learned not to expect much from the majority. They have been disappointed too many times. Promises become meaningless.

In 1972, after Senator George McGovern was nominated for President by the Democratic Party, he chose Senator Thomas Eagleton as his vice-presidential running mate. Shortly thereafter, he dropped him from the ticket. One of the saddest comments surrounding Senator Eagleton's troubles was to hear on television a lovely young lady from Saint Louis who had made a seconding speech for Senator McGovern at Miami say that she was disappointed in Mr. McGovern. At first she thought he represented idealism around which youth could build, but now she saw him as just another politician.

A Father's Words

In his inaugural address, October 13, 1961, Davis Y. Paschall, president of the College of William and Mary, said: "As a boy on the farm in Lunenburg County, Virginia, when we hitched the mules for a long day in the tobacco fields, my father would often say, 'Today we shall walk humbly and plow a straight furrow.' "

God with a Face

The family had gone to the mountains for vacation. Their cottage overlooked a friendly lake. After a swim and dinner, it was bedtime. Tenderly, the mother prepared her little daughter for the night, heard her prayers, kissed her, and left the room. Immediately, Julia called for her to come back. The child raised some difficult questions about God. Patiently the mother listened, and then said reassuringly, "We'll be on the porch. There's nothing to hurt you. God is in the dark as well as in the light." Plaintively the child replied, "But I can't see Him in the dark, Mummy. I want a God with a face."

So do we all. When night comes, trouble knocks, disappointments punctuate the day, and problems pyramid, we all crave a God with a face. In our anxiety and agony, we join David in saying: "Such is the generation of those who seek him, who seek the face of the God of Jacob" (Ps. 24:6).

Hardest Subject

Johnny *could* read! In fact, he was one of the brightest pupils in class. Bubbling with energy and enthusiasm, he was forever getting into trouble. At the end of one testing period he brought his report card home. It revealed that he had made "A's" on everything except conduct. It was marked "D." When Johnny's father asked him why he made such a low grade in behavior, his thoughtful son replied, "Because I guess it's my hardest subject."

And so it is for most of us.

Ingenuity

A news item caught my eye because it happened in my wife's hometown, Milford, Connecticut. According to the report, the one-hundred-seventeen-year-old clock on the tower of the Church of Christ Congregational had been out of order, silent for a decade. The brethren finally decided they should do something about the dead clock. A contractor submitted a bid for a thousand dollars. While members were debating the pros and cons of restoring the clock, a fifteen-year-old boy, Howard Ward III, a member of the congregation, investigated the situation for himself. With twenty-five cents worth of parts, a pair of pliers, and an oil can, he got the clock going.

Ingratitude

Garry Moore had three young men on his show, "To Tell the Truth." It developed that these high school boys were standing by a subway station in New York City when suddenly a man fell on the tracks below. Instantaneously, and without the knowledge of the other, each boy jumped down to rescue the man. They managed to pull him to safety just seconds before the train came sweeping into the station. The mayor presented each young man with a special citation for bravery. Several organizations in New York recognized these extraordinary youths for their heroism. When Gary Moore asked one if he had had any contact with the family or with the man whom he rescued, he said, "No, he never thanked us."

Lonely Children

Bishop Joseph R. Kennedy told the story of giving a schoolboy a ride in Omaha. The youngster was depressed and immediately said, "Are you going a long ways, mister? If you are I wish you would take me along!" "Why?" asked the bishop. "I don't want to go to my house. (He didn't call it 'home.') There won't be anyone there when I get there unless Clara, the cleaning woman, hasn't left. Mother is at a social. My dad won't be home until after I am in bed, and he leaves before I get up in the morning. I tell you, mister, big houses are awfully lonely for little kids."

The bishop declared that he stopped to let the boy out before one of the most beautiful houses in Omaha.

Missing Children

Approximately ten thousand American children are kidnapped each year. It is estimated that fifty thousand children disappear from their homes annually. Not more than one hundred are recovered.

Opening Outward

When William James, noted philosopher, was a little boy, he wrote a friend about their new summer home: "It is a wonderful house, with all the doors opening outward." The Christian life should be lived with openness. Too many of us live behind facades, barricades of mind and mortar. We have interesting ways of turning life inward.

A Practicum in Banking

In 1927 a student bank opened in Topeka, Kansas. It was operated by the Seaman High School. In 1960 the school offered a course in "Money and Banking." Selected according to character and ability, ten students annually operate the bank, which is open during lunch hour. Any student or faculty person can deposit or borrow money. The interest rate in 1983 was 10 percent. At the end of the day, the money is deposited in a local bank. The school bank, said to be the only one of its kind in the country, averages about one-hundred-forty accounts and aggregates one-hundred-thirty thousand dollars a year. The little bank made its "two-millionth-dollar" deposit in 1980.

What a challenging concept and rewarding experience for young people!

Romance and Enthusiasm

Mrs. Ramsey MacDonald, wife of a former prime minister of Great Britain, said to her husband during the latter days of her life, "Whatever you do, put romance and enthusiasm into the lives of our children. With those qualities their lives will be good."

Some Are Brilliant

Sammy Ho earned a bachelor of science degree from the University of Washington in June of 1982 at age thirteen, the youngest to graduate from the one-hundred-seven-year-old institution. Moreover, he received his diploma cum laude. He had mastered undergraduate algebra, trigonometry, calculus, statistics, and numbers theory. Some of his professors said he exceeded *them* in mathematical ability. It was anticipated that Sammy would have his doctorate in numerical analysis by the time he was seventeen.

They Start Early

On February 28, 1981, news media reported that:

A nine-year-old boy suspected of holding up a bank at Rockefeller Center, New York City, for $118, surrendered to FBI agents yesterday." The four-foot-five-inch, ninety-pound youth is believed to be "the youngest bank robbery suspect in city history."

This Thing of Age!

Johann Strauss, Jr., composed his first waltz at the age of six.

John Keats died at twenty-six, but what a legacy of poetry he left!

Upton Sinclair published his first book, *The Prairie Pirates,* when he was seventeen.

John Wesley preached with remarkable regularity and effectiveness when he was past eighty.

Jesus of Nazareth was a young Man. According to our methods of reckoning time, His ministry did not exceed His thirty-third birthday. Albert Schweitzer believed that our Lord's ministry was much briefer than the traditional three-year span. It was not His age, but His identity, relationships, promises, and fulfillment culminating at Calvary and the empty tomb that made Him Savior.

Charles Haddon Spurgeon at nineteen preached to 27,000 persons on a British hillside.

Influence of Young People

By contrast, aged people need youth. Visit any college campus, and nearby you will find some of the youngest old people on earth. These professors, staff members, and other workers have been around youth so long and in such numbers that they think young, act young, and dream like young people.

Notes

Action

1. *The Wall Street Journal,* May 5, 1983, "In Memoriam Mr. B: Dance's 'Public Servant' "

2. Helmut Thielicke, *Being a Christian When the Chips Are Down,* (Philadelphia: Fortress Press, 1979), p. 26.

3. Helen Hayes, *A Gift of Joy,* (Philadelphia, New York: Lippincott, 1965), pp. 44-45.

4. Elton Trueblood, *The Humor of Christ,* (New York: Harper & Row Publishers, 1964), pp. 35-36. Permission requested.

5. Everett Tilson, *Segregation and the Bible,* (Nashville: Abingdon Press, 1958), p. 117. Used by permission.

America

1. Gerald R. Ford, *A Time to Heal: An Autobiography,* (New York: Harper & Row Publishers, Inc. and The Reader's Digest Association, Inc., 1979), p. 202. Used by permission.

2. *Time,* March 23, 1981, "The Duel Over Gun Control," p. 33.

3. Norman Cousins, *Human Options,* (New York: W. W. Norton & Company, Inc., Copyright © 1981 by Norman Cousins), p. 55.

4. *U. S. News and World Report,* July 5, 1982, "The Nation's Real Values—Still Alive," p. 50.

5. Ford, p. 187.

6. *Time,* July 5, 1982, "Insane On All Counts," p. 22.

7. *Parade,* December 5, 1982, "Patrick Henry's Daring Proposal," p. 21.

Awareness

1. Howard Thurman, *With Head and Heart,* (San Diego: Harcourt Brace Jovanovich, 1979), pp. 77-78.

2. *Time,* May 9, 1983, "The Joy of Pure Movement," p. 91.

3. *Richmond Times-Dispatch,* October 24, 1982, "Sweaters Cost $400 but Makers Get $10."

4. Reprinted from "An Insider's View," by Howard Rice, *Pacific Theological Review,* Fall 1982. Used by permission.

5. Mel White, *Mike Douglas: When the Going Gets Tough,* copyright © 1982 by Mel White, p. 212, used by permission of Word Books, Publisher, Waco, Tex. 76796.

The Bible

1. Charles Leber, *Is God There?*, (Old Tappan, N.J.: Fleming H. Revell Company, 1948), pp. 134-135. Used by permission.
2. Roy Pearson, *The Believer's Unbelief*, (New York and Toronto: Thomas Nelson Publishers, 1963), p. 58. Used by permission.

Celebrations

1. *Pulpit Digest*, May 1959, "The Meaning of Our Memorials," by Floyd E. McGuire, p. 60. Used by permission.
2. Permission granted by the University of Virginia, Charlottesville, Va.

Christlikeness

1. *Saturday Review*, Jan. 27, 1962, p. 24.
2. Excerpt from *Love Is Eternal* by Irving Stone. Copyright 1954 by Irving Stone. Reprinted by permission of Doubleday & Company, Inc.
3. G. Ray Jordan, *Religion that Is Eternal*, (New York: Macmillan Publishing Co., Inc., © G. Ray Jordan 1960), pp. 49-50. Used by permission.

Christmas

1. *Christian Century Pulpit*, December, 1957, "Greeting at Christmas," by Fra Giovanni, AD 1513, p. 22. Permission requested.
2. *The Daily Oklahoman*, December 7, 1964.
3. William J. Gaither, Christmas *Lyrics*, (Nashville: The New Benson Company). Permission requested.
4. *Richmond Times-Dispatch*, December 13, 1982, "Santa's Helpers Make Christmas Possible Again."
5. Maxwell Anderson, *The Wingless Victory*, (Hinsdale, N.Y.: Anderson House Publishers, Copyright 1936 by Maxwell Anderson. Copyright renewed 1964 by Gilda Anderson). All rights reserved. Reprinted by permission of Anderson House.
6. Harry Reasoner, *Before the Colors Fade*, (New York: Alfred A. Knopf, Inc., 1981), p. 113. Used by permission of CBS Public Relations, New York, N. Y. 10010.

The Church

1. Kermit L. Long, United Methodist pastor.
2. William Sloane Coffin, *The Courage to Love*, (New York: Harper & Row, 1982), p. 82.
3. Used by permission of the pastor, Charles Jim Marsh, Longboat Island Chapel, Florida.
4. Poem by Arthur Cleveland Coxe.
5. Mathilde W. Duke, "My Church," Nashville, Tennessee. Used by permission of author.

Commitment

1. Robert H. Schuller, *Self-Esteem, the New Reformation,* (Waco, Tex.: Word Books, Publisher, 1982), p. 119.

Courage

1. Editors of the Viking Press, *The Churchill Years,* 1874-1965, (New York: The Viking Press, 1965), p. 102.

2. *Parade,* May 15, 1983, "Amazing Appendectomy," p. 16.

3. *Sarasota Herald-Tribune,* January 7, 1983, "Four Drown Trying to Save Dog," p. 2.

4. Roland H. Bainton, *Here I Stand, A Life of Martin Luther,* (New York, Nashville: Abingdon-Cokesbury Press, 1950), p. 185.

5. Phil Donahue & Co., *Donahue,* (New York: Simon & Schuster, 1979), pp. 66-67. Used by permission.

The Cross

1. Alan Walker, *The Many Sided Cross Of Jesus,* (Nashville: Abingdon Press, 1962), p. 108.

2. Reprinted by permission from *Yesterday, Today, And What Next?* by Roland H. Bainton, copyright 1978 Augsburg Publishing House, p. 41.

Death

1. *The Sarasota Herald-Tribune,* September 13, 1981, "105th Birthday Noted by Convict Jailed in '22."

2. Sheldon Vanauken, *A Severe Mercy,* (San Francisco: Harper & Row, 1977), p. 174. Permission requested.

3. Passages from *George Washington, First in Peace* by Douglas Southall Freeman, edited by Mary Wells Ashworth and John Alexander Carroll, are reprinted with permission of Charles Scribner's Sons. Copyright © 1957 Charles Scribner's Sons, pp. 623-624.

4. Bonnie Ball O'Brien and Dorothy Elliott Sample, *Life in the Fifth Dimension* (Nashville: Broadman Press, 1984), pp. 19-20.

Easter

1. Used by permission of Gilkey's daughter, Margaret Gilkey Richards. Source unknown.

2. Arthur Lichtenberger, Presiding Bishop of the Episcopal Church, USA, *The Day Is at Hand,* "Lenten Rule," (New York: The Seabury Press, 1964), p. 27. Out of print.

3. Bruce Catton, *A Stillness at Appomattox,* (New York: Book-of-the-Month Club, Inc., 1982), pp. 453-454. Permission requested.

4. John Sutherland Bonnell, *I Believe in Immortality,* (Nashville: Abingdon Press, 1959), pp. 86-87.

5. In the sermon, "Amazing Grace," by Bishop Gerald Kennedy. *The Splendor of Easter,*

Floyd W. Thatcher, copyright © page 44-45; used by permission of Word Books, Publisher, Waco, Tex. 76796.

Education

1. Norman Cousins, *Human Options*, (New York: W. W. Norton & Company, Inc., Copyright © 1981 by Norman Cousins), p. 27. Used by permission.
2. From inaugural address, 1978, by Dr. A. Bartlett Giamatti, Yale University. Used by permission.
3. Alistair Cooke, *Six Men*, (New York: Alfred A. Knopf, Inc., 1977), p. 80. Used by permission.
4. *Time*, June 28, 1982, "Head High, Chin Up, Eye Clear," p. 56.
5. Dumas Malone, *Jefferson and His Time: The Sage of Monticello*, Vol. VI, (Boston: Little, Brown and Company, 1981), p. 235.

Evangelism

1. *Time*, May 3, 1982, "Counting Every Soul on Earth," by Richard N. Ostling, p. 67.
2. *Christian Century Pulpit*, August, 1951, "If I Should Die Before I Live," a sermon by John Branscomb, p. 17.
3. *Time*, December 13, 1982, "People," p. 63.

Faith

1. *Parade*, March 6, 1983, "The Many Loves of Bette Davis," by Dotson Rader. Used by permission.
2. *Pulpit Digest*, July/August, 1982, "To Worry Or to Sleep," by Paul C. Mills, p. 48.

Family

1. *Time*, December 6, 1982, "A Wedding Every 20 Minutes," p. 83.
2. *Changing Times*, April 1983, "Facing Up to the High Cost of Kids," p. 28.
3. Joseph E. Persico, *The Imperial Rockefeller*, (New York: Simon & Schuster, 1982), p. 17. Used by permission.

God

1. Monica Furlong, *Merton, a Biography*, (San Francisco: Harper & Row, Publishers, Inc., 1980), p. 265. Permission requested.
2. Malcolm Muggeridge, *Twentieth-Century Testimony*, (Nashville, Toronto, New York: Thomas Nelson Publishers, Copyright © 1978 by Evangelische Omroep). Reprinted by permission of Thomas Nelson Publishers.
3. C. S. Lewis, *Surprised By Joy*, (London and Glasgow: Collins Clear-Type Press, 1955), p. 182.

4. Carl Sandburg, *Honey and Salt,* "God Is No Gentleman," (New York: Harcourt Brace Jovanovich, Inc., 1963), p. 39. Used by permission.

5. Wilbur Rees, *Leadership Magazine,* Winter Edition 1983, "$3 Worth of God," Vol. IV, No. 1, p. 107. Used by permission.

6. C. S. Lewis, *The Joyful Christian* (New York: Macmillan 1977), p. 180.

Heaven

1. *The Sarasota Herald-Tribune,* August 30, 1981, "Noted Roving Broadcaster Thomas Dies at 89," p. 1.

2. Sigalovada Suttanta in *Dialogues of the Buddha,* translated T. W. and C. A. F. Rhys Davids (London: Oxford University Press, 1921), part III, pp. 178-179.

3. *Great Poems of the English Language,* (New York: Tudor Publishing Co., 1935), p. 1155. Unable to locate copyright holder; apparently in public domain.

Hell

1. Arthur E. Travis, *Where on Earth Is Heaven?* (Nashville: Broadman Press, 1974), pp. 109-111.

Hope

1. *Parade,* July 3, 1983, "When Faith is Triumphant," by Cleveland Amory, p. 4. Used by permission.

2. Henri J. M. Nouwen, *Intimacy,* (New York: Harper & Row, 1969), a student's prayer, pp. 59-60. Permission requested.

Humor

1. *Time,* February 28, 1983, "Taking Notes for History," p. 24.

2. Robert E. Goodrich, Jr., *Reach for the Sky,* (Old Tappan, N. J.: Fleming H. Revell Company, 1960), p. 88.

Integrity

1. Bennett J. Sims, Episcopal Bishop of Atlanta, *Purple Ink,* (private printing, 1982), p. 167. Used by permission.

2. Harry Reasoner, *Before the Colors Fade,* (New York: Alfred A. Knopf, 1981), p. 195.

3. *Richmond Times-Dispatch,* February 10, 1982, "Cheating Brings More Rewards than Virtue," by Bob Greene, p. C-2.

Jesus

1. Author unknown.

2. Albert Schweitzer, *The Quest of the Historical Jesus,* (New York: Macmillan, 1948), Agents for A. C. Black, Ltd., of London, 1922, p. 401. Used by permission.

3. Joseph Fort Newton, *River of Years*, (New York: J. B. Lippincott Company, 1946), p. 25.

Leadership

1. *A General's Life, an Autobiography by General Of the Army Omar N. Bradley and Clay Blair*, (New York: Simon and Schuster, 1983), dust jacket.
2. Norman Cousins, *Human Options*, (New York: W. W. Norton & Company, Inc., Copyright © 1981 by Norman Cousins), p. 109.
3. Harry S. Ashmore, *An Epitaph for Dixie*, (New York: W. W. Norton & Company, Inc., 1957, 1958), p. 40.

Life

1. *AARP News Bulletin*, November, 1981, "At 105, This Artist Radiates 'Beauty, Joy' and Wins Friends," p. 9.
2. *Richmond Times-Dispatch*, May 23, 1982, "American Reunion in Alaska," by Richard Reeves.
3. Joyce Landorf, *Irregular People*, (Waco, Tex.: Word Books, Publisher, 1982), p. 30.
4. Author unknown.
5. United Technologies Corporation, Hartford, Conn. 06101, 1982. Used by permission.
6. J. Clifton Allen, *Life Is Worth Your Best*, (Nashville: Broadman Press, 1980), p. 30.
7. United Technologies Corporation, Hartford, Conn. 06101, 1981. Used by permission.
8. From a speech given by Dr. Steven Rhoads at the Medical College of Virginia's Colloquia in Bioethics, October 14, 1982.
9. Bennett J. Sims, Episcopal Bishop of Atlanta, *Purple Ink*, (private printing, 1982), p. 143. Used by permission.

Love

1. *Great Poems of the English Language*, (New York: Tudor Publishing Co., Copyright 1927 by Robert M. McBride & Company), p. 1122. Apparently in public domain.
2. *The Asheville Citizen*, Asheville, North Carolina, July 29, 1981, "It's Celeste's Life That's Important," p. 1.

Maturity

1. From Mel White, *Mike Douglas: When the Going Gets Tough*, copyright © 1982 by Mel White, p. 188, used by permission of Word Books, Publisher, Waco, TX 76796.
2. *Modern Maturity*, December-January, 1983, p. 49.

Ministry

1. James H. Robinson, *Adventurous Preaching*, (Great Neck, N.Y.: Channel Press, 1956), pp. 162-163.

2. Malcolm Muggeridge, *Something Beautiful for God: Mother Teresa of Calcutta,* (New York, Evanston, San Francisco, London: Harper & Row, Publishers, 1971), pp. 88, 107. Permission requested.

3. Helmut Thielicke, *The Trouble with the Church,* (New York: Harper & Row, Publishers, 1965), p. 29.

4. *The Man from Ida Grove;* Copyright © 1979 by Harold E. Hughes. Published by Chosen Books, Lincoln, VA 22078. Used by permission.

5. Reprinted with permission of Saint Paul's Episcopal Church, Richmond, Va.

6. W. A. Criswell, *Criswell's Guidebook for Pastors* (Nashville: Broadman Press, 1980), pp. 21-22.

Missions

1. Fred W. Craddock, *Overhearing the Gospel, Preaching and Teaching the Faith to Persons Who Have Already Heard,* (Nashville: Abingdon, 1978), p. 9.

2. George Eayrs, *Letters of John Wesley, A Selection of Important and New Letters,* (London: Hodder and Stoughton Limited, 1915), p. 244. Used by permission.

3. *Newsweek,* December 22, 1959.

4. *Pulpit Digest,* December 1967, "No Apologies," p. 58. Used by permission.

Money

1. Permission by Kathrine K. White (Mrs. W. L.), *The Emporia Gazette,* Emporia, Ks 66801.

2. Adam Smith, *The Money Game,* (New York: Random House, 1967).

3. John Kenneth Galbraith, *Money, Whence It Came, Where It Went,* (Boston: Houghton Mifflin Company, 1975), p. 3.

4. Peter Collier & David Horowitz, *The Rockefellers: An American Dynasty,* (New York: Holt, Rinehart and Winston, 1976), pp. 182-183.

5. *As I See It: The Autobiography of J. Paul Getty,* (Edgewood Cliffs, N. J.: Prentice-Hall, Inc., 1976), p. 331.

Peace

1. Prepared by David L. Bailey, Jr., The Virginia Council of Churches. Used by permission.

Perseverance

1. Norman Vincent Peale, *The Positive Power of Jesus Christ,* (Wheaton, Ill.: Tyndale House Publishers, Inc., 1980), p. 197.

Power

1. *The Saturday Evening Post,* October 16, 1943; *Fortune* magazine, April, 1945; *American Magazine,* January, 1951; *Holiday,* March, 1952.

Prayer

1. James A. Michener, *Sports in America,* (New York: Random House, Inc., 1976), p. 384. Used by permission.
2. See Robert H. Schuller, *Self-Esteem, The New Reformation,* (Waco, Tex.: Word Books, Publisher, 1982), pp. 158-159.
3. Prayer of an unknown Confederate soldier.

Revival

1. Vachel Lindsay, *Masterpieces of Religious Verse,* (New York: Harper & Brothers, Publishers, 1948), Edited by James Dalton Morrison, p. 504. Permission requested.
2. Lloyd C. Douglas, *The Robe,* (Boston: Houghton Mifflin Company, 1942), pp. 412-413.

Sin

1. *Richmond Times-Dispatch,* July 30, 1982, "Sorry, Ma'm, Nothing Works for Anybody Today," by Bob Greene, p. C-5.
2. Langdon Gilkey, *Shantung Compound,* (New York: Harper & Row, 1966), p. 233.
3. Karl Menninger, *Whatever Became of Sin?,* (New York: Hawthorn Books, Inc., 1973), p. 19. Permission requested.

Sports

1. Red Smith, *To Absent Friends from Red Smith,* (New York: Atheneum, 1982), p. 172.
2. *The Wall Street Journal,* March 30, 1983, "Mind Machines," p. 1.
3. Red Smith, pp. 42-43.
4. Ibid., p. 11.
5. *Sarasota Herald-Tribune,* January 5, 1981, "Olympian Still Swims at Age 94."

Stewardship

1. W. A. Poovey, *How to Talk to Christians About Money,* (Minneapolis: Augsburg Publishing House, 1982), p. 30.

Success

1. *AARP News Bulletin,* Vol. XXIV, No. 3, Washington, D. C., March 1983, "Tobacco Road Lawyer Lives in the Fast Lane," p. 1.

Time

1. Herman Wouk, *The Caine Mutiny,* (Garden City, N.Y.: Doubleday & Co., Copyright © 1951, 1979 by Herman Wouk), pp. 61-62. Used by permission.

Vocation

1. *Parade,* May 16, 1982, "The Blue Jeaniuses," p. 20.
2. *Parade,* May 31, 1981, "Now It Can Be Told," p. 12.
3. J. Paul Getty, *As I See It,* (Englewoods Cliffs, New Jersey: Prentice-Hall, Inc., 1976), p. 88.
4. *Time,* June 28, 1982, "Daydreams of What You'd Rather Be," p. 78.

War

1. Bruce Catton, *A Stillness at Appomattox,* (New York: Book-of-the-Month Club, Inc., 1953), pp. 334-336.
2. *Richmond Times-Dispatch,* February 16, 1982, "$60,000 a Rebel In El Salvador," by Richard Reeves.
3. *Churchill, the Walk with Destiny,* (New York: The Macmillan Company, 1959), Compiled and Designed by H. Tatlock Miller, Loudon Sainthill, p. 148.

World

1. *The Wall Street Journal,* April 29, 1982, "On Key Largo Yachts, Slump Bring Vague Worries but No Discomfort," p. 31.
2. *Richmond Times-Dispatch,* November 29, 1982, "His Christmas Is Tradition."
3. Tim Floyd, *Welcome to the Real World* (Nashville: Broadman Press, 1984), pp. 92-93.

Worship

1. *Pulpit Digest,* May, 1965, "The Meaning of Worship," by W. B. J. Martin, pp. 58-59.
2. Found in an old church in England.

Youth

1. *Richmond Times-Dispatch,* April 7, 1983, "Tech's Good Citizens," editorial page.

Index of Names

L

Laertius, Diogenes 114
Lamb, Charles 33
Landorf, Joyce 213
Lansky, Meyer 18
Larkin, Philip 122
Latimer, Hugh 80
Latourette, Kenneth Scott 364
Lauren, Ralph 23
Lavin, Linda 226
Lazarus 105
Leber, Charles 29
Lee, Robert E. 44, 192-193
Lee, Robert G. 90, 108
Lewis, C. S. 97, 110, 143, 145, 146, 158, 365
Lewis, Francis 37
Lincoln, Abraham 19, 32, 46-48, 131, 191, 214, 232-233, 282, 290, 380
Lindbergh, Anne Morrow 31
Lindbergh, Charles A. 15
Lineacre, Thomas 308
Livingstone, David 88, 183, 257, 261
Lloyd-George, David 169
Lombardi, Vince 326
Longfellow, Henry Wadsworth 7, 21, 104, 375
Louis XV 102
Lowell, James Russell 146, 339
Luccock, Halford 156, 275, 309
Luce, Clare Booth 165
Luke 39, 287
Luther, Martin 71, 74, 85, 96, 119, 123, 130, 133, 174, 267, 299, 303, 376
Lydia 39

M

MacArthur, Douglas 136, 206, 273
MacDonald, Ramsey 390
Maclaren, Ian 151, 196
MacLeish, Arhibald 124, 212, 217
Madison, James 131
Malachi 307
Malone, Dumas 63
Malone, Ted 381
Malone, Walter 158
Mann, Horace 117-118
Mao Tse-tung 184
Marconi, Guglielmo 290
Marney, Carlyle 179, 304
Marshall, John 379
Marshall, Peter 302
Mary 63, 290, 303
Masefield, John 200
Mathewson, Christy 322-323
Matthew 12
May, Julia Harris 228
Mays, Benjamin E. 270
Mays, Willie 327
McClellan, George B. 309
McCracken, Robert 327
McGee, Clyde 360
McGovern, George 386
McLeod, George 35, 296

Mellon, William 306-307
Menninger, Karl 317, 318
Menzies, Robert Gordon 30
Merton, Thomas 143, 273, 274
Michelangelo 342
Middleton, R. L. 185
Miller, Arthur 234, 341
Miller, Basil 193
Milton, John 160
Mitchell, Thomas 159
Moffatt, Robert 261
Moody, Dwight Lyman 70, 124, 148, 300, 310-311, 311-312
Moore, Edward 284
Moore, Garry 388
Moore, Henry Spencer 345
Moore, Thomas 147
Morgan, Angela 56
Morrison, Robert 261
Moses 39, 204, 208, 376
Muggeridge, Malcolm 54, 122, 143

N

Nansen, Fridtjof 162
Napoleon (Bonaparte) 79, 280, 285, 291, 315, 363
Nelson, Thomas 37
Newman, John Henry 272
Newport, Christopher 42
Newton, Isaac 11
Newton, John 194
Newton, Joseph Fort 201, 247
Nicklaus, Jack 328-329
Niebuhr, Reinhold 293
Niemöller, Martin D. 95, 129, 283
Niles, D. T. 75, 118, 304, 330
Nixon, Richard M. 131, 358
Nobel, Alfred 153
Nouwen, Henri 303

O

Orwell, George 249
Osler, William 386
Ott, Mel 327

P

Padarewski, Ignace Jan 355-356
Palmer, Alice F. 254
Parker, Barrington 19
Parker, Francis Wayland 113
Parker, Joseph 147, 151
Parks, Rosa 86, 213
Pascal, Blaise 11, 114, 370
Pasternak, Boris 78
Pasteur, Louis 11, 290
Paton, John G. 262
Paul 8, 21, 25, 39, 82, 104, 119, 165, 225, 232, 307, 317, 355, 376, 383
Peale, Norman Vincent 278, 358
Pepper, Claude 55-56, 230
Perry, Gaylord 321
Peter 21, 228, 241, 288
Phelps, Digger 32
Philip I 100
Phillips, J. B. 75, 83, 196, 203

Picasso, Pablo 342
Pierce, Shanghai 68-69
Pike, James A. 170
Pilate, Pontius 200
Pippin, Frank 54
Pitt, William 250
Poling, Clark V. 241
Poling, Daniel 226
Pope Pius IV 264
Powell, Jake 326
Presley, Elvis 211
Price, Eugenia 101

Q

Quayle, William 146, 182
Quillian, Paul 121

R

Reagan, Ronald 19, 131, 179, 356-357
Reasoner, Harry 191, 341
Rembrandt 253
Reston, James 320
Reynolds, Quentin 360
Rhea, Claude 195
Rhodes, Cecil 48, 207, 266
Rice, Grantland 320, 324
Rice, Howard 25
Richards, Timothy 166
Richardson, Norman 375
Ride, Sally K. 352, 354
Ridley, Nicholas 80
Riegels, Roy 324
Riis, Jacob 240
Robertson, R. B. 7
Rockefeller, John D., Jr. 268
Rockefeller, John D. IV 174
Rockefeller, Nelson A. 141
Rodeheaver, Homer 311
Rodney, Caesar 36
Roebling family 358
Rogers, Will 176, 347
Rooney, Andy 102
Roosevelt family 131
Roosevelt, Theodore 18, 160, 233, 240
Ross, Edmund G. 88
Rubinoff, Benno 75
Rubinoff, David 347
Rudin, Margaret 354
Rukeyser, Louis 265
Ruskin, John 27, 212
Russell, Bertrand 317
Rutledge, Archibald 168, 309

S

Sadat, Anwar 190
Samaritan, Good 48
Sampson, Ralph (allusion to) 177
Samson 165-166, 177
Samuel 376
Sankey, Ira 310
Sanzio, Raphael 21
Sarah 76

403

Subject Index